D1209385

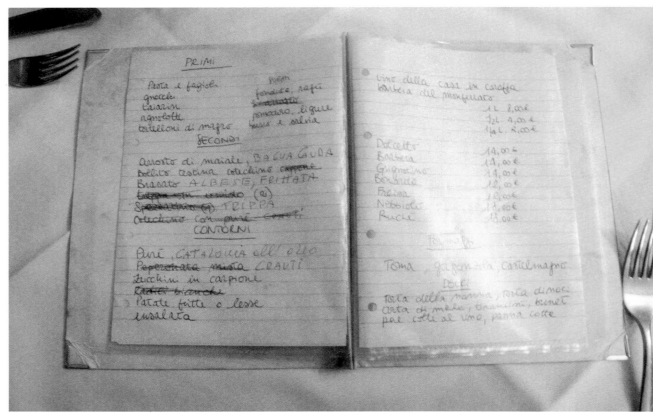

BOCCA

COOKBOOK

JACOB KENEDY

PHOTOGRAPHY BY HOWARD SOOLEY

BLOOMSBURY

NEW YORK · BERLIN · LONDON · SYDNEY

IF FOOD BE THE MUSIC OF LOVE...

FOR VICTOR

INTRODUCTION

I don't eat food, I devour it. The act of consumption, of making something wonderful a part of me, goes rather to my head. In a fleeting moment, I taste that most precious ingredient, the love a great cook has poured so freely into the pot. It is all too easy to forget where the food came from, and the reason it is delicious.

I think there is something particularly alluring about Italian food – don't you? It has special qualities that permeate not only every dish worth eating there, but every aspect of the culture. In Italy, my spirits lift. The architecture seems to enhance nature in the countryside, and to exalt mankind in the cities. Human beauty shines in paintings and sculptures, in the smiles people give to children, in the directness with which they talk, in the food they prepare and eat with such passion and understanding. I am freed from any sense of the guilt or malaise that seem so common in the modern age. It is this freedom, this happiness, which makes Italian food so uniquely delicious and nourishing.

But Italian cuisine is hard to pin down, as each region has its own – which is where the variety originates, and where the joy lies. Here are some thoughts on how this may have come to pass. They may help you understand where I am coming from, and also where I am going to take you.

Isolation My mother lived with her parents in Rome when she was young, and they had a holiday home in nearby Sperlonga, which they still keep. There wasn't at that time a road to the village – they moved in with two pianos, which had to be carried by hand (like a funeral procession) across the Aurunci hills. The outside world had just begun to touch this place – a makeshift cinema was perched outdoors on a cliff-face by the sea. They showed *The Ten Commandments* in 1956, and when Moses parted the waters the audience fled, shrieking – they thought it was real. My mother for a short while dated a local boy who refused to believe she was Jewish because she didn't have horns or a tail. A wild one, she used to run for days in those hills. She occasionally met a bird-trapper (even wilder), who caught tiny robins, finches and starlings in horsehair nooses, taking them to market in a cage on his back. A genuine Papageno, he could speak no human tongue, communicating instead with whistles and trills.

Today, Sperlonga has a road and attracts thousands of Roman and Neapolitan tourists, but a few of the older generation can barely communicate in Italian, speaking only their local dialect fluently. The point I'm trying to make? As in Darwinian evolution, with humanity too isolation leads to astonishing **diversity**.

Diversity Italy was unified only about 150 years ago. Before this, it was divided into independent states, today preserved as the twenty regions. Indeed, so-called *Italian* dialects are in fact dialects of vulgar (spoken) Latin. Modern Italian (based on the Tuscan,

Florentine dialect) became ubiquitous in Italy only with the advent of television in the 1950s. This fragmented history is even more evident in the country's cuisines: Sicilian flavours are as evocative of North Africa as of 'Italy', a vestige of Moorish rule. Whilst a single language permeated the country out of necessity, the food still exhibits a startling diversity, and in its unique culinary tradition each region takes great **pride**.

Pride Regional pride is one thing, but each city, hamlet and household has its own version of a dish, of which it is incredibly proud. This pride is one of the reasons Italian cooking is so very, very good. Indeed, whilst chefs worldwide have the conceit that theirs is the *best* way, the conceit of the Italian cook is that his way (or, more specifically, his mother's way) is the *only* way. Judged on these chauvinistic grounds, not a single recipe in this book is right, let alone **authentic**.

Authenticity Because I am not Italian I may have a more objective view of the country's food. The pride that makes an Italian so very good at cooking his local delicacies, renders him blinkered to the finer points of food from elsewhere, if he cares to consider it food at all. I may not write about Palermitan cuisine with the knowledge of a local, but perhaps I have a better understanding of Venetian cooking than a Sicilian can. I have travelled Italy as much as possible, solely in the pursuit of pleasure – these journeys have, with hindsight, become the research that underpins my work. Though the recipes that follow may not be considered authentic in the strictest sense, they're honest – and I believe well-informed – renditions. At any rate, everyone has their own way of making a dish – it would be a hard task to find two Piedmontese who could agree on how to make *bagna caoda*, but you could bet your bottom dollar they'd agree that mine is wrong. Perhaps the pot is calling the kettle black. In any case the recipes are here for their history, sense of place, and **deliciousness**.

Deliciousness My friends might laugh at me for saying this, as I normally cook far too much, but they can laugh away: I am a minimalist chef. If something can be removed from a recipe and not make the dish worse, I believe that doing so will make it more delicious. Italian food is intrinsically simple – and the simpler food is, the harder it is to get it right. With fewer stages of preparation and fewer elements to combine, you have fewer opportunities to adjust your seasoning, or cover your mistakes: if it isn't perfect you can't hide it. I always try to find the simplest way of doing things, so the making and the eating can be as direct and pleasurable as possible. This is the route to **happiness**.

Jacob Kenedy
London, February 2011

RAW

Indulge me, and consider a fig. Modestly concealed beneath the fig leaf it is surely the original forbidden fruit, a corporeal and vulvaceous red within.

Should the figs you encounter on your shopping rounds look shrivelled, or hard, or powdery, pass them by – they were never any good, and never will be. Any figs that are decent, but a little dry or yellowing in the centre, or slightly firm, can be baked into a tart, or mixed with almonds and prosciutto in a salad. Although they weren't the most beautiful specimens, your art will make them part of a delicious whole.

But when you find the perfect fig, don't mess with it. You are likely holding one harvested in late August or September. Though rather small, inside it is a melting pool of honey. The skin will be pale green and smooth or purple-blushed and cracking. It should not be rinsed, for fear of washing its green aroma away, nor cut, let alone peeled. It will be best of all if you picked it yourself, for no-one but you will have touched it, and you will be that much closer to nature. Eat it in two clean bites, savouring the scent with the first, and the sweetness with the second.

And that is the glory of raw food – it is the embodiment of nature's purity. As a tribesman might eat the heart of a lion to assume its bravery, or a Jew ingest bitter herbs and salt water to symbolise his ancestors' enslavement, so when you consume something raw, you make the goodness of nature a part of you.

Raw flavours are lighter, cleaner and more distinct. So many things are delicious raw – peas, lettuces, young fava beans, fennel, artichokes, scallops, langoustines, sea bream, bass, and tender beef – that it should be a crime to cook them. To consume an ingredient raw is a choice, an act of connoisseurship and humility. It is to acknowledge and revel in nature's supremacy. To cook would be to destroy her perfection.

SHAVED ARTICHOKE SALAD

Artichokes are somehow the closest to my heart of all foods. I have a memory of sitting on my grandfather's knee, pretending to be pirates (he sported an eye patch anyway) as he peeled leaves from a boiled artichoke we shared, before cleaning the heart, which he left all for me. The image is so strong, yet I wonder how much is genuine – I was only two at the time, and shouldn't really remember anything.

With their subtle, nuanced flavour and stunning geometry, artichokes are a reassuring common thread running through Italy's regional cuisines. Sometimes cooked whole (like the one I ate as a pirate), they are more commonly cleaned beforehand (see overleaf). This salad must be made and dressed at the last moment, and can be varied a hundred ways. The addition of truffle oil to the dressing (use 2 tablespoons white truffle oil, and 3 olive oil instead of ⅓ cup in the recipe below) and shavings of Parmesan being one such variant, which can be made even more luxurious with the addition of copious shaved fresh truffle. The salad can be changed in character drastically by plunging the shaved artichokes for a couple of seconds into boiling salted water, before dressing and serving warm. Or salad leaves, arugula and endive can be added, along with a few pomegranate seeds, for a lift. Here it is at its simplest.

Serves 4 as a starter

16 tiny artichokes (*castraure*), or
　8 young ones, no more than 2½in
　across, cleaned (overleaf)

3 tablespoons lemon juice
⅓ cup chopped flat-leaf parsley
⅓ cup extra virgin olive oil

Thinly slice the artichokes lengthways, about ¹⁄₁₆in thick. Dress quickly with the lemon juice to keep them from turning brown, then add the parsley and oil. Toss and season to taste with salt and pepper. Serve straightaway.

TO CLEAN AN ARTICHOKE

It takes a little practice and understanding to clean artichokes well: you want to remove absolutely everything tough, but ensure you take away only the minimum as the tender flesh is precious and in minority. In general, anything bright or dark green is inedible, but you can always check for tenderness either by digging in with a fingernail, or testing a trimming between your teeth.

Use a sharp knife to trim off the tough green parts of the leaves. The tender part of the artichoke, were you to cut it in longitudinal section, would be somewhat kite-shaped, the base making the broader end and the leaf tips the longer point. Keep the knife parallel to the longer sides of this imaginary kite, and cut around the artichoke, removing the tough leaves which will fall away like pencil sharpenings.

Having 'sharpened' the leafy end of your artichoke, do the same to the base. You will cut off the stem in the process, but for most recipes this is no bad thing. Use a paring knife or peeler to trim off any hard-to-reach green bits, like those at the widest point of your kite and at the base of the stem.

Now cut off the tip of your sharpened artichoke (the tops of the leaves are tough), again leaving as much as is tender still attached. The result should look like a pale rosebud.

Put your cleaned artichokes immediately in water acidulated with lemon juice or crushed parsley stalks. This will keep them from blackening and turning bitter, a fate your blade and your hands (try dishwashing liquid mixed with a little sugar) cannot avoid.

Larger artichokes will need to have their choke (the juvenile flowers, which would grow to make the purple glory of this outsized thistle) removed, by scooping it out with teaspoon and a rotating motion. Smaller ones, where even the choke is tender, will be just fine left as they are. They can be kept in their lemony water for a few hours before using.

BAGNA CAODA / WARM ANCHOVY FONDUE WITH RAW VEGETABLES PIEDMONT

Bagna caoda is one of the defining dishes of Piedmontese cuisine. Every family has its own way of making it, and in its eyes the one below will almost certainly be wrong. Others (even one or two renegade Piedmontese) have said it is the best they've ever eaten.

An anchovy fondue with crudités, this dish is an anomaly. It is fish-based, and Piedmont has no sea (anchovies, being salted, feature strongly in inland cooking along with salt cod and stockfish). And it is, largely, a plate of raw vegetables which again bucks the trend in Piedmontese cooking – normally identified by rich dishes full of truffle, meat and butter. My version has a hint of lemon, and uses cream to help it stay in emulsion: neither are common twists, but both are authentic. Apparently you can enhance the dish with shavings of white truffle. This sounds like a nice thing to me – good for the *bagna caoda*, although maybe not the best use of a precious truffle.

Serves 4 as a starter, 2 as a main

Anchovy sauce
1 head garlic, cloves thinly sliced
⅓ cup milk
About 4oz anchovy fillets (start with about 7oz whole salted anchovies, if you can get them)

3 tablespoons butter
½ cup heavy cream
Grated zest of ¼ lemon
7 tablespoons extra virgin olive oil

Soak the garlic in the milk for at least an hour. Meanwhile, fillet the anchovies: rinse off the salt under running water, and use your thumb to open up the two fillets, then pull out the spine. Drain the fillets, then chop.

Put the garlic, milk and butter in a bowl and set over a double boiler. Cook for about an hour, stirring often with a whisk until the garlic has melted to a thick paste. Add the cream, chopped anchovy fillets, lemon zest and plenty of pepper. Cook for up to an hour more until smooth, then slowly stir in the oil. It should emulsify, but if it gets too thick and starts to split add a touch of water, a little at a time. If it splits despite your best efforts, just transfer everything to a blender and purée until smooth. Keep the mixture hot in the double boiler until ready to use, stirring occasionally to keep it from separating. The *bagna caoda* should be liquid, but thick enough to coat.

This sauce may be made in advance, refrigerated and then warmed carefully over a low heat. If it splits on reheating, bring it together with a dash of heavy cream.

To dip in the *bagna caoda*:

Must-haves are
**Cardoons (forced, and nearly white),
  cleaned and stripped of their fibre,
  or artichokes, cleaned and wedged**
Red peppers, cut into strips
Fennel, cut into wedges

Optional are
Treviso leaves, especially *treviso tardivo*

Puntarelle stems or spears
Boiled and sliced beets
Asparagus spears
Celery stalks
Thin slices of raw beef
Carrot sticks
Jerusalem artichokes
**Raw eggs (for scrambling in the sauce
  at the end)**

The *bagna caoda* must be served hot – best in a fondue pot – and the vegetables raw and crunchy. They are just dipped in the sauce, and eaten straightaway or left to simmer in the anchovy loveliness until cooked to your taste, at the table. When the dipping vegetables are finished with, and a small quantity of the sauce is bubbling at the bottom of the pot, a couple of raw eggs may be stirred in to scramble at the end – a real treat.

RABBIT TONNATO WITH RAW FAVA BEANS AND RADISHES PIEDMONT

Vitello tonnato, veal with tuna sauce, is a Piedmontese summer classic, notably served at the feast of Ferragosto (Assumption Day). The sauce is unusual – a tuna-flavoured mayonnaise – and all the more quirky a combination when you think that tuna, in Italy, is also known as 'veal of the sea'. At Masuelli San Marco, my all-time favourite Milanese restaurant, they serve rabbit in the same sauce – there with a little salad of radishes and celery. Here I make the dish with the first fava beans of spring.

Serves 4 as a starter, 2 as a main

½ farmed rabbit (a lengthways half)
1 small onion
2 bay leaves
½ carrot
4 celery stalks
1 bunch radishes
1lb fresh fava beans (or ¾ cup shelled ones)
A few flat-leaf parsley leaves
3 tablespoons salted capers, soaked until tolerably salty
1 tablespoon extra virgin olive oil

Tuna sauce
1 salted anchovy, rinsed and filleted, or 2 anchovy fillets in oil
3oz best-quality canned tuna in oil
A few oregano leaves
1 egg yolk
1 tablespoon red wine vinegar
1 tablespoon lemon juice
1 tablespoon salted capers, soaked until tolerably salty
⅓ cup extra virgin olive oil

Put the rabbit, onion, bay, carrot and half the celery in a pot (cut the rabbit into a couple of chunks to fit, if necessary). Barely cover with water, season with salt and simmer over a low heat for an hour or until the meat is soft enough to be pulled from the bone. Leave it to cool in its liquor, then drain (save a little of the stock) and pull the meat from the bone.

Make the sauce by combining the anchovy, tuna, oregano, egg yolk, vinegar, lemon juice and tablespoon of capers in a food processor. Add the oil gradually, in a steady stream, then season with pepper and slacken with a bit of the stock (3–5 tablespoons) to the thickness of heavy cream. The sauce can be kept in the fridge for up to a day or so, but may thicken over time – in which case, thin it with a little more rabbit stock or water.

Slice the remaining celery on the bias ¼in thick; wash and halve the radishes. Shell the fava beans, briefly blanching and peeling the shell from any larger than a fingernail. Toss the vegetables together with the torn rabbit meat, parsley, 3 tablespoons of capers and the oil. Spread the creamy sauce flat on a plate, and mound the salad on top in a haphazard pile.

BATTUTO / RAW YOUNG BEEF SEASONED ONLY WITH OIL (AND MAYBE TRUFFLE) PIEDMONT

In Piedmont, austerity is in vogue. *Battuto* – simply seasoned raw beef – can be one of the best things in the world, a harmony of raw meat and oil. There they use *vitellone* – young beef, or long-in-the-tooth veal. Only three components make the dish – meat, oil and the cook's hand – but if each is perfect they come together like the Holy Trinity.

I use rose veal when I can get it, which isn't often, or I mix veal and beef in equal proportions to the same end. A fine piece of fillet would be great, but cleaned top-round (also known as top sirloin) is more economical and tasty as long as it is meticulously cleaned of any silverskin outside or within the muscle. It *should* be very finely chopped (not diced) with a very large and very sharp knife, but is *just as good* ground through a ¼in plate on a meat grinder, or judiciously pulsed in a food processor; 1lb of this meat will serve four as a starter, half as many as a main, if combined with 7 tablespoons of fruity, but not too peppery, extra virgin olive oil, a good amount of salt and a little pepper to taste. Fingers or a spoon can be used to mix – the meat should be stirred with the seasonings until the oil emulsifies, its glossy appearance vanishing to a gentle sheen.

I serve this all year round with very thin slices of very crisp toast, a wedge of lemon available for those who need it, although I am not included among their number. In winter, I shave white truffle – ¾–1½oz for four – over the meat. But I am a decadent pig.

TARTARE
VALLE D'AOSTA

I first ate a horsemeat tartare on the southern shore of Lake Garda, in an unpromising shack that turned out to be rather good. Never having eaten horse before, I asked the waiter if it wasn't a little strong when eaten raw. He said it was actually rather mild, and excellent – he spoke with such conviction that I ordered the dish against my own judgement. I am glad that I did: it was delicious.

Horsemeat is not so easy to find in most parts of the world – but, you'll be glad to hear, is unnecessary unless you have an urge to surprise or shock your guests. Beef makes a great tartare in France, a delicious one in Italy, and a superlative one in your home.

Serves 4 as a starter, 2 as a main

3/4 lb beef fillet or lean, tender horsemeat
3 tablespoons finely diced Parmesan
3 tablespoons salted capers, soaked until tolerably salty, then chopped
1/4 cup finely chopped flat-leaf parsley

1/3 cup extra virgin olive oil
A squeeze of lemon juice
Thin slices of bread, toasted until crisp, or thicker slices, grilled, to serve

Clean any silverskin from the meat, which should be dark, dark red and quite supple to the touch. Slice it thinly (1/8 in) with the grain, then stack these slices up and cut into 1/8 in-wide strips, again with the grain. Cut these strips across into 1/8 in dice, then transfer to a bowl along with the other ingredients. Stir together, seasoning with ample salt and pepper. Serve with the toast on the side.

BEEF CARPACCIO WITH ARTICHOKES AND PARMESAN VENETO

Carpaccio, a salad of thinly sliced raw beef, was apparently created at Harry's Bar in Venice and named after Vittore Carpaccio, a Venetian Renaissance painter. A few others lay claim to its invention, notably Savini in Milan, and I have been unable to discover who's telling the truth. Anyway, you can still get it at Savini, I imagine, and certainly at Harry's Bar or Cipriani (same owners, same town). Their way of serving (with a heavy, mustardy dressing) may not have changed since the 1950s, but then again neither have many of the clientele.

Below is a lighter, perhaps more modern version. You could serve it without the artichokes, but as in so many dishes, I prefer it with.

Serves 4 as a starter, 2 as a main

½ lb fillet steak, or veal fillet
4 smallish (2½–3in) artichokes,
  cleaned (page 26)

2oz Parmesan, shaved with
  a potato peeler
2 tablespoons extra virgin olive oil
4 lemon wedges, to serve

Clean any silverskin from the outside of the fillet, then cut it across into ⅛ in-thick slices. Divide into four portions (two if serving as a main course) and spread each of these in a single layer on a piece of parchment paper. Cover with another sheet of paper and smack with the flat of a heavy knife until you have a thin, even *carpaccio* under ¹⁄₁₆ in thick. If you can't get the slices thin enough this way, roll heavily with a rolling pin.

Sprinkle wide, flat plates with a little freshly ground pepper (the dish looks better without pepper on top). Removing the top leaf of paper, overturn each portion on to the centre of a peppered plate, then peel off the remaining sheet. Season with a sprinkling of salt. Thinly slice the artichokes lengthways, and scatter these over the *carpaccio* along with the Parmesan shavings. Drizzle with the oil, and serve with wedges of lemon on the side.

OYSTERS WITH CAPERS AND WHITE BALSAMIC
VENETO

A South African friend of mine once described swimming on the Cape beaches at Clifton – the jarring ice-cold salty sea in contrast to the baking sun – as 'like eating an oyster'. Well, eating a raw oyster is just like jumping into the cold sea on a hot day – saline, and shockingly refreshing.

Here paired with capers, watch out for the saltiness. Some oysters are saltier than others, but in any case make sure your capers are well soaked, lest the dish cross the line between refreshing and desiccating your mouth.

Serves 1 (as a large starter) to 12 (as a canapé)

12 small, plump oysters in their shells
3 tablespoons salted capers (best the fat ones from Pantelleria), soaked until only mildly salty
3 tablespoons white balsamic vinegar

3 tablespoons finely chopped chives

To serve
Crushed ice
Lemon wedges

Shuck the oysters: you'll need either an oyster knife, or a medium flat-headed screwdriver and a paring knife. Hold an oyster in a carefully folded kitchen towel to protect your hand. Force the tip of the oyster knife or screwdriver into the hinge of the oyster and twist sharply to pop it open. Slide the blade of your knife along the inside of the flatter shell to cut it off. Use the tip of your knife to carefully cut the body of the oyster from the bowl-shaped shell, taking care not to disturb the delicate fringe-like lips, nor to spill the delicious juices.

Make a bed of crushed ice on a deep plate, and balance the opened oysters on this. Top each one with a couple of capers, a few drops of vinegar and a tiny sprinkling of chives. Serve with lemon wedges.

CRUDITÀ DI MARE / RAW LANGOUSTINE, SHRIMP, BREAM AND SCALLOP VENETO

At Da Fiore in Venice (where I have eaten a few of the seminal meals of my life, see pages 127 and 296), I once had a *carpaccio* of sea bass with a hint of rosemary. I cannot begin to tell you how good it was, or indeed how good the dish below is. You need very fresh seafood, of course, but other than that you can't go wrong.

Serves 4 as a starter, 2 as a main

4 live langoustines
8 small raw shell-on shrimp
  (preferably *gamberi rossi*, red ones)
4 fresh, large dry-cut scallops
  (i.e. not soaked)
1 skin-on fillet of a small sea bass or sea
  bream (a 7oz fillet)

Lemon wedges, to serve

Rosemary oil
1 tablespoon finely chopped
  rosemary leaves
¼ small garlic clove, sliced
¼ cup extra virgin olive oil

First make the rosemary oil. Pound the rosemary and garlic in a mortar and pestle with a good pinch of salt and a small one of pepper. Transfer to a tiny teacup (or tiny pan), add the oil and heat for a few seconds in a microwave (or on a low flame) until it only just begins to bubble, but doesn't really fry (the idea being to take away the aggressive rawness of the garlic and herb, but leave the flavour fresh and seemingly uncooked). Let cool before using.

Take the langoustines and put them out of their misery by splitting their heads in half with a knife. Blanch the tails (holding the heads above water) in boiling water for *literally* 3–4 seconds: this leaves them raw, but makes them easier to peel. Refresh in iced water, and either split in half (to serve on the shell) or don't, instead peeling the tails but leaving the end tail-fin attached for presentation.

Now attack the rest of the seafood. Shell the shrimp, again leaving the tail attached. Remove the tough ligament from the scallops, and discard along with any corals. Slice the white meat across into perfect, 1/16in-thick discs. Pin-bone the fish and place it skin-side down on a board. Using a razor-sharp knife, cut at a shallow angle to the board towards the tail end of the fillet, to make a *carpaccio* of the fish – thin, even slices, about 1/16in thick.

Arrange the seafood flat on a cool plate. Sprinkle lightly with salt (except the langoustines, which come perfectly seasoned from the sea), drizzle with the rosemary oil and serve with wedges of lemon on the side.

CASTELFRANCO, TREVISO AND ALMOND OR HAZELNUT SALAD VENETO

Bitterness, almost a negative word, is highly prized by the Italian palate. The *radicchio/endive* family is a homage to bitterness and is full of the crunchy, refreshing and delicious. In this salad I use *castelfranco* (from Castelfranco Veneto), whose yellow leaves marbled with purple-red specks remind me of the variegated tulips that were once worth entire fortunes. To rival it in beauty and deliciousness, *treviso tardivo* (from Treviso) has long, curling leaves like a cock's tail with purple blades and bone-white quills.

Serves 4 as a starter, or 4–8 as a side

1 head *castelfranco* (or *radicchio*)
1 head *treviso tardivo* (or *arugula*)
⅓ cup shelled hazelnuts or skin-on almonds, toasted and very roughly chopped

Dressing
1 shallot
1 garlic clove
¾ cup red wine
3 tablespoons red wine vinegar
1 tablespoon thyme leaves
½ cup extra virgin olive oil

To make the dressing, slice the shallot across into thin rings, and the clove of garlic lengthways, both as thinly as possible. In a small saucepan, boil these in the red wine until it has reduced to all-but-nothing, a bare teaspoonful or two remaining. Remove from the heat, add the vinegar, thyme leaves and oil and season with salt and pepper. Let cool before using.

Break the leaves of the *castelfranco* and *treviso tardivo* from the base of the lettuces, but be sure to leave them whole and undamaged – they are things of beauty! Wash them gently and only if necessary. When you are ready to serve, toss with the dressing, and season with additional salt to taste. Serve piled on a plate, scattered with the toasted nuts.

SHAVED RADISH AND CELERIAC SALAD WITH POMEGRANATE, PECORINO AND TRUFFLE OIL

Unlike most of the recipes in this book, this dish is an original contrivance. I had a flash of inspiration years ago, at Boulevard (the Great Restaurant in San Francisco, and once second home to me) where I had to make something new for the menu and had only glorious watermelon radishes to work with. I made a salad of these red-and-green wonders, shaved thinly, with slivers of fresh truffle and Parmesan and dressed simply with olive oil. Necessity is the mother of invention, and I have been making versions of this salad ever since. The earthy flavours of this dish (ewe's milk cheese, radish, celery root and truffle) evoke central Italy to me, and in particular Umbrian soil. These low tones contrast well with the highs of pomegranate, parsley and vinegar.

The vinegar in particular is worth mentioning. White balsamic is, depending on your viewpoint, either a modern interpretation or a modern corruption of a traditional product. I always felt ambivalent about it, until I tasted a particularly fine one, aged for five years in ash barrels, that rubbished its detractors.

Serves 4 as a starter

1 bunch radishes (about 8)
½ black radish, or scant 2in daikon radish, about 5oz in either case
A chunk of celery root, about ¼ very small bulb, peeled (about 2oz)
A little chunk of Pecorino Romano cheese (about 2oz)
¼ pomegranate, seeds picked out, or ½ cup seeds

Leaves from a few sprigs of flat-leaf parsley

Dressing
1 tablespoon white truffle oil
7 tablespoons extra virgin olive oil
1 tablespoon white balsamic vinegar
Juice of ¼ lemon (or 2 more teaspoons white balsamic)

Make a dressing with the oils, vinegar, lemon, salt and pepper. Taste for seasoning.

Do the following just before you serve, as radishes dry out, and celery root blackens with time. Wash the radishes (both red and black, don't peel either), and shave thinly – best on a mandoline. Use a potato peeler to shave the celery root and Pecorino. Toss the lot with the pomegranate seeds and parsley, and dress lightly.

Serve in haphazard but tall piles on individual plates, or in a bowl to share from.

RAW AND COOKED FAVA BEANS WITH LEMON, MINT AND RICOTTA LE MARCHE

I like fava beans best as they start to swell, when they are neither tiny nor over-ripe and starchy. Inevitably, the shells yield some little ones and some bigger ones. This simple salad has a pleasing economy, as both are used to best effect – the large beans boiled until just cooked, and the baby ones raw, crunchy, and slightly bitter. I dress the salad with lemon and mint, as it is a favourite not only of mine, but also of David Cook – once my right-hand man – who put this dish on the menu as soon as the first *fave* hit the market. In Le Marche, it is often served with an anchovy dressing instead, like the one I serve with *puntarelle* (page 323).

Serves 2 as a starter, 2–4 as a side

2 ³/₄lbs fresh fava beans in their shells (or 2 cups shelled)
1 lemon
1 sprig mint

¼ cup extra virgin olive oil
3 tablespoons fresh or smoked sheep's milk ricotta (optional)

Shell the fava beans, separating the little (smaller than a fingernail) from the large. Boil the large for 1 minute in unsalted water, until the flesh within has turned from a pastel to a deep green. Refresh in iced water, then shell the cooked bigger beans (leave the raw tinies in their skins).

Only when you are ready to serve, toss all the beans together with the juice and a few scrapings of zest from the lemon, the shredded mint leaves, the oil, salt and pepper. Serve with the ricotta crumbled on top.

RAW OVOLI, PORCINI OR CREMINI SALAD WITH CELERY LAZIO

Ovoli mushrooms, *Amanita caesarea,* have a delicate taste and are wonderful. Picked young, as the bright orange cap emerges from its white sarcophagus, they look just like hatching eggs. To say they are hard to find would be a gross understatement, but other mushrooms can make this salad just as good. In particular *porcini* (as pictured here, also known as ceps), if young and firm, are delicious raw; even the humble cremini mushroom would make this a pleasing dish.

Serves 4 as a starter, 2 as a light main

½lb *ovoli*, *porcini* or cremini mushrooms, no more than 2½in long
4 celery stalks

Leaves from 3–4 sprigs flat-leaf parsley
⅓ cup extra virgin olive oil
3 tablespoons lemon juice, or a little more to taste

Clean any dirt from the bases of the mushrooms with a paring knife, and wipe the caps gently with a damp cloth if necessary – don't wash them. Slice them finely, around ⅛in thick, and also slice the celery stalks on the bias to around the same thickness.

Spread the celery and mushrooms thinly on a plate, scatter with the parsley leaves, salt and pepper to taste, then drizzle with the oil and lemon. Serve quickly, before the salt draws the juices from the vegetables and leaves the salad wet and limp.

MOZZARELLA
CAMPANIA

The trick to great mozzarella is finding it. I only eat buffalo mozzarella raw: with its creaminess, slight acidity and incredible texture it must surely be one of the finest things on earth, or at least when it is good. But so many things can go wrong – the milk may not be pure, it may be under-salted, the curds cooked to too high a temperature before shaping, worked too much or too little, and worst of all it may not be fresh.

Purists say to eat mozzarella on the day it's made, preferably still a little warm. At this point, it can be so firm as to squeak against your teeth, and I have to say I normally prefer it the day after. It is marginally better without being refrigerated: and on those occasions I can buy it fresh, I keep it out of the refrigerator and eat it within 36 hours. Most, if not all, of the Italian mozzarella you can buy has been refrigerated, and this should be kept in the fridge until you use it. Buffalo mozzarella should always be sold swimming in its whey; it should be bright white with a smooth, glossy skin. Avoid any that look wrinkly, or whose skins peel like bad sunburn when rubbed – they are old. The texture should be quite firm, bouncy, and fibrous when torn. When you cut one open, a milky white liquid should ooze out – but more on that later.

In the UK and the US I have come across a number of companies farming and making their own buffalo mozzarella. I applaud the sentiment (local and fresher), and wish them luck, but have yet to taste a product that compares with a top-quality Italian one.

Most importantly, when you find a mozzarella that you like, make mental note both of the brand you buy and the shop it came from – and stick to it! Even in the mozzarella capital of the world – Campania, around Mondragone and Caserta – quality varies, and everyone has a personal favourite. Some are firmer, others more giving, some stronger, etc. Unless you are lucky enough to obtain mozzarella on the day of making, eat it as soon as you buy it, as it will never be as great tomorrow.

I eat my mozzarella simply, with good oil, or with arugula and good oil, or with tomatoes and more good oil (and maybe a leaf of basil too). The first bite is bliss, but the very best comes at the end, when I dip a thick, chewy, almost burned crust of bread in the mixture of buffalo milk and oil that swims in the bottom of my plate, sometimes peppered with stray tomato seeds. This is the ambrosia that spurs me on to take yet another gleaming sphere of cheese from the bowl of whey in the centre of the table, just so that I can savour that final moment again.

RICOTTA WITH WALNUTS AND ARUGULA
PUGLIA

The combination of ricotta, walnuts and oil is one of those perfect things. I first met it in its natural habitat at a rather glorious restaurant, Oasis in Puglia, in the form below. There they served little wicker baskets of ricotta, still warm from the making. Be sure to use the best you can find – pure sheep's milk if possible. Just as good as fresh ricotta is the lightly salted and smoked ricotta *affumicata* that is less readily available but stores better.

Serves 4 as a starter, 2 as a main

³/₄ lb fresh or smoked sheep's milk ricotta
2 bunches wild arugula, washed
  (about ¼ lb)

²/₃ cup shelled walnuts
½ cup extra virgin olive oil

Serve the ricotta in thick slices, mounding the undressed arugula and walnuts in separate, adjacent piles. Sprinkle salt and drizzle the oil over everything; serve with or without bread.

SEA URCHINS
PUGLIA

I am a realist: you are not going to find urchins at your local fishmonger's. But I hope this recipe (if it is even a recipe) may help some readers, next time they see urchins on a menu or find their own whilst paddling or snorkelling on holiday, to pluck up courage and tuck in. They are best from September until March, getting progressively riper until they spawn and empty.

You will need urchins, scissors, lemon and a teaspoon. You will not need gloves, unless you are clumsy.

Pluck an urchin from the sea. Hold it upside-down (the underside is flatter with shorter spines), gently cupped in your hand. Do not squeeze, for obvious reasons.

The mouth is at the centre of this underside (urchins live with their bottoms up). Plunge one blade of your opened scissors into the mouth, and snip to reach the outside, then around to cut out a circle of spiny shell, which you discard.

Rinse out the shell gently, in the seawater the urchin just came from. Clinging to the inside of the shell, in the shape of a star, should be five tongues of orange. Squeeze a little lemon and eat the orange bits with your spoon. Delicious, if risky work.

The orange gonads are also delicious stirred through pasta (*tagliolini* or *spaghetti*) with butter and lemon zest, a hint of nutmeg and a scattering of toasted breadcrumbs.

TUNA TARTARE WITH ORANGE, CAPERS AND PINE NUTS SICILY

Sea and sunshine. This dish is about as Sicilian as it gets: capers (the best are from nearby Pantelleria), oranges, pine nuts and the tuna that gets these islanders so excited. The flavours are fresh, zingy and intense. It is impossible to say if this recipe is traditional, or one I made up – everything is so typical, it would be hard to imagine it hasn't been done before.

The tartare is very simple, so the quality of the ingredients is of utmost importance. Your tuna must be ruby-red and bright, best cut from the eye of the loin – any other parts will be sinewy and fiddly to dice. The capers should be fat and ripe, packed in salt. The olive oil should be fruity, preferably from Sicily, and the pine nuts Italian or Spanish (look for long ones, much more resinous and flavoursome than their Chinese counterparts).

Serves 4 as a starter, 2 as a light main

Some bread, preferably *ciabatta* or the like (enough for 12 very, very thin slices)
3 tablespoons pine nuts (preferably long ones)
3/4 lb prime tuna loin*

3 tablespoons salted capers, soaked until tolerably salty
1/4 cup extra virgin olive oil
Grated zest of 1/4 orange
1 tablespoon chopped flat-leaf parsley

*The ethics of eating tuna are confusing at the time of writing. I use 'sustainably' line-caught yellowfin or skipjack. You may prefer to use mackerel, which is also delicious, and undoubtedly plentiful.

Cut the bread into a dozen incredibly thin (1/16in) slices, and toast in a slow (320°F) oven until pale gold. Toast the pine nuts to the same colour. It is better to fry them barely submerged in oil, then drain them, but they can be done in the oven at the same time as the bread, even if this will dry them a little.

Dice the tuna into even 1/8in cubes. Practice and a sharp knife help.

Drain the capers, squeeze them dry and chop coarsely, then stir in the olive oil and orange zest along with a pinch of black pepper.

When you are about ready to eat, stir together the tuna, caper dressing, pine nuts and parsley. Taste for seasoning. Serve with the toast on the side.

CURED / SAUSAGES

Too often I've been told, on tasting the most delicious *salame*, of how this or that particular rare breed of porker was fattened for months on a diet of pears and acorns, or Parmesan whey, or mermaid's tears, which gave it its special delicacy, complexity and sweetness.

True, acorns fed to the *salame*-pig make the flesh subtly nutty, and dairy makes it subtly sweet, while mermaid's tears might render it salty, or lend a bouquet of sardines... But if you're making a *salame* it is *your* hand that will make it sing. The fennel seeds you add to the meat make it fennely, chili makes it hot, fat makes it rich and salt makes it salty. Subtleties are all well and good, but the big things count for more. Here process is crucial: which cut is selected, how it is ground, seasoned, kneaded and cured. Understanding and care are even more precious than the ingredients themselves. With decent pork, a decent recipe and a lot of time you can make a sausage as good as any you could buy – and it will taste better still to you, perfumed with that most elusive and valuable spice, the satisfaction of creating something yourself.

Pigs were long the mainstay of household livestock. This may be because their flesh is so well suited to preserving, or perhaps we have come up with so many ways of keeping the meat because it was such a common and important beast. But we have long salted, dried, cured and pickled everything: leaves, seeds, flowers, mammals, birds and fishes. All types of curing are ancient, far pre-dating the Age of Refrigeration. That they remain current is testament to how refined they have become.

Serving *salumi*, cheeses, cured fish and pickled vegetables is always a delight. They work in almost any combination, in any season, and at any time of day. They can be enjoyed as a whole meal, or but a small course amongst many, with wine red or white or sparkling, or with beer. They are the least lonely food to eat alone, the most convivial to share. To prepare a meal that anyone can enjoy often leads to dumbing it down, eliminating idiosyncrasy and quality – look to the high street for proof. Cured foods are the opposite – the highest common denominator, food for everyone.

LARDO AND WALNUTS
PIEDMONT

Lardo, cured pork back fat, is one of those insanely naughty foodie delights. Famously from Colonnata in northern Tuscany, and also Arnad in Valle d'Aosta, it is made in most of the northerly regions. With a texture and flavour between *prosciutto* and butter, the unctuous pigginess marries beautifully with walnuts, each accentuating the other's taste. I first had this combination at Trattoria Valenza in Turin, and put it on the menu the moment I returned home.

Serves 4 as a starter

5oz *lardo*, thinly sliced
¼ cup shelled walnuts

Cover a plate with the slices of *lardo* in a single layer, and dust this with the walnuts, coarsely grated. It would be wise to have bread on the table.

SOPRASSATA DEI MEDICI / MUSCAT AND ORANGE BRAWN TUSCANY

When my parents spent a heavenly year in Panzano, Tuscany, they befriended a local butcher, about whom I loved to hear stories as I was growing up. He was a poet, musician and absolute vegetarian (or so I was told by my mother, who cannot tell a story without exaggerating – his vegetarian, macrobiotic phase actually lasted only eight weeks). Years later I paid homage to him with my father. Entering his white marble temple to meat, I met the high priest himself.

Dario Cecchini is a huge, looming, ursine, grinning joy to behold. Known as the poet-butcher of Chianti, he is now world-famous, and we have a few foodie friends in common. I ate his *soprassata dei Medici* – an ancient, heavily porky and headily aromatic brawn he has revived – and fell in love with it. I never managed to spend time with him to learn his secrets, but Dario has offered the next best thing, and sent over the very recipe he uses, in what is known to the *cognoscenti* as the best butcher's shop in the world. He tells me it has never been written down before, so here is a world exclusive... In Dario's words, '*My version belongs to the Renaissance tradition, when taste called for contrasts as much as well-balanced flavours. Ingredients include sea salt, strong black pepper, four Tuscan herbs (clove, cinnamon, nutmeg and coriander), orange zest and Vin Santo. Prepared plain and simple without the addition of any preserving agents, it is superb served cut into cubes and sprinkled with Vin Santo and/or orange juice.*'

Serves 20 as a starter

The feet and head of a pig	**Ground black pepper**
10 bay leaves	**Ground cloves**
Salt	**Ground nutmeg**
Vin Santo	
Oranges	*To serve*
Ground cinnamon	**Grated orange zest**
Ground coriander	**Orange juice or Vin Santo**

Put the pig's feet and head in a large pot with the bay leaves – add no salt. Cover with cold water and set over a medium heat. When the pot comes to a simmer, turn the heat down so low that only the occasional bubble comes to the surface, and cook for 5 hours, until the meat is falling from the bone. Top up the water if it runs low. Lift the pork extremities from the water, leave to cool until you can handle them, and pick all the meat, skin, and tendon fastidiously from the bone. Make sure you get the tongue, jowl, snout and ears – everything other than bone, nail or brain.

Weigh this picked, gelatinous mess. Per 2 generous pounds, add generous 2 tablespoons salt, 3 tablespoons Vin Santo, the grated zest of an orange, ½ teaspoon each of cinnamon, coriander and black pepper, a rounded ¼ teaspoon of clove, and ¼ teaspoon of nutmeg. Mix together well.

Take a sheet of muslin (or an old sheet) and drape it over a bowl. Put in the meat, and bring together the edges of the cloth, twisting them together ever-so-tightly to make a taut sphere. Put this between two plates, and press it under a weight in the fridge overnight.

Serve the *soprassata* cut into rough ½in cubes, sprinkled with just a touch of orange zest, doused with either orange juice or Vin Santo; have a hunk of toast on the side.

Variation: Warm *Soprassata* Salad Put the cubes of *soprassata* in the bottom of a soup bowl – around 3oz per portion. Spoon boiling hot cooked chickpeas, drained of their liquor, over the top and leave to sit for a minute, so the gelatin can melt, before serving with a little sliced red onion on top.

TONNO DEL CHIANTI / 'TUNA' MADE FROM PORK TUSCANY

Another of Dario's recipes, this one for Tuscan 'tuna'. It is made from pork, but then Chianti is not exactly close to the sea, and therefore not exactly famous for its seafood. Cooked slowly, like tuna is in the can, the taste is remarkably similar. I serve it as a tepid salad with white beans and onion (overleaf).

Again, the recipe has never been written down before – but Dario sent the description from his official trademark, which is rather detailed, and I have tried to elicit from it a recipe that works at home. Note the meat cooks for a good eight hours – best to start it in the morning, so you can finish the preparation that night, or the morning after.

Serves 20 or so, as a starter

1 pork shoulder or leg, boned
20 bay leaves

1 bottle white wine
Olive oil or sunflower oil

Take the pork, and rub it liberally with salt – about 3 tablespoons per 2lbs. Find something it can drain on (say, an upturned plate stood in a bowl) and leave it in the fridge for 3–4 days.

Rinse the pork under running water, pat it dry, and put it in a snug-fitting pot or metal container. Tuck 10 of the bay leaves around it, add the wine, and just enough water to cover. Weigh the meat down with a couple of small plates, and cover with a tight-fitting lid. Set this pot inside a larger one, filled with water, and cook either on top of the stove or in the oven. In either case, as soon as the water jacket comes to a simmer, turn the heat down to low (low flame under pot, or set the oven to 275°F) and cook for 8 hours, checking hourly that the outer pot hasn't boiled dry. At the end of this day's cooking, turn off the heat and let cool at room temperature in the pot – a few hours, or overnight if you prefer.

When cool enough to handle, lift out the meat. Save the stock, which is a flavoursome base for a future soup or stew. Working carefully with your fingers, start to clean the individual muscles from the joint – remove and discard all traces of fat and skin. Try not to break them, but leave them intact and beautiful.

Put these separated muscles in a heatproof container, tuck the remaining bay leaves between and cover in the oil. If you wanted to sterilise the meat, and keep it for months, you could recook it in canning jars, or sealable vacuum bags, in a boiling water bath, until very hot through. I just warm it in a saucepan so the flavours infuse, then keep the meat under oil in the fridge until it's used up – the work of a week or two.

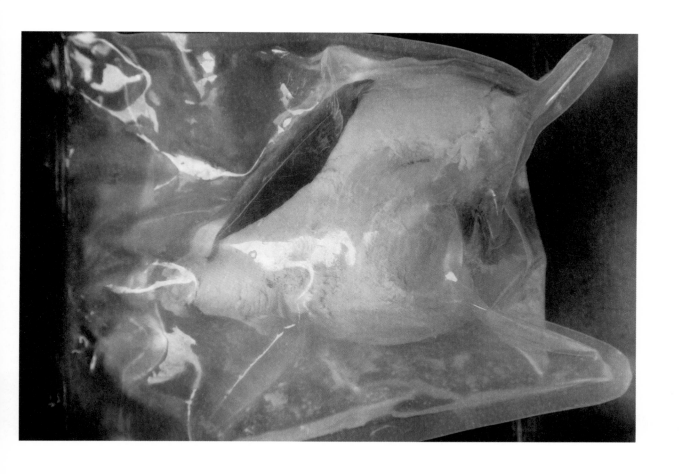

TUNA AND BEAN SALAD
TUSCANY

This simple salad is a true Tuscan classic, and is a wonderful choice for a summer lunch, especially a picnic. It can be made with quality canned tuna, or with *tonno del Chianti* (previous page). In season, ripe tomatoes make a satisfying addition; around the same time of year use fresh cannellini beans if you can get them, otherwise canned or dried will be fine.

Serves 4 as a starter, 2 as a main

3 cups drained cooked cannellini beans (room temperature)
1/3 cup chopped flat-leaf parsley
1/2 cup extra virgin olive oil
1/4 cup red wine vinegar

1/3 cup finely chopped red onion
7oz drained *tonno del Chianti* (previous page), or canned *ventresca* (tuna belly)

Dress the beans with the parsley, oil, vinegar and half the onions, seasoning with salt and pepper to taste. Crumble the 'tuna' or tuna into chunks over the beans, and serve with the remaining onion on top.

SARDINE 'IN SAOR' / SARDINES PICKLED WITH ONIONS VENETO

This recipe is one of the great classics of Venetian cuisine, and you'll find it in almost every *bacaro*, *osteria* and restaurant in the region, from the humblest to the most aloof. The preparation varies a little (some add pine nuts and raisins, some don't), but the combination of the sweet onions, biting vinegar and strong oily fish is irresistible. The quantity given here is not the smallest, but the fish are pickled by the end of the preparation and will keep for 5 days in the fridge.

Serves 8 as a starter, 4 as a main

2 ½lbs fresh, smallish sardines
3 teaspoons fine sea salt
All-purpose flour, for dusting
½ cup extra virgin olive oil
7 medium white onions
1 ¼ cups white wine vinegar

¼ cup raisins (optional)
¼ cup pine nuts, the long Italian or Spanish ones (optional, but compulsory if using raisins)
Toasted bread, to serve

First clean the sardines: rub them with your thumb from tail to head under running water to remove any scales, and pull out the guts with your fingers, leaving the heads on. Blot them dry with a paper towel and season with half the salt. Coat in the flour, then shake off any excess to leave only a light dusting. Heat half the oil in a wide pan over the highest heat until smoking hot, then brown the sardines for under a minute on each side – they must be coloured on the outside, but not cooked through. Set aside.

Slice the onions across into ¼in-thick half-moons, and fry with the remaining salt in the remaining oil for around 10 minutes over a medium heat, until softened and translucent but still as white as ivory. Remove from the heat and add the vinegar, and the raisins and pine nuts if using. Layer this marinade with the fish in a non-reactive dish (ceramic, Pyrex, plastic or stainless steel), being sure to start and finish with a layer of marinade. Refrigerate for at least 12 hours.

Remove as many sardines as you need along with their fair share of marinade from the fridge half an hour before serving, so they may reach room temperature before being consumed with toast.

ANCHOVY, HERRING, RADISH AND BUTTER
LOMBARDY

I ate this plate at Masuelli San Marco in Milan. The restaurant is staunchly traditionalist and wonderful, a real must on any visit. The combination of cured fish, butter and radish seems more Scandinavian than Italian. But as you travel further north in Italy, so the people seem less sunny, almost less 'Italian', and so does their food. Preserved fish (salted, smoked or dried) is still more prevalent than fresh in Lombard cooking, despite Milan being home to Italy's largest fish market today. The local cuisine dates from a time when fresh fish was hard to transport without spoiling.

Serves 4 as a starter

2 large, cold-smoked (uncooked)
   herrings
6 whole salted anchovies

8 radishes
¼ cup unsalted butter, chilled
Bread, perhaps toasted, to serve

Fillet the herrings and taste a little bit. If they are very salty, soak them for half an hour in water. Fillet the anchovies under gently running water, using the tip of your thumb and prising the fillets off the spine, starting from the belly. Drain them immediately. Wash and halve the radishes.

Arrange the filleted fish, radishes and slices of butter on a plate, and sprinkle a tiny amount of salt over the radishes and butter. Serve simply with fresh or toasted bread, a knife and a glass of light red wine.

SAUSAGE-MAKING, AN OVERVIEW

Most sausages are made from pork, with a fairly high fat content to keep them succulent. Seasonings are simple (predominantly salt) and delicate – a little spice goes a long way. Whilst the British banger contains a good deal of starch (normally as rusk), Italian sausages are pure pork, and all the better for it. Making sausages at home could be seen as a hassle, or a delight. I was scared of the process until I studied it, but now find sausagery to be one of the most rewarding pastimes. It is very primal, and the results breathtakingly delicious.

Rural families across Europe still slaughter their pig in autumn. They consume some of the flesh roasted or grilled, turn some into fresh sausages, and preserve the rest as *salami* and cured joints of meat. That used for sausages is high in fat (perhaps 20 percent by weight, which appears an even higher content on visual inspection): belly and shoulder are common inclusions, along with the otherwise-hard-to-use neck and cheek. The pig, an important part of the household economy, will be fattened especially, fed on fruits and nuts that happily abound at the right time of year. Sausage-makers place real emphasis on this fattening process, and on the subtle flavours imbued by the particular foods provided to the pig (acorns in Tuscany, Parmesan whey in Emilia-Romagna).

This was a worry to me when I began making the odd sausage at home (something I now do almost daily at my restaurant): how could I make a great sausage without that 'special' meat? I was pleasantly surprised. Ingredients are important, but the process is even more so: using my own, lovingly developed recipes and ordinary (albeit ethically raised and good-quality) pork from everyday breeds produces an astonishing product, and one which truly amazes me every time I taste it. Results are achievable at home that knock the competition for six. There are a few distinct steps to making sausages.

Grinding and seasoning If you don't have a meat grinder, you can ask your butcher to grind the meat for you, in which case you should add the seasonings when you knead the meat. Otherwise, weigh your seasonings out before you grind – it is best to grind them in with the meat for an even mix.

The primary seasoning of all sausages is salt – simple rock or sea salt for fresh sausages. For cured sausages, a curing salt ('normal' salt mixed with nitrates or nitrites) is added. These minerals preserve the red colour of the meat and reduce the chances of bacteria (in particular, *Clostridium*, the cause of botulism) spoiling it. Nitrites give an instant cure – they are used for meats that won't have a long time to hang and develop the culture of bacteria and fungi that turns sausage into *salame*. Nitrites can be safely cooked at high temperatures. Nitrates, on the other hand, don't directly cure the meat but are gradually converted into curing nitrites by the living culture in a *salame* – think of them as a slow-release option. Nitrates have the disadvantage of turning into poisonous nitrosamines at high temperatures, so shouldn't be used to cure meats destined for the pan – *cotechino*,

guanciale, pancetta and the like. Both nitrites and nitrates are safe in concentrations below 200 ppm, but toxic in large quantities. To avoid poisoning your family, buy a proprietary curing salt, where the nitrous salts are mixed with sodium chloride (table salt), and any accidental overdose will render the meat inedible – intolerably salty. In the following recipes, 'curing salt for *salame*' indicates one such blend, based on nitrates, and 'curing salt for cooked meats' the nitrite equivalent. In modern *salame*-making, a culture of freeze-dried bacteria and fungal spores is also added, to give the 'good' microbes a head-start, and further diminish the chances of spoilage.

Spices (pepper, chili, fennel seed, nutmeg, cloves, etc) are also used to season sausages. Their flavours somehow amplify in the meat, so precision is vital when measuring them. An excess of only 2g, when measuring 2g of a spice, will double its quantity and dramatically affect the taste of the finished sausage. If you need a quantity smaller than your scales will be able to measure with precision, weigh more than you need (say four times – 8g in our example) and either divide it by eye (to take a quarter); or, with your scales, dilute the 8g spice in a known quantity of salt (say 40g), and weigh out the proportion needed (here, 12g), remembering to take account of the extra salt (use 10g less salt in the remainder of the recipe).

Precision also has its role to play in grinding – the grind of the meat (the size of the holes in the meat grinder plate, the metal disc the meat passes through) is important. Bigger holes give a coarser, more rustic texture – so be sure to specify if your butcher is grinding for you. If doing it at home, make certain that the meat is nice and cold before you start. Cut it into long strips, just narrow enough to fit into your grinder, then rub these with your seasoning. The grinder will draw such broad ribbons through with ease if the blade is sharp and the plate flat, and in doing so mix the seasonings evenly through the meat. The meat should be passed through the grinder once only.

Kneading The most important characteristic of a fine sausage is its bind – the way the particles of meat are attached to each other by kneading. The bind is what makes a sausage a succulent whole, as opposed to a little bag of ground meat that would, on cooking, turn to a mass of dryish meat particles drowning in their own liquid. It takes quite some effort to knead any quantity of meat properly (although by my reckoning, a sausage-maker of little experience can make his or her own body-weight in a day of grinding, kneading, stuffing and hanging). Sausage meat can be kneaded by machine – in a mixer with a dough hook – but the result will never be quite as lovely, nor your pride so great – so I recommend this only to the elderly and infirm, who have a good excuse. At the restaurant, I make batches of up to 300lbs at a time, so there really is no justification for the domestic cook to shirk at a couple of pounds. For that matter, it is worth making reasonable quantities at a time – I have scaled the recipes that follow down to what I deem to be the minimum practical, but at home I would never bother with less than 12lbs – if you concur, scale the recipes up.

The meat will only bind properly with the addition of salt and a little water (or wine), so be sure all the seasonings are in before you start. Turn the meat out in a great pile at one end of a clean work surface, preferably a sanitary one – marble or stainless steel. The best way to knead a quantity of meat reliably is to smear it repeatedly against the surface. Working with the palm of your hand against the worktop, gradually smear mini-handfuls of the meat along the work surface, working from one end of the mass of meat to the other until your whole pile has been transferred across the table. Repeat this process, back and forth, until the meat is well kneaded. That is to say the texture should have altered, the colour become paler, the mixture a little sticky, and there should be no notable change in its nature between kneadings (i.e. you reach a point where further kneading won't alter it). In general, eight times across the table will be right, by which time your arms and shoulders will be sore and your brow sweaty.

Stuffing Traditionally, sausages are stuffed into casings made from different sections of the intestine. Sheep's intestines are used for very thin sausages, and pigs' for fatter ones. Cured sausages (*salame*, *cotechino*, etc) are stuffed into cows' guts with unusual names – middles, bungs, and open ends. Commercial sausages are more often made in artificial (collagen or cellulose) casings, but I always use natural ones for texture and appearance, which should be soaked for an hour to de-salt and re-elasticise them. Running a little water through the casing will clean the inside, and keeping it, your hands and the worktop wet will provide lubrication and make the process almost inconceivably smoother: keep a small bowl or squeeze bottle to occasionally bathe work surface, sausage and nozzle in water. One end of the prepared casing is tied, and the other ruched over the nozzle of a stuffer – a mechanical piston that forces the sausage meat through its wide spout, packing it into the casing that feeds off the end. You should stuff your own sausages *if* you have a stuffer, but your butcher, if friendly and compassionate, will likely be willing to do this for you. Beef casings for *salami* are wide enough to fill by hand, if you prefer. In any event, it is critical that no pockets of air form inside sausages for curing, or the meat will spoil. Making sure the meat is well kneaded, and packing it firmly into the stuffer, should prevent this.

Linking Most fresh sausages, and some cured ones, are 'linked' – the long stuffed casing (1) twisted to make separate, smaller sausages. Some butchers just twist between each section, then tie a piece of string around each twist to keep the sausages separate, but I prefer a string-free technique, like making balloon animals. Starting from the tied end of the stuffed casing, twist (2) at three evenly spaced points to make three sausages. Fold the second and third of these together (3), then twist to join them into a pair (4). Make a fourth twist and fourth sausage, then feed this (and the long, trailing, unlinked length of filled casing) through the twisted pair (5) until the fourth sausage becomes a trio with the second and third, the twist at the top of the fourth sausage snapping in place (6) against the one between sausages two and three. Repeat this process (7, 8, 9) to make a chain of sausage-trios, each sausage holding another in place, until the entire length has been linked and the far end tied shut. Broad *salami,* rather than being linked, are tied around and around tightly with twine, to keep the meat from falling to one end as they hang. Small air bubbles between the meat and the skin can be removed by pricking with a toothpick, but this has to be done when the skin is wet or it will never adhere properly to the meat.

Curing Even 'fresh' Italian sausages are often hung for a few days to develop a more pungent flavour. Thin sausages (up to 1½in wide), carefully hung so as neither to touch each other nor anything else, will gradually ripen until aromatic and firm even at room temperature or in the fridge. Properly cured *salami* may be hung from anywhere between one and six months, during which period fungi and bacteria will ferment the meat, creating a mild acidity and converting the added nitrates into the nitrites that protect the meat. A white or pastel mould will grow over the skin, aiding the drying process and improving the flavour, while the sausage may lose up to one-third of its weight. Specific conditions are needed: neither too warm (the meat would rot) nor too cold (it wouldn't ferment fast enough), neither too wet (again, it would rot) nor too dry (the meat would lose water too fast, forming a hard crust on the outside and later becoming hollow and mouldy within). The ideal environment is the same as for storing wine: 57–61°F, 60–70 percent humidity.

Eating Sausages and *salami* are served in a number of ways (pages 90, 144, 158, 198, 207, 212 and 238) but always generously and with a wine light and refreshing enough to cut through the fattiness.

ITALIAN SAUSAGES AND SPICY SAUSAGES

Italian sausages have a very distinctive flavour – or at least the ones from central Italy do. A certain strength of pigginess results from a period of maturation, and a certain piquancy from the wine and from the chili. They are often very coarsely ground, although this is a matter of taste, and frequently flavoured with fennel seeds, which can only be a good thing. They are sometimes seasoned with curing salts, which makes them stay pink when cooked and look a little freaky. Outside of Italy, very tasty ones can be bought vacuum-packed in the better delicatessens, but be sure they have been imported from Italy. Outside of the country, no-one makes a great Italian *salsiccia*. No-one, that is, except *you*...

Makes about 10 fat sausages, enough for 5 as a main

1½lbs pork meat from the leg or shoulder
¾lb fatty meat from the belly (skinless)
¼ cup red wine
Generous 2 tablespoons salt
Scant ¼ teaspoon hot red pepper flakes
Scant ¼ teaspoon ground black pepper
¾ teaspoon whole fennel seeds

4 yards hog casing, soaked and
  run through with fresh water

Spicy sausages (optional)
An additional ¾ teaspoon hot red
  pepper flakes
1½ teaspoons unsmoked paprika

I like these sausages relatively coarse, for which the meat should be ground through a 5/32 in plate. Blue-blooded aristocrats may prefer it a little finer, say ¼in, whilst the coarsest of people might like the coarsest of grinds – 3/8 or even ½in. The meat could even be hand-cut with a knife. In any event, it must be mixed with the wine, salt and spices, then kneaded very well (page 68) until strongly bound. Left uncovered overnight in the fridge by purists, it may also be stuffed into casing immediately, then linked (page 70), and pricked only where necessary. The sausages are hung by professionals for 3–5 days in a cool cellar, but they do equally well spread out on a towel if you haven't room to hang, as long as they are uncovered and refrigerated. In this time, they will dry out slightly, darken and start to smell slightly sharp, when you'll know they're ready.

Such flavoursome sausages are versatile, and fantastic for making *ragù* (page 144), or braising with ribs (a similar recipe, page 212), or in a soup (page 191). They are decent for breakfast, great crumbled on pizza, but come into their own for a summer's lunch or dinner, split open (butterflied) and grilled over hot coals, then served with grilled *treviso* or *radicchio* (page 238), with *broccoli rabe* (page 336), wet polenta (page 303), grilled polenta (page 304), *panzanella* (toasted bread salad, page 311), *cannellini* or *borlotti* beans (pages 310 and 313), or a hunk of bread and good wine. In short, they go with almost anything.

LUGANEGA / AROMATIC SAUSAGE BY THE METRE VENETO

Luganega is a thin sausage, coiled like a snake – sheep's casing, being from smallish animals, should make it a scant ½in in diameter. Seasoned with *porcini*, cinnamon, nutmeg and cloves, it always makes me think of Christmas – but the lightness and delicacy of the meat is appropriate year-round.

The name derives from *Lucania*, the ancient name of today's Basilicata, but the sausage has gradually migrated towards the north. It is now available all over Italy, but more so at higher latitudes, and is celebrated in the Veneto. There it is eaten raw, or grilled, or crumbled up into *risotti*, or hung and dried and eaten as a snack. If you want to eat yours raw, be sure to use the freshest pork from a reputable supplier – if he looks like he might even have known the pig by name, it can only be a good thing. The recipe below will also be delicious cooked, but to use it in *risotti* replace one-quarter of the pork shoulder with belly meat, to add a little fat. When grilling the sausage, leave it pink (medium) in the middle, for extra succulence.

Makes 3 yards, enough for 4 as a main, or 8 as a starter or in a risotto

2lbs pork shoulder meat (skinless and boneless)
Generous 2 tablespoons salt
Scant ¼ teaspoon ground cloves
Scant ¼ teaspoon ground nutmeg
Scant ½ teaspoon ground cinnamon

1 teaspoon ground black pepper
1½ teaspoons dried *porcini* powder (if you can't get this, grind dried *porcini* mushrooms to a dust)
4 yards sheep's casing, soaked and run through with fresh water

Grind the meat through a ⅛in plate, and knead it (page 68) with the salt, spices and mushroom powder. Stuff it into the washed casing and coil it up into a giant spiral – there is no need to link it into individual sausages (indeed, to do so would somehow defeat the point). This will keep for a few days in the fridge – it is not hung and partially dried like other Italian sausages. If it is to be consumed raw, do so the day it is made, or the day after, but no later.

Break off sections of the sausage and use them as you need. A small nugget will do raw, as a snack – perhaps with toast. Longer pieces (about 14in for a starter, 30in as a main) should be coiled up tightly and secured with toothpicks before cooking on a very hot grill. Two minutes on each side will be long enough to leave the meat deliciously pink inside and the skin browned. Let them rest for a minute or two somewhere warm before serving, to make sure they aren't actually cold in the centre.

COTECHINO / BOILING SAUSAGE
EMILIA-ROMAGNA

Cotechino is an unusual sausage. Made partly from pig's skin (*cotica*), mixed with meat, fat and sometimes a little beef, it is cured like a *salame* for a minimum of a few weeks before being boiled for hours, until the tough pig's skin ground in with the meat turns soft, velvety and gelatinous, binding the sausage into a tender, aromatic whole. Few Italians would make their own these days, but it is well worth the effort – even in Italy, where one can purchase good raw, cured *cotechino* to boil oneself, a home-made version always comes up trumps. *Cotechino* is traditionally served in the festive period, especially with lentils and a fiery sweet *mostarda* (page 207) at New Year. It is also an essential part of *bollito misto* (page 198). *Cotechino* is made throughout the north of Italy; my recipe below, pure pork and made with pig's cheeks, is based on the Bolognese version.

Makes 3 x 12in *cotechini*, each enough for 6 as a starter or 3 as a main (the whole recipe serving 18 as a starter, or 9 as a main)

1¼lbs skin-on pig cheeks
1¼lbs skinless pork meat from the leg or shoulder
1¼lbs pork skin, with a little fat (¼in thickness) attached
3 tablespoons curing salt for cooked meats

2 tablespoons salt
Scant ¼ teaspoon nutmeg
1 teaspoon ground black pepper
3 x 16in lengths beef middle casing, soaked and run through with fresh water

The ingredients are a little unusual – some butchers apparently refuse to believe that pig's cheeks exist with the skin on – but they are very tasty indeed, with lots of glands and gnarly bits in the jowl that give an incredible roundness of flavour. If you can't get them, replace with a mixture of half skin and half meat.

The ingredients are also quite tough – pigskin makes excellent leather, after all – so some people boil the skin for a few minutes to soften it before cutting and grinding. I feel somewhat uneasy about mixing cooked and raw meat, let alone if they are to be left to hang together for a month – so I always grind everything from raw. Raw skin is too much for many meat grinders to cope with (the blade must be sharp and the motor strong as a pig), and I advise the domestic cook to have their butcher grind the meat and skin together, through a ⅛in plate. If you want to do it at home, use a razor-sharp knife to cut the cheeks, meat and skin into long, thin strips, make sure they are very cold indeed, and then pass them slowly through a good grinder to obtain fine, ⅛in grind.

Combine the ground meat with the salts and spices, and knead well as described on page 68: the mixture may become mushier than normal as a result of its high fat content. Tie one end of a length of casing and stuff it tightly, then tie the other end. A spiral of twine along the length of the sausage should be enough to help keep its shape – nothing too tight, as it won't lose a lot of volume when it hangs. Prick the skin anywhere you see little bubbles beneath the skin while it's still wet – even the most diligent of sausage-makers will get a bubble or two. Hang the *cotechini* for a minimum of 2 weeks and a maximum of 6 (perhaps 20 days or so – see page 70 for details of the ideal hanging environment), until the skin has a little mould and the texture is partially firmed. If they dry too much you'll only have to boil them longer, and too fresh will result in an only slightly milder-than-ideal flavour – so don't worry too much. When you judge them ready, cook what you need and freeze the rest.

Cook the sausages by simmering in water with a few vegetables for flavour – carrot, onion, celery and bay perhaps. One lone sausage in a lot of water will need salt added, but a potful of sausages will likely season their cooking water sufficiently by themselves. The sausages are simmered for around 1½–2 hours, depending on how dry they are – but are done when they are tender to the point of a wooden skewer. Peel the skin off when they're cooked, and slice the *cotechini* into ½in-thick rounds. They should be served in winter, hot, with plenty of lentils (page 207) or mashed potato (page 211) and something piquant like *mostarda* (as on page 306) or *salsa verde* (see *bagnet vert*, page 198). Leftovers are delicious grilled or pan-fried the next day.

CACCIATORE / THIN SALAMI FROM NORCIA
UMBRIA

Norcia, in Umbria, is a town so famous for sausages and *salami* that across Italy you might find, from time to time, shops called *Norcinerie* (sausage shops). They make every kind of sausage – from fresh little ones to massive *salami*. The easiest of their cured sausages to make is *cacciatore* – named after the hunter who might carry it as a snack. Its thin diameter means it cures quickly, with less time to spoil and a greater tolerance for less-than-perfect (cooler, warmer or drier than ideal) hanging conditions.

Makes around 1½lbs *cacciatore*, enough for 15 people to nibble on

1 garlic clove, crushed but whole
⅓ cup red wine
1lb pork shoulder or neck meat, ground scant ¼in
1lb pork belly meat, ground scant ¼in
A pinch of *salame* culture (optional)

2¾ tablespoons curing salt for *salame*
Scant ¼ teaspoon freshly ground black pepper
½ teaspoon hot red pepper flakes
32in beef middle casing, or 48in-wide hog casing, soaked and run through with fresh water

The day before, steep the garlic in the wine overnight, then discard the clove. (If you forgot, don't worry – omit the garlic and the sausage won't suffer.)

Combine all the ingredients (except the casing) and knead well (page 68) until the mixture is pale and sticky. Stuff it into the casing, being sure to exclude any air in the middle, and prick the skin with a toothpick anywhere you see bubbles between the skin and the meat (you must do this while the skin is still wet). Tie the ends very firmly – I use a single length of string running twice along the length of the sausage to help take the weight when it is hanging. A length of twine spiralled around this thin sausage should be enough to keep the meat in place. Hang it in a cool, dryish and pest-free place (a cellar or larder would be ideal) for a month or two, until firm, mouldy and delicious.

When ready, the sausage is best sliced quite thickly (⅛in) at an angle – *salame* always looks more elegant in longer slices. Serve it with bread and olives, perhaps some cheese and certainly some wine – something bubbly, or a refreshing red.

FINOCCHIONA / FENNEL SALAME
TUSCANY

Finocchiona is, to me, the perfect *salame,* delicately yet distinctly aromatic with fennel seeds, redolent of the Tuscan hills. This is a proper *salame,* broad and bold, requiring specialist ingredients, perfect drying conditions and a practised hand.

Makes 1 very large *finocchiona*, which should last a family a month of sporadic eating

7lbs pork leg meat, trimmed
2lbs pork belly meat
2lbs pork back fat
Generous 3/4 cup curing salt for *salame*

3/4 teaspoon *salame* culture (optional)
2 tablespoons whole black peppercorns
2½ tablespoons whole fennel seeds
1 beef 'open end' or 'bung' casing

For a fine texture, grind meat and fat through a ⅛in plate; for a coarse one, grind the leg and belly meat at 5/16in, and dice the fat by hand into rough ½in cubes. Add the seasonings and knead the meat (page 68). Soak the casing, and stretch it with your fist to its full width (this is rather gross, especially if you think about it). Tie one end firmly with thin but strong twine, and pack the filling in with force. Tie the other end tightly.

Before proceeding further, prick the sausage anywhere you see even the smallest bubble under the skin. Take a length of string five times longer than your sausage, and firmly tie it to one end of the *salame.* Twist to make a loop of the string, a little wider than the sausage, and feed it over the end of the salame, close to where it is tied on. Pull on the trailing end to tighten, and form another loop of string as before. Work this second loop around the sausage, 1½in further down from the first, tighten again and repeat until you reach the end of the salame, then tie it firmly. Cut two more lengths of string, each about three times as long as the *finocchiona*, and tie one at each end, like a long tail. Take one and start to feed it along the sausage, twisting it around the encircling string each time it crosses a loop. Pull it tightly, so the sausage pokes between the gaps in the string like cellulite through fishnets. When you reach the end of the sausage, work your way all the way back, then repeat with the other string. Make two short loops from the strands left at either end, by which to hang the *finocchiona*.

The *finocchiona* is best hung until just firm (normally 3–4 months – see page 70 for details of the best hanging environment), turning (upending) once a month to keep the meat evenly distributed, but not hard to the touch as, to my taste, it is better when still rosy pink and slightly moist. It should be sliced straight across, very thinly, and is delicious alone with bread, or in spring served with a slice of Tuscan Pecorino and some raw fava beans in their shells.

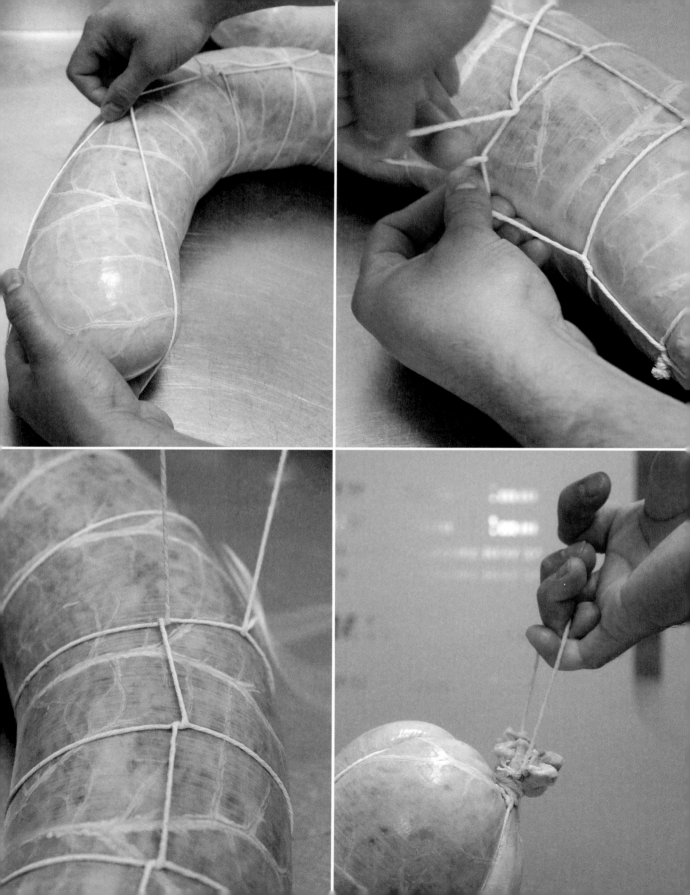

'NDUJA / EXTREMELY SPICY SALAME
CALABRIA

I have had the opportunity to work with a few Calabrians, elsewhere in Italy and back in Britain. They have been the salt of the earth, with deep black eyes, good wit and a fiery intensity that must surely be fuelled by chili. *Bacio di satana* (kiss of the devil), *diavulillo* (li'l devil) and other demonic names pepper dishes like *'nduja*, a soft *salame* made with as much as 30 percent chili *by weight*. Even Calabrian 'caviar' is hot – tiny white fish fry cured in salt and chili – but not as hot as *'nduja*...

I use smoked (Spanish) paprika, as *'nduja* is best lightly smoked, and this avoids the need to build a smoke-house.

Makes 1 large salame

2lbs skinless pork belly
4½lbs pork back fat
2lbs fresh red chilies
1⅓ cups hot red pepper flakes
Generous ½ cup smoked paprika
Generous ¾ cup curing salt for *salame*

Generous 2 tablespoons crushed
  black pepper
Generous 2 tablespoons whole
  fennel seeds
1 beef 'open end' or 'bung' casing

Grind all the pork finely, through a ⅛in plate. Cut the tops from the chilies but leave the seeds in (this sausage is to be *extremely* spicy – mine is even spicier than the Calabrian), and work them finely in a food processor. Combine all the ingredients (except the casing) and knead well – just as usual, but wearing rubber gloves as this is thermonuclear hot stuff. Prepare, fill and tie the casing as for *finocchiona* (previous page).

Hang for 4–6 weeks, until partially firmed but still malleable to a squeeze. (Longer won't hurt – look at the 3-month-old beauty opposite.) The sausage inside will be spreadable – great on toast, or pizzas, or in a pasta sauce (page 158). Given its fortitude, it should last quite a while, but I tend to eat it quickly (it is delicious) and do my stomach damage in the process.

FRIED

At my favourite little spot in Rome, the first course arrives: olives stuffed with veal and pork, artichokes opened like flowers, buffalo mozzarella, sticks of salt cod, zucchini, their golden blossoms, tender blood-red shrimp from the deepest waters and pale squid landed that very morning in tiny day-boats... Each and every one is deep-fried, delicious, and light as a feather.

Fried food does not have to be heavy. The fish and chips or fried chicken joint fries slowly in a stiff batter, to make a thick and crunchy coating, laden with oil, which keeps the encased flesh moist during the long cooking time and for hours under the heat lamps. But fry quickly in a thin coating and you will achieve the opposite, a dish which must be eaten immediately, but that is delicate and has absorbed a minimum of oil.

The type of fat you use for frying is important. Lard is tasty, and works at high or low temperatures, but imparts a distinctive flavour to the food. Olive oil is delicious, but tastes repulsive if scorched, so should never be used to fry above 300°F. Vegetable oil (rapeseed, sunflower, corn or grapeseed and the like) is neutral in taste and can be heated safely to 375°F: this is the commonest and normally best choice.

Frying is safe *if you know what you're doing*. The most common mistake I see is the apprehensive cook dropping ingredients from a height into the hot oil they so fear. The resulting splash is exactly what they're afraid of: food lowered in gently poses much less of a threat. As always, cook with confidence and you'll be fine. Water is your enemy, as even a small drop can boil violently and send the oil explosively everywhere. I always heat my pan first before adding oil, to make sure it's dry, and use dry utensils to transfer food to and from it. Frying food tends to bubble a lot, so never fill the pan more than one-third full of oil lest it go over the edge. Always get the oil to temperature before putting the food in. Should it all go to pot, turn off the heat and cover the very same with a lid. Try to do so calmly and, disaster averted, pretend it never happened.

Frying is not difficult, if you understand three things: temperature, seasoning and coating. *Temperature* is the most critical. Flash-fried foods are cooked at 375°F (as hot as oil can get safely), so they crisp quickly without over-cooking. Larger items are fried at 300–320°F, so they can cook longer before browning. Food poached under oil at around 210°F is called *confit*, and this is about the gentlest way to cook there is (oil holds less than half the heat of water at the same temperature). *Seasoning* early is vital. All but the tiniest of things (where a sprinkling of salt on the outside will suffice) should be seasoned before they're coated and fried. *Coating* protects the food from the oil, and is the bit that gets crispy. Batters can be delectable, but more often I use a *dredge* – a mixture of flours to coat with – for an infinitely thinner and lighter exterior. A delicate coating makes for a delicate dish: fish that remembers the sea, and vegetables that remind you of the sunshine.

FRITTO MISTO ALLA PIEMONTESE / MISCELLANY OF LAMB, SEMOLINA AND APPLE PIEDMONT

This dish is in fact a pared-down version of the Piedmontese classic, which might see a list of fruits and meats as long as your arm fried into a heart surgeon's nightmare. The recipe below may be somewhat simplified but it still requires considerable effort and planning. Do not be fooled into thinking it is any healthier.

Serves 4–6 as a starter, 2–3 as a main

¼lb calf's or lamb's sweetbreads
1 lamb's brain
4–6 frenched lamb chops
   (chops with the bones cleaned)
Vegetable oil, for frying
12 cubes *semolino dolce*
   (recipe below)
⅓ cup all-purpose flour
2 eggs, beaten
½ cup breadcrumbs (made from real bread)
1 small apple, or ½ big one
12 large sage leaves
3 tablespoons thick balsamic
   vinegar

Semolino dolce
¾ cup milk
3 tablespoons superfine sugar
1 strip lemon zest
6 tablespoons semolina flour
1 egg

Batter
Scant ½ cup all-purpose flour
3 tablespoons cornstarch
2 teaspoons extra virgin olive oil
A pinch of salt
1 teaspoon baking powder
Scant ½ cup beer

To make the *semolino dolce*, bring the milk and sugar to the boil with the lemon zest. Remove the zest and beat in the semolina over the heat with a wooden spoon. It will thicken quickly, but cook until it will thicken no more. Take it off the heat and beat in the egg while the semolina is still hot. Spread out ½in thick on a plate covered with plastic wrap to cool. When solidified, cut into ½in cubes.

Poach the sweetbreads and brain in a pan of already simmering salted water – a couple of bay leaves or sprigs of thyme might not go amiss. After 6–8 minutes, when just underdone, turn off the heat and leave to cool in their liquor. Peel off any gnarly membranes. Separate the two lobes of the brain and cut each in half again. Cut the sweetbreads into similar-sized pieces. Beat the chops out a little (they should end up like ¼–½in-thick lollipops). Make sure you have everything ready before you make the batter, and have started to heat a 2in depth of oil in a saucepan that's large enough to accommodate all the ingredients with room to spare.

To make the batter, mix together all the ingredients, adding the beer slowly and beating well to remove any lumps. When you have a thick paste, stir in the rest of the liquid. If you prefer a yeast batter, see page 94.

Heat the oil to 350°F – hot but not smoking. While it's warming, prepare the *fritto*.

The sweetbreads should be seasoned with salt and pepper, then well dusted in the flour. The brains, chops and *semolino* should all be seasoned, lightly dusted with flour and then dipped in the egg before being finally breadcrumbed.

When the oil has reached temperature, slice the apple into eight thin wedges. Dip these in the batter and lower into the oil. After they have fried for 2 minutes and are starting to look promising, add all the meats and *semolino* cubes (you can cook in batches if your pan's on the small side). Now coat the sage leaves in batter on one side only and lay them, batter-side down, on the surface of the oil. Fry everything for a further 2–3 minutes, until the breadcrumbs have turned golden brown and the sage leaves are crispy all the way through. Drain well and pile on to a serving dish. Drizzle with the vinegar and serve straightaway.

Variations Lambs' tongues should be boiled in a similar stock to the sweetbreads, but for over an hour until tender, and then peeled. Lamb's kidneys, pulled free of the caul fat, should be split in half and their white core removed. Lamb's liver can just be cut into fingers, if you remove the largest veins. All three can be breaded in addition to those above, for a more complete selection of a lamb's anatomy.

MOLECHE / TINY SOFT-SHELLED CRABS
VENETO

Venetians are renowned for their *moleche* – tiny soft-shelled crabs that make you believe God truly did create the natural world for our pleasure, even if only for a moment before they are all gone and a vague malaise kicks in.

Moleche are hard to find, even in the Veneto – but look out for them in good restaurants when you visit. The starting material for *moleche* is not your typical eating crab, but tiny green ones – like those that scuttle across rocks, scaring children but posing no threat – that live in the Venetian lagoon. As they swell to their peak autumn or spring size they become fat crabs in small shells, like fat men in thin suits. Fishermen collect them, and watch them like a hawk. When they shed their shells, they are whisked to market and sold, live, within a day or two before their new shell starts to harden. Their tiny size (that of a large spider) makes them come out so crisp, an ethereal crab popcorn, after a few minutes in oil. *Moleche* are a hundred times as appealing as the soft-shelled crabs you find elsewhere.

On those rare occasions that I am in a position to purchase and cook raw *moleche*, I moisten them in milk, then dust with flour and fry at 350–375°F for 3–4 minutes until very crispy, and serve either with wet white polenta (page 245) and $1/32$–$1/16$ in-thick slices of orange, dusted in flour and fried until crunchy, or raw blood oranges and mâche (page 296) – another combination picked up at Da Fiore (pages 39 and 127). Occasionally, I treat myself to a cheap ticket to Venice, just to eat them by the lagoon – as they simply cannot be found anywhere else.

CRESCENTINE FRITTE / FRIED BREADS WITH CURED MEATS AND CHEESE EMILIA-ROMAGNA

I was keen to see the kitchen at Autotreno, my favourite restaurant in Bologna, to study the local cuisine *in situ*. At its helm are two gorgeous ladies, there since the restaurant was kitted out in the 1970s attire it still wears so splendidly today. They are now bent double under the weight of the years, of all the meals they have cooked, of all the customers they have satisfied. And yet they go on, cooking as only they know how, that is to say, deliciously. But they are shy of the outside, and it took the persuasive powers of my friends Angela and Gianni of Gelatauro (page 415) to arrange an audience.

Once we were in, these doyennes of Bologna showed me how to make their *crescentine* – featherlight breads fried in lard. They served us a giant platter, a symphony of animal fats – the lard from frying, the melting fat on the *prosciutto*, and the tangy unctuousness of the Squacquerone cheese. They gave us a big bottle of sparkling Pignoletto. It was 9am, and that was breakfast. I knew it was going to be a good day.

Serves 4 as a starter, 2 as a main

Crescentine dough
1½ tablespoons dried yeast,
    or 2½ tablespoons fresh
Generous 1 cup lukewarm milk
3¾ cups Italian 00 flour
½ teaspoon salt
2oz lard

To fry and to serve
A mixture of lard and vegetable oil,
    14oz of one and 1½ cups of the other
¼lb Squacquerone or Stracchino cheese
8 thin slices *finocchiona* (fennel *salame*,
    page 80) and 4 thin slices *speck* (smoked
    prosciutto*), or 8 slices *prosciutto crudo

First make the *crescentine* dough. Disperse the yeast in the milk, then combine with the flour, salt and lard to make a dough. Knead it well until smooth and glossy, then let rise for about an hour until doubled in bulk.

Roll the dough out on a well-floured surface to make a sheet 3/32in thick. Cut out four diamonds, about 2¾ x 6in (trimmings can be used to make a simple bread, or extra *crescentine* that will be eaten in moments, I guarantee). Let rise for 20 minutes before cooking.

Heat the lard/oil mixture to 375°F (almost smoking). Fry the *crescentine*, turning when golden on the first side – a minute and a half or so in total. Drain well.

Dollop the cheese on to plates, and arrange the puffed breads alongside. Drape them with the *salumi* and serve immediately. Bound to put a smile on anyone's face.

OLIVE ASCOLANE / FRIED OLIVES STUFFED WITH PORK AND VEAL LE MARCHE

There is something decidedly retro about the idea of olives stuffed with mixed meats and fried: an image of something grey and tasteless from the 1970s comes to mind. These stuffed olives are the pride and joy of Ascolanans – they take a while to prepare properly, and some dexterity on the part of the cook (which, as you will read, I have yet to fully master). When made by hand with care and taste, they are sublimely delicious, with a complex, layered taste that titillates the palate.

In Rome, where the average traveller is more likely to meet them, these olives are a staple component of the *fritti* one might be served at any *pizzeria*. Even at the finest (my very favourite is Dal Paino on Via di Parione, where a simple *pizza bianca* strewn with zucchini flowers and sausage is manna from a fiery heaven), the *olive ascolane* aren't quite as good as those we can make ourselves. Often, one is under the impression they come to restaurants pre-prepared, perfectly spherical and frozen – not entirely unlike the 1970s dish I imagine. Mine are never perfect, as I can't figure out how to get enough stuffing inside one olive, or indeed how to get the stone out cleanly. Instead, I pare the flesh from the stone, then press it around a large marble-sized ball of filling. The resulting irregular form, like a cracked, fossilised dinosaur egg, is a very tasty nugget indeed.

Makes 20 stuffed olives, enough for 4–5 as a starter, but best in combination with some or all of the *fritti romani* on pages 94–102

40 very large green olives
   (in the absence of the Ascoli variety,
   use Cerignola or the like – they should
   weigh 12oz)
½ lb ground pork
½ lb ground veal
2 tablespoons butter
2oz *prosciutto* or *speck*, finely chopped
A pinch of grated nutmeg
½ cup rich beef stock (or water)

½ cup white wine
3oz Parmesan, freshly grated
1 teaspoon very finely chopped rosemary
   leaves
2 teaspoons finely chopped sage leaves
3 eggs
All-purpose flour, for dusting (about 1 cup)
1 cup breadcrumbs (made from real
   bread), for rolling
Vegetable oil, for frying

Pare the olives' flesh from the stones with a small, sharp knife, keeping the pieces as large as you can. Finely chop half of the pitted olives; set the rest aside.

In a skillet, fry the pork and veal in the butter over a high heat, stirring occasionally until all the meat is cooked, some of it has browned, and it starts to spit at you. Add the chopped *prosciutto* and nutmeg and let it fry for a minute more, then add the stock and the wine and allow it to boil away until the meat is still moist, but there is no visible liquid left. Transfer the mixture to a bowl and let it cool before adding the Parmesan, herbs and one of the eggs. Taste for seasoning, and check the texture – it should be moist, but stiff enough to form a ball that doesn't fall apart (if too runny, a judicious addition of breadcrumbs will solve the problem). Chill it in the fridge.

Take a lump of the filling, the size of a large marble, or a walnut's-worth, work it into a ball and press a few pared slices of olive on to the outside to cover it as best you can. Repeat until you have used up the filling and the olives. Spread the flour in a wide bowl or tray, the remaining two beaten eggs in another, and the breadcrumbs in a last. One-by-one, roll the re-formed olives in the flour, then the egg and finally the breadcrumbs. They can be refrigerated in this state until you are ready to use them, or fried straightaway in oil deep enough to cover them, slightly less hot than you might use to fry fish – 320–325°F should do the trick. After 4 minutes, when the outside is golden and the middle piping hot, they are ready to drain and serve – but only to your most favoured guests.

FRITTI ROMANI – FILETTI DI BACCALÀ / FRIED SALT COD LAZIO

Fried salt cod is one of many utterly delicious Roman *fritti*, and best at Filetti di Baccalà, a tiny restaurant near Campo de Fiori that bears the name of its signature dish. I prefer to salt my own cod (in fact, I now use pollack as it is just as good, cheaper and more world-friendly). I pin-bone the fillets before they are salted, which is much easier than after, then layer them with copious quantities of coarse salt for a few days before soaking them.

This recipe uses a yeast batter, which takes a little time to rise. For an instant alternative, use a tablespoon of baking powder in place of the yeast, and beer instead of water. The batter will be ready to use immediately this way.

Serves 4 as a starter, or more in combination with the other *fritti romani*

14oz salt cod or salted pollack fillet, soaked for 24 hours in two changes of fresh water
Vegetable oil, for frying
Lemon wedges, to serve

Batter
1 cup all-purpose flour
½ cup cornstarch
1½ tablespoons extra virgin olive oil
1 tablespoon dried yeast, or 2 tablespoons fresh
1 cup lukewarm water

Pin-bone the cod, unless you had the foresight to do it before salting, and cut it from the skin (place the fillet skin-side down on a board and use a thin knife, almost parallel to the board, working from the tail end). Cut it into batons about 1in wide by 4in long. Taste a little bit of it (it is delicious and safe raw). If it's too salty, return it to fresh water for a while. When it tastes good, blot it dry.

Make a batter by combining the flour and cornstarch in a bowl with the olive oil and yeast. Stir in enough of the water to make a thick paste that you can work just enough to get rid of any lumps, then add the remaining liquid in a steady stream. Let it rise for an hour, or until light and fluffy: once risen, it will keep at room temperature for a further 5 hours or so.

When you're ready to eat, heat a wide pan not more than a third full of vegetable oil, but deep enough to submerge the fish. You should let it reach 375°F – hot, but not quite hot enough to smoke. Dip the batons of fish into the batter, which should be thick enough to coat, but thin enough to do so thinly, then lower them gently into the oil. Fry for 3 minutes until golden brown, and serve on paper towels with lemon wedges and a cool beer. Delicious with fried zucchini (page 321).

FRITTI ROMANI – SUPPLÌ AL TELEFONO / TOMATO RICE CROQUETTES *LAZIO*

I love these Roman rice and mozzarella croquettes – not least for their name, which refers to the molten mozzarella's tendency to form unmanageable strands as you eat, not unlike telephone wires trailing from your mouth. The combination of tomato, basil and mozzarella is classic, and this dish is a staple appetiser at Roman *pizzerie*.

Makes about 20 *supplì* (enough for 5–7 as a starter)

1 smallish onion, diced
½ garlic clove, sliced
Generous 2 tablespoons salt
¼ cup extra virgin olive oil
1½ cups risotto rice (*vialone nano, arborio* or *carnaroli*)
¾ cup white wine
1½lbs fresh tomato, blended (seeds and all)

3 tablespoons freshly grated Parmesan
10 basil leaves, chopped at the last minute
1 whole egg
5oz mozzarella, cut into 20 even pieces
About 2 cups fine breadcrumbs (made with real bread)
Vegetable oil, for frying

Sweat the onion and garlic with the salt in the olive oil until tender, around 5 minutes, then add the rice and gently fry for another couple. Add the wine and cook until absorbed, stirring frequently, then the tomato and continue until the mixture is thick and dryish again. Add about ½ cup water and continue cooking (it should be just enough to make a fairly thick, and very *al dente* risotto). Remove from the heat and beat in the Parmesan, and finally the chopped basil, with pepper to taste. Spread the rice out on a tray to cool.

When you are ready to make the *supplì,* stir the egg into the rice. Take a portion of the rice mixture (about 1 tablespoon, or one-twentieth of the lot), shape into a ball and use your thumb to make a hole. Stuff a piece of mozzarella in, and close the rice around it. Press the ball together firmly, and form a fat, elongated croquette. Coat in breadcrumbs, and refrigerate until you are ready to eat.

To cook, heat at least 2in depth of oil until hot, but not smoking (300–350°F). Fry the *supplì* in batches, then drain on paper towels for a minute or so and serve immediately. It is vital they are hot through for the cheese to melt – about 4 minutes in the oil should do. The long strands of cheese that inevitably form as you eat encourage charming *Lady and the Tramp* moments...

FRITTI ROMANI – FIORI DI ZUCCA / FRIED ZUCCHINI FLOWERS LAZIO

The flowers of pretty much any edible pumpkin or squash are suitable for this dish, although zucchini flowers are the most traditional, and most readily available. Male flowers are best (they are cheaper, as their harvest does not take from the crop of zucchini – and they are lighter to eat). You could stuff them with almost anything (ricotta or goat's cheese are common fillings), but my firm favourite is the Roman classic, with mozzarella and anchovy.

Serves 4 as a starter, although I could probably eat the lot – these are very moreish...

8 zucchini flowers (male if possible)
¼lb mozzarella
4 anchovy fillets (approximately, anchovies vary in size, as do people's appetites for them)

4 basil leaves
Batter from the fried salt cod (page 94)

Remove the yellow stamens from the centre of the flowers, trying not to break the trumpet of petals. If the petals do rip, it isn't the end of the world – nor is leaving the stamens in if the flowers are fragile or your fingers all thumbs. Leave the stems on.

Cut the mozzarella in eight pieces, twice as long as they are wide, and drain any excess liquid. Cut each anchovy fillet in half, and halve the basil leaves. Make a little parcel of one piece of each, grind black pepper over liberally and stuff gently into the centre of a flower. Gently twist the petals together at the ends to hold the stuffing in, trying to avoid any exposed filling – the petals contain it within the batter, and any breaches can lead to molten mozzarella escaping into the oil. Repeat with all the flowers.

Heat at least a 1½in depth of oil until very hot (375°F). Pick up the first flower and coat it in the batter, then allow most to drip off (a thin coating is best – the dish, for all its calories, should seem light). Holding the flower by the stem, dip the head into the oil for a few seconds to set the batter before releasing – they look best if the twisted petals stay together and form a point. Fry, turning once until golden and crispy. Drain and eat quickly. A mixture of these and *supplì al telefono* makes a great and impressive *fritto misto*.

FRITTI ROMANI – BOCCONCINI FRITTI / FRIED BABY MOZZARELLA LAZIO

So simple, so delicious, and so messy – milky juices are spurting everywhere, and strands of molten cheese entangle the dinner table like an edible spider's web. I am in heaven, and will have just one more… and another…

Serves 4–5 as a starter, but best with other *fritti romani*, or *olive ascolane* (page 92)

20 buffalo mozzarella *bocconcini*, weighing 1– 1½oz each
All-purpose flour, for dusting (about 1 cup)
2 eggs, beaten

1 cup breadcrumbs (made from real bread), for rolling
Vegetable oil, for frying

Drain the *bocconcini* (baby mozzarella, literally 'little morsels') from their whey, dust them in flour, dip them in beaten egg, then roll them in breadcrumbs. At least, that's what I do – others dip them in a batter like the one on page 94.

Fry them in oil, heated to 350°F, and be attentive – they must cook until the coating (batter or breadcrumb, up to you) is golden, and the cheese more-or-less melted. But a minute too long and the milk they exude will boil, the steam forcing the liquid cheese from its hard and crispy shell into the oil and – disaster – you will be left with empty shells and cheesy oil. To avoid this, fry for about 2–3 minutes, and drain all the fried *bocconcini* as soon as they start to sizzle loudly after a minute of relative peace – a sign that the first drops of liquid are starting to escape, and the cheese within is cooked enough.

Rest for a minute in a warm place before serving, to give any cold cheese in the centre a chance to warm through, even if it doesn't melt fully.

FRITTI ROMANI — CARCIOFI ALLA GIUDIA / FRIED WHOLE ARTICHOKES LAZIO

I have always loved artichokes — my mother (who thinks she's Jewish) does, and her father (who was a Jew) did. My father (who is a Jew but doesn't realise he is one) does too — he probably acquired his love of these edible flowers from my mum, who in turn grew up with them almost as a staple food in 1950s Rome — so I guess they flow in my blood. I first encountered, and fell in love with, these *carciofi alla giudia* ('artichokes in the manner of the Jews') at Piperno in Rome. This preparation is at the core of Roman Jewish cuisine — a rich heritage, and one which is itself at the very heart of my own.

The artichokes should be as large as possible without having any tough choke. You are looking for buds about 2½–3in across, with tightly closed leaves.

Serves 4 as a starter or a side, best with fried sweetbreads (page 102)

8 artichokes
Juice of 1–2 lemons
About 2 quarts sunflower oil

Clean the artichokes (page 26) and keep them in water acidulated with lemon juice.

Drain the artichokes well — best if you blot them dry with a cloth. Season generously with fine salt and deep-fry slowly in at least a 2in depth of sunflower oil at 250–275°F (about 2 quarts in an 8in pan) for 15 minutes until completely tender when tested with a toothpick to the heart, but not falling apart. Remove from the oil and let cool.

These first two steps (cleaning and par-cooking) can be done in advance, the artichokes then keeping for a few days in the fridge. They even freeze well once cooked.

When you are ready to eat, reheat the artichoke oil until almost smoking (375°F). This is the hottest temperature it can safely be — great for flash-frying. Open the artichokes out into flowers by inserting your thumb in the middle, and gently working the leaves out flat like an open chrysanthemum. Fry them upside-down in the oil (lower them in gently to keep them from turning over) for a few minutes until the leaves turn an autumnal brown. Drain the artichokes well. As the oil may get trapped between the leaves, it is best to shake the artichokes as you lift them from the oil with a pair of tongs, then to blot upside-down on paper towels. Sprinkle with crunchy salt, and eat immediately.

FRITTI ROMANI – ANIMELLE FRITTE / FRIED SWEETBREADS LAZIO

Sweetbreads are rich enough as it is, and frying them takes the matter to a whole new level. With a very thin and crispy crust, however, they seem somehow lighter and more approachable: appearances can be deceptive. Everyone seems to think sweetbreads are the nuts or the nut – testicles or brain. Actually they are neither: sweetbreads are the thymus gland, present in all prepubescent mammals; they atrophy as we mature and their function is taken over by the thyroid. For such a seemingly obscure part of the offal they command an exceedingly high price – but that is because they form such a small part of the animal, and are so very delicious.

This recipe calls for calf's sweetbreads. Lamb's may be used too, and at a fraction of the price. In the latter case cook them *confit* (simmer gently under oil) for only 5 minutes, don't press them, and don't cut them into sticks. Otherwise, proceed as below.

Serves 4 as a starter, best with *carciofi alla giudia* (page 100)

1lb calf's sweetbreads
6 sprigs thyme
2 garlic cloves, broken open
1 lemon, cut into 8 wedges
Olive oil to cover the sweetbreads
  in a small pan (about 2 cups)

½ cup all-purpose flour
6 tablespoons semolina flour
Enough vegetable oil to fry them in –
  just over a quart, or a generous 1in
  depth in a wide pan

Pull off any thick membranes or exceptionally gnarly bits from the sweetbreads. Season them well with salt and pepper, and lay in a small saucepan with the thyme, garlic and half the lemon wedges. Cover with the olive oil and cook over the lowest of flames – glance at the clock when bubbles start to rise to the surface, then cook for a further 15 minutes or until the sweetbreads are somewhat firmed, but still a little wobbly and blushing pink. Let cool until tepid in the oil, then drain and place on a tray lined with parchment paper. Cover with another sheet of paper and then another tray, then refrigerate under a weight (you want to press them to a thickness of about ½in) until cool – a couple of hours, or overnight.

When ready to eat, cut the sweetbreads into sticks ¾in wide, and dust in a mixture of the flour and semolina flour. Heat the vegetable oil to 375°F, slip in the sweetbreads and fry until a pale golden brown. If you do as I counsel, and serve these with artichokes *alla giudia*, fry both in the same oil, artichokes going in first as they take longer. In any case, drain the fried, crisp sweetbreads well, sprinkle with salt, and serve with the remaining lemon wedges.

FRITTATA IN THE MANNER OF CARBONARA
LAZIO(ISH)

I invented this *frittata*, although I know it has been done before and it is so good – naughty but nice – that it will be done again. In essence, it is just an over-eggy *spaghetti carbonara* fried in a pan until it sets. Doesn't that just sound like the best idea? Necessity may be the mother of invention, but I believe this one is better explained by divine inspiration.

Guanciale, pork cheek and jowl cured like *pancetta*, is like bacon only better – more fatty, more piggy, more indulgent. Whilst it is hard to find, it is the correct ingredient for *carbonara*, *gricia* (page 148) and *amatriciana* – all the classic Roman pastas. *Pancetta* or unsmoked streaky bacon are acceptable substitutes.

Serves 4 as a starter, 2 as a main

5oz *spaghetti*
¼lb *guanciale*
1 tablespoon olive oil
4 large eggs

¼lb Pecorino Romano (or Parmesan,
   if you must), freshly grated
2 teaspoons (!) ground black pepper

Put the pasta on to boil in plenty of well-salted water. Heat an 8in non-stick or well-seasoned black iron pan over a high flame. Trim and discard the skin from the *guanciale*. Slice it thickly (¼in), and then across into ¾in-wide lardoons. Fry it in the oil over a high heat until the fat has blistered and browned a little on the outside, but is still soft within. The pan will smoke profusely. Take it off the heat.

Beat the eggs with the cheese in a large bowl, seasoning heavily with the black pepper. There is so much salt in the cheese you mightn't need to add any more, but taste to check.

When cooked, but a minute on the too-hard side of *al dente*, drain the pasta and toss it (still hot) into the eggs with the *guanciale* and almost all its fat. Heat the pan over a high heat again until it smokes, then tip in the *spaghetti* mixture. Shake the pan for a moment, reduce the heat to minimum and fry for 2 minutes. Turn the *frittata* out on to a plate, heat the pan until it smokes again, and slide the *frittata* back in. Cook the other side for 2 minutes more, shaking the pan for the first few seconds – the *frittata* should be almost set. Turn it once or twice more if you need to, but it is best fractionally underdone, and rested for a few minutes to finish cooking. Practice makes perfect here.

Serve hot, warm, or at room temperature – great with a little salad, and maybe an extra sprinkling of cheese.

WILD ASPARAGUS AND SHRIMP FRITTATA
LAZIO

I have fond childhood memories of the Aurunci hills near Sperlonga, the resort near Rome where my mother also spent the best parts of her early years. We still follow these walks together in the springtime, trying to find the little boulder where the cork oaks and olive groves meet, where we scattered half of her father's ashes a few years ago. He had a tumultuous time after his death – he was almost smuggled into Israel disguised as blood and bonemeal fertiliser (my mum decided against this at the very last minute, for fear he would be impounded), and languished on her bookshelf in his fertiliser box for a couple of years. Later we attempted to scatter an unfortunate half in the Mediterranean from a boat off the coast of Sicily, which instead blew into our faces. At least a part of him rests in idyllic peace, in one of the most beautiful places we know.

Our walk to this spot takes us past a ruined house, where the irises around have run amok, across fields of wild orchids, and through a cork oak forest where we meet ivory cattle and a small drove of goats. We try not to tread on the delicate wood anemones, our eyes peeled for wild asparagus – the tender shoots of the native asparagus fern. These thin, dark tendrils lie somewhere between green, purple and black, their taste intensely sweet, bitter and above all asparagussy. We rarely find enough to eat, and often ask the sisters who run Poco-Poco, the greengrocer's opposite my grandmother's apartment, to bring us a bunch the next day. This is the bunch I turn into my *frittata*.

I chop the wild asparagus into 3/4–1 1/4 in lengths, discarding the tough stalks, and peel a handful of shrimp fresh from the sea (you could use 5oz fine asparagus and 5–7oz whole shell-on shrimp, shelled). In a non-stick pan, I heat a pat of butter until it sizzles, then gently fry the asparagus and shrimp together for under a minute, until half-cooked. I break three eggs (to make only a thin *frittata,* enough for one on its own, although we inevitably share it at lunchtime with leftovers from the night before), and beat them with a fork and a few torn leaves of basil. I season the asparagus and shrimp with enough salt and pepper to do the eggs as well, which I pour into the pan. I stir very tentatively with the back of my fork until I can see large, wafty curds of egg throughout, then leave the pan alone for 2 minutes, until half-set and coloured on the underside. I turn this out on to a plate, then slide back into the pan and fry for 1 minute more (2 if the pan is small and the omelette thick) until I know it's coloured and think it's set. I don't mind if it's a little runny. I savour the sweet and brine of the shrimp, the sweet and bitter of the asparagus, the sweet and rich of the eggs. The meeting of land and sea, in Sperlonga, where the Aurunci roll gently into the waves.

SPAGHETTI AND CURED MULLET ROE
FRITTATA CAMPANIA

A pasta *frittata,* such as this or the one on page 103, is a great way to use up leftover *spaghetti*, but is hard to cook if the *spaghetti* are cold. If the pasta is undressed, heat it for 5 seconds in boiling, salted water, or if already covered in sauce, heat it in a frying pan with a dribble of water to moisten. The result will always be best with freshly cooked *spaghetti*, though – you can leave it slightly undercooked, as it will continue to absorb moisture and soften in the egg.

       Kitty Travers (ice-cream doyenne) turned me on to this as a way of using leftover *spaghetti* with *bottarga*. Leftover *spaghetti* with *bottarga* doesn't happen often (being delicious, it's normally finished, and being made with such a rare ingredient, is not a common staple meal), but this *frittata* is so good that I devised a simple recipe to make it straightaway, without the hassle of making leftovers first.

Serves 4 as a starter, 2 as a main

5oz *spaghetti*	2 tablespoons extra virgin
¼ cup butter	olive oil
4 large eggs	
3 tablespoons chopped flat-leaf	*To serve*
parsley (optional)	A little salad
3oz *bottarga*, coarsely grated	Lemon wedges

Put your pasta on to boil, in already bubbling water seasoned with abundant salt. Balance a bowl over the pot and allow the butter to just melt in it. Remove from the heat and beat in the eggs, parsley and *bottarga*. Season with a little salt and lots of pepper.

Drain the pasta when still rather *al dente* and stir well, still hot, into the egg mixture. Have already heated (very hot) an 8in frying pan, one that your *frittata* will pretty much fill. Reduce the heat to low, add 1 tablespoon of the oil, swirl it around and pour in the pasta. Shake for a few moments and fry for 3 minutes or until golden brown. Turn out on to a plate which just fits the pan, return the pan to the heat, add the remaining oil and slide the *frittata* in. Cook the second side gently for another 2–3 minutes. Poke it a little to try to assess if it is done or not; if not, turn the *frittata* twice more, cooking for 1 minute each time. It should be just about cooked but slightly runny in the middle; serve with a little salad, and a wedge of lemon if you like.

MONTANARA / FRIED DOUGH WITH TOMATO AND MOZZARELLA CAMPANIA

Better even than a fried pizza (overleaf), and available from the same stalls in Naples, is *montanara* – fried dough topped with tomato sauce, mozzarella and Parmesan. It is incredibly messy to eat, but that's half the fun.

Serves 4 as a starter, 2 as a meal

1 quantity dough from the *pizza fritta* recipe (overleaf)
Vegetable oil, for frying

Topping
1 garlic clove, broken but whole
¼ cup extra virgin olive oil
½ lb of the best tomatoes you can get – or good canned ones

A tiny pinch of hot red pepper flakes (optional)
12 basil leaves
½ lb buffalo mozzarella, cut into ⅛ in-thick discs
⅓ cup freshly grated Parmesan

While the dough is rising, make a simple tomato sauce. Fry the garlic clove in the oil until it starts to brown, then discard the garlic and add the tomatoes (chopped), pepper flakes, salt and pepper and cook over a medium heat for about 15 minutes, until the sauce is no longer watery, but not exactly thick either. Take off the heat, add two-thirds of the basil (torn), and let cool.

Divide the risen dough into four balls, and stretch each out into a 5in-wide approximate disc. You will need a heavily floured surface and hands. Let the discs of dough rise again for 20–30 minutes until puffy, then dust or blow off the excess flour and fry like the *pizze fritte* (in hot oil until golden on both sides).

Drain and immediately douse the fried dough with the cool tomato sauce, then top with the mozzarella, a basil leaf on each disc, and a sprinkling of Parmesan. Serve straightaway, or let it cool to room temperature if the weather's hot.

PIZZA FRITTA / FRIED PIZZA STUFFED WITH RICOTTA CAMPANIA

Pizza, a staple food in Italy and abroad, is such a wonderful thing when done right. This is unfortunately a rare event – even in Rome, home of my favourite style of pizza (thin, crispy and charred), I can think of only a handful of *pizzerie* I truly rate. The gradual homogenisation of cuisine that we are seeing worldwide has started to bite in Italy too, whilst pizza is a deeply personal thing – one *pizzaiolo's* pizza might be perfection to one customer, flawed to the next. The same situation exists in Naples, where locals will each go to only one or two establishments and spurn the rest. If most of the thousands of *pizzerie* in Italy can't get it right, with wood ovens that reach temperatures in excess of 750°F, and practised hands that knead dough made from local, specially ground flours and spring water, what sort of hope have we poor souls at home?

To every problem, there is a solution, and in this case it comes from the home town of pizza itself. In Naples, street vendors sell *pizza fritta* – notably in the market on Via Pignasecca, small stalls sell fried envelopes of pizza dough, blistered without, elastic within, enclosing simple stuffings. My favourite (given below) is filled with plain ricotta, but other classics include ricotta mixed with mozzarella and fried pork lard; *salame* and mozzarella; *prosciutto* and ricotta. You simply can't bake a perfect pizza at home, but you can make a perfect fried one.

Makes 4

1½ teaspoons dried yeast, or 1 tablespoon fresh

1 cup lukewarm water

2¼ cups bread flour

1 small potato, boiled, cooled and riced

1 teaspoon salt

3/4 lb fresh ricotta (sheep's milk is best)

1/3 cup freshly grated Parmesan

Oil, for frying (either pure vegetable oil, or mixed 2:1 with a half-decent olive oil)

First make the dough. Mix the yeast with 1/3 cup of the water and 1 tablespoon of the flour to make a sponge. Leave in a warm place until frothy (20 minutes or so). Combine the remaining flour and water with the potato, yeast sponge and salt and knead well to make a soft, elastic dough so wet it's almost liquid (you may need to beat it with your hands in a bowl). It will take about 10 minutes to achieve a result that should be supple, shiny and cohesive. Let rise in a lightly oiled bowl covered with plastic wrap for 1½ hours until more than doubled in bulk.

When well risen, divide the dough into four rough balls (it will collapse, but don't worry) and place on a heavily floured surface. Being careful not to get too much flour on the top of each ball (you need the dough to stick to itself later), but with floured hands, stretch each ball into an approximate disc 7in in diameter, 3/16in thick in the middle and maybe a touch thicker at the edges.

Mix the ricotta with the Parmesan, season with salt and pepper, and spread a half-moon shape on one side of each disc of dough, leaving a 3/4in border. Fold the dough over to enclose the filling, and press gently to seal. Leave these *pizze* to rise for 20 minutes.

The oil needn't be particularly deep – a generous 1in will do, and the wider the pan the more *pizze* you can fry at once. Heat it to 350–375°F (hot, but not smoking), and slide the risen *pizze* in one-by-one. Handle them gently, as the soft dough is delicate – a large metal spatula may help, if used like a mini pizza peel. Fry for 2 minutes on each side until golden and blistered, then drain on paper towels. Eat hot (best), or not (like they do on the streets of Naples), with your hands.

FRIED GARFISH OR ANCHOVIES (OR OTHER TINY FISH) CAMPANIA

Pesce azzurro, oily fish, forms an integral part of the Mediterranean diet. It is healthy, delicious, and guilt-free. Just enough guilt may be added by deep-frying my favourites, garfish or anchovies.

Fresh anchovies can be hard to find, and must be at their very freshest to be any good – bright and firm, glistening like jewels. Friendly fishmongers will be able to get them for you in season (from midsummer) if you ask nicely. Garfish are even more fabulous. I love to see them swimming, like blades of green-blue steel just under the water's surface. I love to cook them, and even more so to eat them. The best part is lifting away the succulent flesh to reveal the amazing skeleton, as long as a snake's, and blue as only plastic or stained glass can be. They can be hard to find, often thrown back as by-catch – my supplier in Bristol buys them from local teenagers who swap their catch for pocket money.

Serves 4 as a starter

About 1lb garfish, anchovies or other tiny ocean fish
Vegetable oil, for frying
½ cup all-purpose flour
⅓ cup cornstarch
About ⅓ cup semolina flour
A little milk
Lemon wedges, to serve

Garfish range in weight from around 2oz to around 2lbs. They should be scaled and gutted, but leave the head and tail on. Massive ones may be cut into manageable lengths, whilst smaller ones can be curled, their tail put in their mouth to help them fit the frying pan. Anchovies look and eat best with their heads off – pinch between thumb and forefinger to break through the spine and flesh at the nape of the neck, then pull the head – it should come off with the guts attached. Rub the bodies gently under cold water to remove any scales. Season the fish with salt a few minutes before you cook them.

When you're ready to eat, heat the oil to 375°F. You'll need at least a 2in depth in a fairly wide pan, which must be three times as deep as the oil. Mix the flours and cornstarch together. Dip the fish in the milk to moisten them, then into the flour mixture. Shake them around to make sure they're well coated before dusting off any excess, and then lower the fish into the hot oil. For anchovies or small garfish, fry for 1–2 minutes, until pale golden, just crisp outside, just cooked within. Large garfish will take longer – about 1 minute for each ½in diameter.

Drain the fish on paper towels, sprinkle with salt and serve with wedges of lemon.

FRIED SHRIMP AND SQUID WITH EGGPLANT AND LEMON CAMPANIA

This subtle combination of the fruits of land and sea requires a careful, precise and loving hand. The result is a truly spectacular plate of fried food, combining a fragile vegetable with equally tricky seafood, all set off by bitter-sour-crunchy discs of lemon. It is an exercise in delicacy – both of touch (the trick being not to overcook the squid), and technique (the lightest dusting of flour and a quick, hot fry means little oil is absorbed). I almost always have a version of this glorious plate on the menu at Bocca di Lupo – sometimes with anchovies or tiny red mullets, occasionally baby octopus or squid, or sliced orange in place of the lemon – it's all good. The vegetable may be absent, or I might replace the eggplant with zucchini or artichokes, depending on mood and season. I could eat it every day, and very nearly do.

The shrimp are fried in their shells, to eat whole. There is no point in doing this unless the shrimp are small, flavoursome and thin-shelled. In Italy, and when I'm lucky in Britain, I use small Sicilian red shrimp (crimson ones from the deepest waters) or local, transparent Poole prawns, like I used to catch in rock pools as a kid. Readers elsewhere, whose shrimp are larger than mine, will be forced to shell them, and should use the most flavoursome ones they can find. Peeled rock shrimp are always nice, even if you can't eat the shells.

Serves 4 as a starter, 2 as a main

4 medium squid
1 large eggplant, or 2 small
12 small shell-on shrimp
1 lemon, cut across into ¹⁄₁₆in-thick
   pinwheel slices

⅓ cup all-purpose flour
⅓ cup fine semolina flour
⅓ cup cornstarch
Vegetable oil, for frying

Clean the squid, taking the skins off but leaving the wings attached to the bodies. Make sure that nothing slimy is left inside the tubular body. Cut the bodies across into chunky ¾in rings, and leave the tentacles in a bunch (but be sure to remove the beak).

Trim the eggplant, cut it across in half, then lengthways, and then into little batons. Submerge the prepared eggplant batons in salty cold water (about 3 tablespoons fine salt per quart, until almost as salty as the sea): this will season them, keep them fresh, and give the flour something to stick to. Toss together the all-purpose flour, semolina flour and cornstarch to make a dredge, seasoning it with salt and pepper.

When you're ready to eat, heat the oil to 375°F in a wide pan. Use a ferocious flame – a thin pan (such as a wok) will help you to get the heat back up once the seafood is in. Don't be afraid to cook in two or even three batches if need be – this is in fact recommended if you're not sure the oil will stay hot enough. Drain the eggplant batons, then toss into the flour, shake off the excess and lower them into the oil. Fry for 2 minutes until they begin to bubble slightly less ebulliently. Flour the shrimp and add them to the oil, and let them fry with the eggplant for 60 seconds more. Meanwhile, quickly toss the squid and the 12 nicest slices of lemon in the flour, then add both to the pan. Fry for a further 60 seconds or so, again until the bubbles start to diminish, the squid only just beginning to colour – it should still look plump and juicy. It takes courage to draw the squid from the oil so quickly, but this is the only way to keep it as tender as butter.

Season the drained squid, shrimp, eggplant and lemon with a sprinkling of salt as they blot dry on paper towels, then serve piled high on a warmed wide dish. Delicious with a squeeze of lemon, or without.

Variations You can replace the eggplant with 4 small artichokes (globe, cleaned as on page 26), sliced across ⅛in thick, or with 2 medium zucchini, cut just like the eggplant. Artichokes, with their firmer texture and complex flavour, offer a delicious contrast to the seafood. They should be kept whole in acidulated water until the last moment, then quickly dried, sliced, seasoned, floured and fried before they turn brown, at the same time as the shrimp. Zucchini freshens the flavours of the dish. Like the eggplant, it should be kept in salty cold water after it has been cut, but it cooks much faster – add it, floured, at the same time as the shrimp.

PANELLE / CHICKPEA FRITTERS
SICILY

These chickpea fritters are a staple of the Sicilian table – a simple use of a basic, poor man's ingredient that is textural heaven. They are served as a snack, as a side, instead of bread, or as a filling for a *focaccia* sandwich conceptually not dissimilar to a chip buttie. Crunchy on the outside and soft on the inside, their subtle, earthy flavour is homely and pleasing.

Makes about 24 *panelle*, serving 8 with some sliced meats or other morsels

1⅓ cups chickpea flour
¼ cup chopped flat-leaf parsley
Vegetable oil, for frying

Put the chickpea flour into a large bowl, and run it through well with a whisk to make sure it doesn't start off lumpy, or it will end that way. Gradually add 1 quart cold water, whisking all the time, almost like a mayonnaise: start off slowly, then speed up once you have achieved a homogeneous paste. When you have added all the water, transfer the batter to a saucepan, add a pinch of salt and bring to the boil over a high heat, whisking continuously. As soon as it starts to bubble (it will thicken suddenly), decrease the heat to low and continue to cook for 20 minutes, now whisking occasionally, just to prevent sticking. Taste for seasoning.

Stir in the parsley, remove from the heat, and pour the now thick batter on to a tray, lined with parchment paper and greased with olive oil. Spread it by shaking the tray and using a spatula to get as even a layer as you can, between ¼ and ½in thick – roughly 9½ x 14in in total. Let cool until fully set – about half an hour.

Cut the sheet of chickpea dough into about 2½in squares, and fry these in hot vegetable oil (350–375°F), moving them around with a spoon so they cook evenly until golden – about 6–7 minutes. Drain on paper towels and eat hot.

FRIED RED MULLET WITH PESTO TRAPANESE
SICILY

If I had to name my favourite fish, it would be red mullet. Having said this, I have a tendency to think that what I'm eating at the moment is actually *the* most delicious thing in the world. Anyway, suffice it to say that red mullet, with its delicate flesh, glamorous colour and almost prawny-tasting skin, is right up there.

Pesto *Trapanese* is, of course, from Trapani where it is spooned over *busiati* (a peasanty semolina pasta), into fish stews, and to the side of fried fish. Few sauces going by the name of 'pesto' are worth eating, other than the *Genovese* (page 136). This is one of those rare exceptions.

Serves 6–8 as a starter, 4 as a main

4–5 tiny, 2 smallish or 1 medium-large red mullet *per person* as a main course, 2–3 tiny or 1 smallish *each* as a starter
A little milk
A 1:1:1 mixture of all-purpose flour, cornstarch and semolina flour (about ⅓ cup of each will be plenty)
Vegetable oil, for frying
Lemon wedges, to serve

Pesto *Trapanese*
½ cup blanched almonds
2 garlic cloves, crushed
Small bunch basil leaves
¾lb ripe cherry tomatoes
About ½ cup extra virgin olive oil

To make the pesto, grind the nuts and garlic in a food processor until fine, then add the basil followed by the tomatoes. When you have a fine but still textured paste, stir in the oil by hand. Season with salt and pepper to taste.

Season the fish with salt a few minutes before you fry them, then moisten them in milk and dredge in the flour mixture. Deep fry in hot oil (350°F) until golden without and just cooked within – about 4 minutes for small mullets (2–4oz), 6–7 minutes for bigger ones (5–9oz).

Serve with a generous spoonful of the pesto on the side, perhaps a few leaves of arugula, and a wedge or two of lemon on each plate.

OFFERTA!!
€ 3.
LETTERATURA
LA LINGUA
BRAMANTE EDITRICE
PETTA
IL TEATRO
ANTONIO ROT
RBI NA
ovvero
filosofia di u
Franco Di Mauro
ANNA E PIERO SERRA
A ROMA
SE MAGNA COSÌ
Franco Di Mauro Editore

PASTA

'Simple people will never understand our art,' barked the great Chef at his brigade of eager young cooks. No-one noticed Lorenzo, who had snuck in at the back while he was supposed to be peeling garlic and seeding chilies. 'My menu, elegant and intellectual, serves two purposes – it discourages the ignoramus from even entering these hallowed premises, and it is testament to my prowess.'

The entire brigade worked for free, happy to be repaid in Chef Legross' wisdom – knowing also that, with six months under their belts, they could land any job in the country. One set about preparing a terrine of foie gras and lightly smoked raw mackerel in aspic, another the signature 'moon foam' that would adorn it. A third began desiccating lobster tails: these would be crushed to a powder and served with a silver straw, Legross' wry comment on modern excess. Legross himself sat in his office and pondered over a brandy whilst his daughter Délice oversaw the preparation with expressionless eyes.

Lorenzo was a long way from the remote mountain village that was his home. He missed his mamma's stews, her soups, her cakes and her pasta, but wanted dearly to learn from his Master. His wide-eyed gaze followed the others around the kitchen as he tried to decipher what they were doing and, more importantly, why? Lorenzo had never seen food of this calibre, and could not yet understand it. With heart in mouth, he whispered, 'Excuse me, Chef?' Ignored, he repeated, louder this time, 'Chef Legross!'

'What do you want?' came the taut reply.

'Pardon me – I came here only to understand. Why would your esteemed clientele want to inhale a lobster?'

Legross turned as red as the lobster itself. 'Filthy Wop! How dare you question me, or the taste of your betters who *can* appreciate my artistry. You are barely a fetus! Get out – I don't want to see your face again.'

Lorenzo went home, and slumped behind drawn curtains for three days as he contemplated the early end of his career. He was startled by a knock on the door. There stood Délice, looking beautiful even in the dim light of the corridor. She was holding a small box. 'A gift from my father,' she said, with a look of apology in her eyes.

Lorenzo untied the golden ribbon to reveal a head of garlic and two shrivelled, dried old chilies. A card bore two words: 'Your future.'

Délice silently started to weep. Lorenzo gently ushered her in. He dried her face, and set a pot of water as salty as her tears on the stove. He boiled some *spaghetti*, drained them, and dressed them with the spiteful garlic and chili, a little oil, and nothing else.

They ate the *aglio e olio* together without speaking. Délice started to cry again as she ate – she had never encountered food so delicious, food that nourished body and soul rather than mind and ego, food made with more love than technique. She leaned across the table and, her lips glossy with oil and tingling with chili, kissed Lorenzo in silence.

MALFATTI / SPINACH AND RICOTTA DUMPLINGS
LOMBARDY

My dad always used to cook these for me as a kid, and I used to love them. In fact, he still does, and I still do. The flavour is incredibly delicate, the texture soft, with all the comfort of eating baby food, thanks to the ricotta. Not truly a cheese, ricotta is a by-product of the cheese-making process: whey that has been cooked and drained. So you find buffalo ricotta in Campania and Puglia (very rich, creamy and wet); sheep's milk in the far south, the islands, Tuscany and Piedmont (my favourite, creamy and farmyardy); and cow's milk, the commonest everywhere. As by-products go, this is to my mind the very best.

Serves 4–5 as a starter, 2 as a main

10 cups fresh spinach
9oz fresh ricotta (sheep's milk is best)
½ cup freshly grated Parmesan,
   plus plenty extra to serve
1 large egg

3 tablespoons Italian 00 flour,
   plus plenty extra for rolling
Nutmeg (a few grates)
24 sage leaves
5 tablespoons butter

Boil the spinach in well-salted water until tender, refresh it under cool running water and squeeze as dry as you can. Chop it very finely with a knife and mix with the ricotta, Parmesan, egg and flour to make a very soft dough. Season with nutmeg, salt and pepper, but not a heavy hand – the flavours are very subtle, and so too should be the salt.

Bring a pan of salted water to the boil (the spinach water is fine if you still have it). Drop a walnut-sized lump of dough in a bed of flour and roll it into a rough ball: it will be too soft to make a perfect sphere, but that is why the dumplings are called *malfatti* – 'badly made'. Cook it in the water to see if it holds together. If not, add a bit more flour to the mixture and test again. Once the dough is just (but only just) firm enough to withstand cooking, roll the remainder into about a dozen golf balls, again coating them in plenty of flour. Simmer for 7–8 minutes for a slightly oozing middle, counting from when they rise to the surface.

While they are cooking, fry the sage in the butter until the leaves are crisp and the butter hazelnut brown and foaming. Drain the *malfatti*, and serve with the butter and sage poured over, and a liberal sprinkling of grated Parmesan.

Variations A light tomato sauce works well if served under the *malfatti* rather than over them, and dotted with tiny pats of butter. Or try draping the freshly cooked *malfatti* with thinly sliced *lardo* (cured pork back fat), still serving with butter, sage and grated Parmesan.

VEAL AND PORK AGNOLOTTI
PIEDMONT

Agnolotti, tiny stuffed parcels of pasta made from a single, folded piece of dough are, along with *tajarin* (*tagliolini*), the signature pasta of Piedmont – and a source of pride for the locals. They can be made *dal plin* (with a pleat) for special occasions, or plain in a simple half-moon, as I describe here. They may be filled with any manner of stuffing, and whilst they are rather fiddly to make, are also most rewarding to consume.

Serves 8 as a starter, 4 as a main

Filling
2 cups cabbage or escarole
2 tablespoons butter
14oz leftover braised or pot-roasted
  veal or pork, or both*
4 sage leaves
½ cup freshly grated Parmesan
1 egg
Nutmeg (a few grates)

Pasta
1½ cups all-purpose or Italian 00 flour
1 large egg
3 egg yolks

Sauce
3/4 cup butter and 24 sage leaves
or
1 quantity walnut sauce (page 134),
  plus crumbled walnuts
Freshly grated Parmesan, to serve

*If you need to make braised meat specifically for this dish, start with about 1¼lbs of mixed raw pork shoulder and stewing veal, brown it in butter, add some herbs and white wine and simmer with a lid on for 2 hours. The pasta will be delicious served in the juice of this stew (a third alternative to the two specified above), and doubly so with shaved white truffle as well if you can afford it.

To make the filling, boil the greens in salted water until tender. Drain well, let steam dry spread out on a cloth. Chop finely, squeeze any extra water out in your hands, then fry gently in the butter for a few minutes. Let cool, then combine with the other ingredients in a food processor until quite smooth.

To make the pasta, start by kneading the flour well with the eggs. Pass the dough a few times through the widest setting of a pasta machine, folding it in three and giving a quarter turn each time until it looks silky, then roll it progressively thinner until just under 1/32in thick, the second-thinnest setting on most machines.

For the *agnolotti*, cut the rolled pasta into scant 2in rounds with a pastry cutter and dab a piece of filling the size of a chickpea in the centre of each. Working quickly, pick up each disc and fold into a semi-circle to enclose the filling, pinching the edges to close and exclude air. If too dry to stick to itself, or if you've got flour on the dough (you shouldn't need any flour to roll the pasta at all), mist with a little water before you start picking up the discs. Keep the *agnolotti* on a tray dusted with semolina flour until ready to cook.

If serving with butter and sage, fry the sage in the butter in a wide pan until the leaves are crisp and the butter nutty – you'll need to start this just before you put the pasta on. Boil the *agnolotti* in plenty of salted water (I use generous 1 tablespoon per quart water to cook all pasta, but normally judge this by tongue rather than measuring). They will only take 2 minutes. When the sage butter is ready, add a small ladleful of the pasta water to emulsify the sauce. Allow it to boil down until the consistency of light cream, then add the drained *agnolotti* to the pan and toss over the heat until well coated (the sauce will continue to thicken). Serve with Parmesan on top.

To serve with walnut sauce, make the sauce and dress the pasta with it as for *pansôti* (page 134). Sprinkle with crumbled walnuts. This is my favourite. I used to eat *agnolotti alle noci* at least once a week when I lived in Rome, at my local *trattoria*, Marcello on Via dei Campani.

TAGLIOLINI AU GRATIN WITH SHRIMP AND TREVISO *VENETO*

While a few other dishes in this book, I am unashamed to say, have been inspired by the inimitable Da Fiore in San Polo, Venice, this one is an attempt to replicate exactly one of their signature dishes. So great is the feeling of discovery when you find a special restaurant serving a special dish, you somehow take emotional ownership of it. But credit where credit is due, and it clearly isn't due to me.

Serves 4–6 as a starter, 2–3 as a main

¼lb dried *tagliolini,* or 5oz fresh
3 tablespoons butter
½ smallish red onion or 1 shallot, thinly
  sliced across the grain
1 medium head *radicchio di Treviso* (or a
  small *radicchio,* around 7oz), shredded
  ⅛–¼in

½lb shelled rock shrimp
¼ cup white wine
¾ cup heavy cream
⅓ cup freshly grated Parmesan

Melt the butter over a medium heat. Add the onion and a pinch of salt and fry for a few moments, then add the *radicchio* and gently sauté for 4 or 5 minutes until wilted. Add the shrimp, then the white wine and let it boil for a couple of minutes until most of the liquid has evaporated. Add the cream to the sauce, at about the same time putting the *tagliolini* in a pan of boiling, salted water. Let both pots boil until the *tagliolini* are still somewhat undercooked (just over half the recommended cooking time, which is already very short), and the sauce just runnier than cream.

Drain the pasta and add it to the sauce; toss together over the heat for a minute until the pasta is well coated by the cream, season with salt and pepper and transfer to an 8 x 12in baking dish, or a number of smaller individual ones. Sprinkle with Parmesan and brown the top, either in a fiercely hot oven (on maximum) or under the broiler. Serve immediately.

LINGUINE WITH SPIDER CRAB
VENETO

Spider crabs (*granseole*) are impossible to find in the States, but are so good as to make a trip to the Veneto worthwhile. The larger they are, the fewer you'll need – and therefore proportionally less time to pick out the flesh. They seem to become worthwhile at about 2 pounds each. Hold them in your hands to assess their weight – surprisingly heavy ones will be full of meat, whilst surprisingly light ones may be unsurprisingly empty.

Spider crab meat has an incredibly rich, deep, complex fishy taste – something you simply must try if you haven't before. If you can't get it, use 10–12oz 'normal' crab meat – about half brown and half white. A number of other variations work well with this basic method – see the note at the end. This recipe is incredibly authentic, incredibly oily, incredibly good. Some might baulk at the calorific content, or indeed the oiliness of the plate, but those of my persuasion will find it as enticing as honey to a bee.

Serves 4 as a starter, 2 as a main

7oz *linguine*
4–5lbs live spider crabs (2 medium spider
  or Dungeness or large snow crabs)
2 large garlic cloves, broken but whole
3/4 cup extra virgin olive oil

1lb baby plum or cherry tomatoes, the
  ripest, darkest ones you can get
A pinch of hot red pepper flakes
3 tablespoons chopped flat-leaf parsley
  or basil (optional)

Cook the crabs. A fishmonger in Chioggia taught me to stack them, one atop another, in a tall pot just wide enough to accommodate them (if you make a larger quantity, you can stack up to 6 crabs in a tower). Place about 2in depth of water in the pot – just enough to come part-way up the bottom crab – cover tightly with a lid, bring to a fast boil and cook over a high heat for 15 minutes. Spread the crabs out to cool before you pick them.

Pick the meat from the shells: be sure to empty every segment of every leg, every crevasse within the body (especially where the legs join it), and to keep all the liquidy brown meat. You should get at least 5oz meat (up to 7oz) per generous 2lbs of crab.

Start making the sauce when you put the pasta on to boil. Fry the garlic in the oil in a skillet until it is browned outside, then discard the garlic and add the cherry tomatoes, halved lengthways. Fry for 6–7 minutes over a high heat, tossing the tomatoes only occasionally to turn them. Some should start to brown on the outside – this fast frying will concentrate the flavour. Add the pepper flakes, then all the crab meat and the herbs if using. Fry for a minute, stirring gently, just to warm through, then add a splash of the pasta water to make the thick sauce.

Drain the pasta *al dente*, add it to the sauce, and cook the two together for a minute. Taste for salt and pepper and serve straightaway.

Variation: *Linguine* **with Langoustines (and Clams)** This method is also excellent for preparing *linguine* with langoustines, or langoustines and clams. For the above quantity, instead of the crabs take 20 small live langoustines (about 18oz), or 12 small langoustines and 16–20 clams. Halve the langoustines (do not be tempted to rinse out the heads, as it is the squishy bits that make the sauce nice). Add the raw shellfish to the pan after the tomato has fried and sauté together for 3 minutes, until the langoustine shells are opaque, most of the flesh white, and most of the clams cooked. Add the herbs if using (I wouldn't in this case) along with the drained pasta and a splash of its water, and cook for a minute more.

TAGLIATELLE WITH PIGEON RAGÙ
VENETO

For me, the three pillars of Venetian cuisine must be seafood, *radicchio* and wildfowl. Duck is used to great effect (roasted, braised, or as a pasta sauce), whilst pigeons provide an affordable and delicious meat, with their dark flesh and rich yet mild flavour. Normally roasted elsewhere, in which case young (squab) birds are preferred, in the Veneto they make appearances in a baked bread soup (*zuppa coada,* page 177) or here in a rich, alluring sauce. For such preparations older (also happily cheaper and more available) birds are better – they have a deeper, richer flavour, whilst any toughness is slowly cooked away.

Serves 4 as a starter, 2 as a main

7oz dried *tagliatelle,* or 9oz fresh
Freshly grated Parmesan, to serve

Pigeon ragù
2 pigeons
3 juniper berries
10 black peppercorns
2 bay leaves
2 sprigs rosemary, leaves finely chopped
6 tablespoons butter

1 small onion, chopped
1 small carrot, chopped
2 celery stalks, chopped
1 garlic clove, thinly sliced
5oz ground pork
2 sprigs sage
5oz fresh or canned tomatoes, chopped
3/4 cup white wine
3/4 cup whole milk

Roast the pigeons first. Crush together the juniper berries, peppercorns, 1 bay leaf and half the rosemary with a pinch of salt and rub this into the birds. Smear them with a third of the butter, and roast for 15–20 minutes in a hot oven (425°F). When cool enough, cut the breast and leg meat from the bones, keeping the skin on the meat, and chop it into rough 1/4in dice. Use the hearts and livers, too, if they're still in the pigeons.

Make a stock with the bones. Put them in a small saucepan with half of each of the onion, carrot and celery and cover with 1½ quarts water. Simmer for an hour, then strain – you should have a generous 2 cups stock.

Fry the remaining onion, carrot and celery in the remaining butter with the garlic and a good pinch of salt, stirring for 10 minutes over a medium heat until tender. Add the pork and fry, chopping and stirring with a spoon to break up the meat, until the meat just starts to brown and spit. Add the remaining bay leaf and rosemary, the chopped sage and the pigeon meat. Fry for a minute more before pouring in all the liquids – tomatoes, wine, milk and about 1 cup of the stock. Season it lightly with salt and pepper – you can always add more later on. Bring to a simmer and reduce the heat to its lowest. Leave the *ragù* to slowly braise for about 2 hours, during which time it should become as thick as porridge (if it dries out too much you can add a splash of stock). Taste again for seasoning, and set aside until ready to eat (this sauce can be refrigerated for a few days, or frozen if need be).

When you're ready to eat, put the pasta on to boil. Heat the sauce up in a wide pan with a splash of the pigeon stock, or pasta water if the stock is finished – you want the liquid part of the sauce to have the consistency of light cream. When the pasta is a little more *al dente* than you like and the sauce boiling, drain the *tagliatelle* and add them to the sauce. Cook together until the sauce coats the pasta well. Serve immediately with Parmesan on top, and a supple red – Bardolino or Valpolicella, to keep it all in the Veneto.

SPAGHETTI 'COL NERO' (WITH CUTTLEFISH AND ITS INK) VENETO

Cuttlefish stewed in its ink is a staple in Venice – and should be here too. It is delicious, rich and above all black; there is a joy in eating midnight-coloured food that brings out the child in every one of us, resulting in besmeared shirts and blackened smiles.

    Seppie col nero is served in all manner of ways around the lagoon – in pasta, with polenta, or in risotto (page 175). I heartily recommend all three to the home cook. The same basic cuttlefish stew is the basis of them all – if making it especially for this recipe, cut the cuttlefish smaller, into 3/4 x 3/4in chunks.

Serves 4 as a starter, 2 as a main

7oz spaghetti
1 quantity cuttlefish cooked in its ink
  (page 204)

2 tablespoons chopped flat-leaf parsley
2 tablespoons butter

When you're ready to eat, put the pasta on to boil – as ever, in a large pan of boiling, well-salted water. Heat up the stew with the parsley, adding a splash of the pasta water if it looks dry. Drain the pasta a mite on the hard side of *al dente* (it will cook for another minute in the sauce) and add it to the cuttlefish stew along with the butter. Cook until the pasta is chewy and well coated in the sauce, by now thick enough to stick to the *spaghetti*, and not to fall to the bottom of the pan.

DANDELION AND CHARD PANSÔTI WITH WALNUT SAUCE LIGURIA

Pansôti, little triangular stuffed pastas, are typically filled with *preboggion*, a mixture of wild herbs from the Ligurian hills. If you fancy a stroll in the countryside in spring or early summer, you may as well gather your own wild beet, borage, wild celery, wild endive, dandelions, nettles, young poppy shoots and rampions (bellflower shoots). City dwellers can easily gather young stinging nettle tips (note to the foolhardy: wear rubber gloves), as I do for the recipe below. The lazy can use a mixture of arugula and chard or spinach, and still feel proud that they at least made their own pasta.

Serves 8 as a starter, 4 as a main

Pansôti
**Egg pasta dough made with
   2¼ cups Italian 00 flour
   and 3 eggs
¼lb Swiss chard
¼lb dandelion leaves
½ medium onion, finely chopped
¼ cup butter
A good grating of nutmeg (about
   one-fifth of a whole one)
2 sprigs oregano, leaves chopped
1 egg yolk
¼lb sheep's milk ricotta
About 1 cup freshly grated Parmesan**

Walnut sauce
**⅔ cup shelled walnuts, plus extra,
   crumbled, to serve
2oz bread (weighed without its crust)
⅓ cup milk
1 tablespoon oregano leaves,
   or 5 sage leaves
About 2 cups freshly grated Parmesan,
   plus about 2 tablespoons extra to serve
⅔ cup extra virgin olive oil**

To start the *pansôti*, separate the stalks from the leaves of the chard, and roughly chop both. Set a medium pan of well-salted water on to boil. When up to temperature, add the chard stalks and cook for 5 minutes until they are almost done, but still a little crunchy. Leaving them in the pan, add the chard and dandelion leaves and boil together for a further 5 minutes until everything, stem and leaf, is meltingly tender. Drain, refresh in cold water, drain again and squeeze as dry as you can. Chop the cooked vegetables finely.

Fry the onion in the butter with the nutmeg and a good pinch of salt until very tender and amber coloured: 15–20 minutes over a low heat. Add the chopped chard and dandelion and the oregano and fry for a couple of minutes, then turn the mixture out on to a plate to cool. In a bowl, mix this preparation with the egg yolk, ricotta and Parmesan, seasoning with salt and pepper to taste.

Roll the pasta quite thinly (a bit under $\frac{1}{32}$ in thick, or the second-thinnest setting on a rolling machine – see page 124 for a little more detail), taking care not to make the surface floury, and probably working with half the dough at a time. Cut it into about 3in squares, put a teaspoonful of filling in the centre of each, and fold over to make triangles. Pat their fat little bellies down (*pansôti* means 'big bellies' in Ligurian dialect) to flatten slightly. If the pasta isn't wet enough to stick to itself, lend a helping hand by means of a light misting of water. Spread the *pansôti* out on a tray dusted with semolina flour until ready to use.

Make the walnut sauce. Only if they look dark and likely bitter, pour boiling water over the walnuts and let them soak for 15 minutes, then drain and pick off any extraneous bits of dark skin. Soak the bread in the milk, then combine with the nuts, oregano or sage and Parmesan in a food processor. Grind well to achieve a finely textured, creamy sauce. Add the oil and then, gradually, 1¼ cups water. Season with salt and pepper.

Put your pasta on to boil, as ever in water that is already salted, and already boiling, and heat the sauce in a wide pan. It will do an amazing thing: the greenish hue from the herb will turn purple, from the walnut skins. Add a touch of water if need be – when cooked, the sauce should be as thick as cream. Drain the pasta *al dente*, and toss into the sauce. Cook until well coated, and serve with grated Parmesan and crumbled walnuts sprinkled on top.

TROFIE WITH GREEN BEANS, POTATO AND PESTO GENOVESE LIGURIA

Trofie are joyous little spirals of semolina pasta dough. You can buy them dried but, as with *orecchiette* (page 154), I advise you not to – they take too long to cook, the outside becoming mushy before they are done within. (If you don't want the hassle of making your own fresh *trofie*, I suggest using dried *linguine*, adding the vegetables 5 minutes before the end of cooking.) You can occasionally buy *trofie* fresh, but they can be made at home quite easily, with a practised hand and a lot of time – this is an ideal daydreaming activity, something that lets the mind wander like tending the garden or knitting. The result is sublime – quick to cook, and silky-chewy all the way through, their consistency and shape quite sexy on the tongue. *Trofie* are, to my mind, *the* pasta to serve with pesto *Genovese* – the classic basil one. In Liguria, they often cook a few green beans and slices of new potato with the pasta, which add fantastic flavours and textures to the dish.

Serves 4 as a starter, 2 as a main

6oz fine semolina (or 8oz fresh *trofie*,
  or 7oz dried *linguine*)
3 tiny new potatoes
1 cup fine green beans
4oz pesto *Genovese* (see below)

Pesto *Genovese*
4oz bunched basil
1 garlic clove
2 cups freshly grated Parmesan
2 cups freshly grated Pecorino Romano
2/3 cup pine nuts (the long Italian ones)
3/4 cup extra virgin olive oil
2 tablespoons butter, softened

For the pesto, remove the basil leaves, wash them gently and only if you have to, then let them dry naturally, spread out on a cloth. Crush the garlic to a paste with a little salt. Put the cheeses, basil and garlic into a food processor and work until a fine paste, then add the pine nuts and continue until quite fine, but with some texture from the nuts. Add the olive oil and butter, some salt and pepper. It is best to let it stand for a few minutes before you finally taste for seasoning. This recipe is enough for about ten – there's no point making a smaller quantity, and the sauce freezes very well, especially in little packets for two.

For the *trofie*, put the *semola* out on a wooden board, make a well and add 1/3 cup water at room temperature. Bring together to make a firm dough, knead and let rest, covered, for at least 15 minutes. Make sure your board is completely free of any flour. Break off a walnut-sized lump of dough and roll to make a long, 3/16in-wide strand. Cut it into 3/4–1in lengths. One-by-one, quickly roll each of these lengths between the flat of your hand and the board to make a 1½ in-long strand, ⅛ in wide at the middle and tapering at either end. Use something flat, long and straight (palette knife, ruler, back of a knife) and hold it at a 45° angle to the board, and a 45° angle to the little piece of pasta dough. Slide it, in a single motion towards you, rolling along and across the dough. You need some friction between the pasta and the board to flatten and twist the pasta into a tapering helix – if you're skidding, dampen the board slightly. Without too much practice, it should take about 15 minutes for this quantity. They don't all need to look the same – they are home-made! Leave the *trofie* spread out to dry slightly for about 20 minutes, until just a little leathery outside.

Peel the potatoes and slice very thinly and evenly, ⅛ in thick. Top the green beans (I like to leave the tails on), and cut in 1–1½ in lengths. In a pan of well-salted water, boil the pasta, beans and potato together for 5 minutes* or until cooked. Drain, and serve with the pesto on top to stir in at the table.

*If using bought, dried *linguine*, be aware they will likely take longer than 5 minutes to cook. To avoid the unthinkable choice between undercooked potatoes and overcooked pasta, add the vegetables 6–7 minutes before the end of the cooking time predicted by the packet.

TORTELLINI IN BROTH
EMILIA-ROMAGNA

Tortellini are the pride of Emilia-Romagna. You can't escape them – and everywhere they are filled with the same mixture of *mortadella, prosciutto,* Parmesan and pork or chicken. Their origin has become enshrined in folklore – depending on whom you ask, they were invented by an innkeeper in Bologna or Castelfranco Emilia who was smitten by the beauty of a guest (Lucrezia Borgia or Venus herself). So aroused was he that he crept up to her door and peered through the keyhole: all he could see was her navel. But what a navel it was – he rushed to his kitchen and created a pasta in the exquisite belly-button's image.

    Tortellini are delicious served *con panna* – with cream, butter and nutmeg – but here I serve them in broth instead for a more delicate dish, one where you can really experience their erotic mouth-feel to the full.

Serves 12 as a starter, 6 as a main

**5oz *tortellini* per person as a main,
  2¹⁄₂oz as a starter**
**2 cups flavoursome, clear chicken broth
  per main, 1 cup per starter**

Tortellini
**Egg pasta made with 3¹⁄₂ cups Italian 00
  flour and either 5 large eggs, or
  3 eggs plus 7 extra yolks**
¹⁄₄lb pork loin, diced ³⁄₄in

2 tablespoons butter
¹⁄₄lb *mortadella*
¹⁄₄lb *prosciutto crudo*
¹⁄₄lb Parmesan
1 egg
A grating of nutmeg

To serve
Freshly grated Parmesan
1 fresh white truffle (optional)

For the filling, gently fry the pork loin in the butter until just cooked and lightly browned. Turn off the heat and let cool in the pan. Combine the pork and its juices with the other ingredients in a food processor and process until a smooth paste. Refrigerate if not using immediately.

For the *tortellini*, roll a quarter of the pasta (keep the rest covered with an upturned bowl until you're ready to use it) just under ¹⁄₃₂in thick (see page 124 for more detail), making sure there is no flour on the dough, and lay it out flat on a clean, very lightly floured table. Cut into 1¹⁄₂–2in squares, and dot a tiny (hazelnut-sized) piece of filling in the centre of each. Check that the pasta is tacky – it must be wet enough to stick to itself when you come to make and seal the *tortellini*. If it isn't, spray with a light mist of water from a plant mister. Cover loosely with plastic wrap, to keep the pasta from drying as you work. You should have a well-organised space, a precise checkerboard of pasta squares, neatly dotted with filling and protected under plastic. Nothing else should be on the table.

Take one square of pasta from under the plastic wrap. Close it diagonally, to make a triangle, and gently squeeze the sides to seal and exclude any air. Fold the top of the triangle down, to make a trapezoid, with the tip of the triangle just sticking out. Put a finger gently against the lump where the filling is (keep the folded triangle on the outside), and wrap the two longer corners around your finger so they meet. Press together to join, then remove your finger. Do this again with another little square of pasta, and again, and again, until it's time to roll out another fresh sheet of the remaining pasta dough.

For the finished dish, bring the chicken broth to the boil and season it to taste with salt. Cook the *tortellini* in this until they swell and rise to the surface – about 2 minutes. Serve swimming in their broth, with a tablespoon of grated Parmesan in each bowl, and (on special occasions) a generous shaving of white truffle.

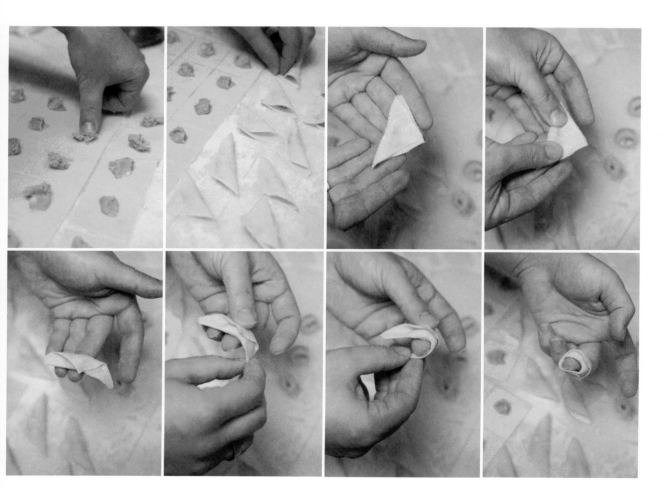

PAPPARDELLE WITH CHICKEN LIVER RAGÙ
TUSCANY

I ate this dish somewhere in Tuscany, at an old convent where they served a few plates of food. I cannot remember exactly where, but it was idyllic – we sat outside, under an old oak tree which shaded a hill from the summer sun. I think I was twelve, perhaps a year or two older; it is a happy memory.

Serves 4 as a starter, 2 as a main

7oz dried *pappardelle*, or 9oz fresh
Freshly grated Parmesan, to serve

Chicken liver ragù
½lb chicken livers
⅓ cup extra virgin olive oil
½ small onion, chopped

1 celery stalk, chopped
1 garlic clove, chopped
⅔ cup dry Marsala
½ cup white wine
1 scant tablespoon chopped rosemary
3 tablespoons chopped flat-leaf parsley
3 tablespoons butter

Heat a wide frying pan over a high heat until smoking profusely. Toss the chicken livers in a bowl with 1 tablespoon of the olive oil and some salt and pepper, then pour into the hot pan, spreading them out as much as you can. Let them fry without moving them for 2 minutes, until well browned on one side. Turn them over, and fry the second side in the same way, then transfer to a plate to cool. When safe to handle, chop them finely with a knife, reserving any juices that oozed on to the plate as they sat.

Fry the onion, celery and garlic in the remaining oil with salt and pepper in a small saucepan over a medium-low heat. After 10 minutes, or when very soft, add the chopped chicken liver and its juices and fry for a couple of minutes until hot through. Add the Marsala and wine and cook at the gentlest of simmers until the sauce is very thick (almost like a pâté) with a little oil risen to the surface, at least an hour. For such a small quantity, you may need to add ½ cup or so of water during the cooking – don't let it fry. Stir in the rosemary and take off the heat: this sauce can be refrigerated for a few days, or used straightaway.

When ready to eat, put the pasta on to boil in lots of salted boiling water, and heat the sauce in a wide frying pan. Add a splash of the pasta water to thin the sauce slightly (the liquid part should be creamy). When the pasta is *al dente*, drain it and add to the sauce with the parsley and butter. Cook together for a few moments, until the butter has melted and the pasta is well coated in the sauce, then serve with a light sprinkling of Parmesan.

POTATO GNOCCHI WITH SAUSAGE RAGÙ
LAZIO

This dish is similar in flavour and technique to the *polenta con spuntature* (ribs and sausages) on page 212 – it is perhaps even more humble than that already humble dish. But it is an exuberant plate: intense flavours of pork, tomato, rosemary and Pecorino against a subtle foil of potato. With comforting textures and exciting tastes, it is a truly great example of the Roman approach to flavour.

Serves 8 as a starter, 4 as a main

Sausage ragù
14oz Italian sausage (fennel-seedy and slightly spicy if possible, page 72)
⅓ cup extra virgin olive oil
3 garlic cloves, sliced
½ teaspoon hot red pepper flakes
1¼lbs chopped canned tomatoes
1 tablespoon finely chopped rosemary

Gnocchi
About 1¾lbs russet potatoes
2 large eggs
About 1 cup all-purpose flour
A few grates of nutmeg

Freshly grated Pecorino Romano, to serve

To make the sauce, cook the sausages in 1 tablespoon of the oil – either in a frying pan or a blazing hot oven. They don't need to be cooked through, but set firm and slightly browned. Cut into ¾in chunky rounds, and keep any pan juices.

In a fairly small pan, fry the garlic in the remaining oil until browned, but nowhere near burned. Add the pepper flakes, then immediately the tomato, the sausages and their juices. Cook at a bare simmer (on the stove-top, or in a slow oven) for 50 minutes until rich, condensed and delicious. Add the chopped rosemary as you remove the pan from the heat.

For the *gnocchi*, boil the potatoes whole, skin on, in salty water. When cooked all the way through (test with a thin skewer or toothpick), drain and let cool for a few moments until you can handle them. Peel them with your fingers, and put them through a ricer/mouli.

Weigh out 1¼lbs of the riced potato. While still slightly warm, add the eggs, flour and nutmeg and season to taste with salt and a touch of pepper. Mix just as well as you need to make an even blend, but work as little as possible or the texture will become doughy. Take a small lump, roll on a well-floured surface, cut off a tiny nugget and test in boiling water to make sure it will withstand cooking. If not, add a bit more flour to stiffen the mixture and test again until you are satisfied – remember, they shouldn't be too firm, more cloud-like.

Shape the rest of your *gnocchi*: again on a well-floured board, roll a sausage of the dough to become as thick as a finger (up to you whether you use thumb, index or little as your guide). Use a table knife to cut the sausage into small dumplings, as long as they are wide. A quick flick of the knife as it hits the board will move one just aside before you cut the next.

Handle the *gnocchi* very gently. Drop them into boiling salted water, and cook for 2 minutes (start timing when they bob to the surface). Once cooked, they can be used immediately, or spread out on an oiled plate to chill. They can be reheated in water or directly in a sauce when you're ready to eat.

For the dish, warm the sauce with a splash of water. When bubbling, add the *gnocchi* and toss to coat (if you're adding cooked *gnocchi* from cold, allow them to warm in the sauce over a low heat for a couple of minutes). Serve with a heavy-handed sprinkling of Pecorino.

PAPPARDELLE WITH ZUCCHINI AND THEIR FLOWERS LAZIO

My dad and I once found ourselves with time to kill at Ciampino Airport – a result of general neuroses about flying with small children, and certain others specific to my family (we're early for everything). Taking a random punt on a nearby lake that looked nice on a map, we headed to Castel Gandolfo, which happens to house the Pope's summer residence. It sits on the edge of a volcanic crater filled with water, Lago Albano. Luck was clearly with us, as we were the only people in a small restaurant perched over the water, where I ate one of the best pastas of my life, made with zucchini flowers.

Serves 4 as a starter, 2 as a main

7oz dried *pappardelle*, or 9oz fresh
½lb zucchini
12 male zucchini flowers (the ones with no zucchini attached – much cheaper than the female)
1 garlic clove, thinly sliced

3 tablespoons extra virgin olive oil
4 basil leaves
2 tablespoons butter
3 tablespoons freshly grated Parmesan, plus extra to serve

Sweet zucchini are the key to this dish – *zucchine romane* are best (long, ridged and pale green), otherwise young, firm zucchini are a safe bet. Slice two-thirds of them across into ⅛in discs, and shave the rest as thinly as you can. Season the shaved ones lightly with salt a few minutes before you start to cook, to soften them slightly.

Prepare the flowers by tearing the petals, including the green bases, from the stalks. Discard the stalks and tear the flowers in half lengthways (many discard the stamens at this point, but they won't do any harm left in).

Cook the thicker discs of zucchini with the garlic, oil, and 3 tablespoons of water for 10–15 minutes over a medium heat in a wide frying pan until the water has evaporated and the zucchini are very tender. Meanwhile, add the pasta to another pan of boiling, salted water, such that it should be ready when the zucchini are done (a minute before they are cooked for fresh *pappardelle*, dramatically longer for dried ones). To the frying pan, just before the pasta is done, add the shaved zucchini, blossoms and torn basil leaves and cook for maybe half a minute, seasoning with salt and pepper. Drain the pasta (as ever, reserving a little of the cooking water) and add to the sauce, along with the butter, Parmesan and a couple of spoons of the pasta water. Cook for 30 seconds more, adding a touch more water if the dish looks dry. Serve immediately with a light sprinkling of extra Parmesan.

GRICIA CON LE FAVE / PASTA, GUANCIALE, FAVA BEANS AND PECORINO LAZIO

This concoction was a recent discovery, at Da Enzo in Trastevere, on the south side of the Tiber river in the heart of Rome. They proudly displayed a sign in the window – '*in questo locale si usano solo le fave fresche*' (here we use only fresh fava beans) – a joke, as restaurants are legally required to advertise where they use frozen products. Our rather wonderful and very proud waitress guided us to a few off-menu options, and when she mentioned *gricia con le fave* my ears pricked up. *Gricia*, or pasta with cured pork cheek and Pecorino, is one of the great, very basic Roman pastas. Fava beans are one of my favourite vegetables – the harbingers of summer. To eat them together I knew would be heaven.

Serves 4 as a starter, 2 as a main

6oz *rigatoni* or *tortiglioni*
1 cup shelled fava beans (1¼lbs in their shells, or just use frozen)
3 tablespoons extra virgin olive oil

1½ teaspoons ground black pepper
2¾ cups spinach or chard leaves
¼lb *guanciale*
1¾ cups freshly grated Pecorino Romano

Set any fava beans smaller than a fingernail aside (you won't have any of these if your fava beans came frozen), and pile the rest into a small saucepan. Add the oil and cover with water, add half the pepper but no salt. Cover tightly with a lid and simmer for 2 hours, until the beans and their shells are a rich brown and very soft, and almost all the water gone (make sure it never reduces to less than a tablespoonful at the bottom of the pan). Add the chopped raw spinach leaves and braise for half an hour more, adding a splash of water if the vegetables start to fry rather than steam.

Trim the skin from the *guanciale* (you'll be left with around 3oz of fatty flesh, having discarded the skin or kept it for a soup). Cut the flesh into ¼in-thick slices and then across into ½in lardoons.

Cook the pasta as usual – and add any tiny, raw fava beans in with it for the last minute.

While the pasta is boiling, fry the *guanciale* in a wide pan over a high heat until fiercely smoking and starting to colour – crispy outside but still soft within. It will release plenty of fat, which makes the sauce. Add first the slow-cooked fava beans and spinach (take care – the fat may spit) and the remaining pepper, then the pasta. Sauté for a few moments, adding just enough of the pasta's cooking water to partially emulsify the sauce. Serve with the grated Pecorino on top.

SMOKED MOZZARELLA AND PESTO LASAGNE
CAMPANIA

Alberto Comai, sage friend and colleague, made this dish for me on a whim. It is homely cooking, rooted more in familial than regional cuisine and, whilst it uses pesto *Genovese*, the flavour of smoked mozzarella and basil couldn't be more Campanian if it tried. Use buffalo milk cheese if you can get it, but cow's will do just fine in this dish.

Serves 8 as a starter, 4 as a main

11oz fresh lasagne, or 7oz dried (best if it's green*)
1 tablespoon extra virgin olive oil
1 cup freshly grated Parmesan
7oz pesto *Genovese* (page 136)
1lb smoked mozzarella (fresh, or Scamorza or Provola), thinly sliced

⅔ cup pine nuts (look for long ones)

Béchamel sauce
10 tablespoons all-purpose flour
5 tablespoons butter
3 cups milk
A little grated nutmeg

*To make green pasta, take about 4 cups spinach and boil until tender in salty water. Drain, refresh and squeeze dry. Measure it again – you should have about ⅓ cup. To this add 1 large egg and a pinch of nutmeg. Blend finely, add 1¼ cups 00 flour, and knead to an emerald dough. The amount yielded will suffice for the recipe above, rolled just under 1/32in thick.

Make a béchamel sauce first: fry the flour in the butter, then add the milk all at once (if you're brave), or very gradually (allowing the pan to come back to the boil with each addition). In either case, whisk until the mixture comes to the boil, and season with salt, pepper and nutmeg to taste.

Blanch the pasta by immersing it for 30 seconds in boiling water, then refresh in cool water and spread out to dry on a cloth. Grease the inside of your baking pan (about 8 x 12in) with the oil and sprinkle with a quarter of the Parmesan. Dot the bottom with a little of the béchamel, then start to build the dish: put in a single layer of pasta, smear sparingly with pesto, put thin slices of Scamorza over the top, spread thinly with béchamel, scatter pine nuts, then cover with another sheet of pasta. Remember this is a dish of pasta with sauce, not sauce with pasta – keep the toppings thin and sparsely distributed. The uppermost layer should be white – just Scamorza and béchamel, sprinkled with the remaining Parmesan.

Bake in a 350°F oven for 45 minutes, until browned on top and bubbling everywhere. Let cool for 15 minutes before serving, or someone will get hurt.

LINGUINE WITH CLAMS
CAMPANIA

Clams are one of the best things about seaside holidays in the Mediterranean. Fresh, sweet, salty, small yet plump – but perhaps their best feature is that even the frustrated summer resort cooks aren't tempted to mess with them too much. Italians love their pasta with clams – *spaghetti*, *spaghettini* or *linguine* – and this simplest of pastas is at once one of the fallbacks and greatest points of pride for many a Campanian chef. Eateries at every level serve this dish, from a beachside shack to a refined establishment like Da Dora on Via Palasciano in Naples, which is my favourite old-school fish restaurant in the world. At each and every one you will see diners, rich or poor, young and old, all with platefuls of *linguine alle vongole* and happy smiles.

Serves 4 as a starter, 2 as a main

7oz *linguine* (or *spaghetti* or *spaghettini* – up to you, as even Italians can't agree)
⅔ cup extra virgin olive oil
1¼lbs clams (manila or littleneck), otherwise mussels, cleaned
1 garlic clove, thinly sliced

A good pinch of hot red pepper flakes
A handful of flat-leaf parsley, chopped
A tiny pinch of all-purpose flour (¼ teaspoon, optional)
⅓ cup white wine

While your pasta is cooking, heat a wide frying pan over a high heat. When smoking hot, add ½ cup of the oil and then, quickly and all at once, the clams, garlic and pepper flakes. Fry for a few moments (I like my garlic to just start to colour at the edges, but this is a matter of taste), then add the parsley and the flour (optional, to emulsify the sauce). Stir together and then add the wine. Let the pan bubble away – the clams will let out some liquid as they start to cook. Once they have begun to open, they shouldn't fry – if your pan gets too dry, add a little water, but remember that in the finished dish the sauce should be more oil than water.

When most of the clams have opened, add the drained pasta and remaining oil and cook together until the last ones pop. Serve immediately.

SPAGHETTINI WITH RAW TOMATO
CAMPANIA

Classic from southern Lazio all the way down to Sicily, raw tomatoes make one of the simplest and tastiest sauces. My grandmother, who prepares this pasta almost every day when in Italy, calls it *primavera* – but it is a far cry from the Ital-American sauce of the same name. Why she calls it *primavera*, 'spring sauce', I'll never know. This dish is a true taste of summer, packed with ripe tomatoes, olive oil, basil – all great, zingy flavours. The rawness makes this a most refreshing and uplifting dish.

Serves 4 as a starter, 2 as a main

½ lb *spaghettini*
1lb ripe tomatoes
⅓ cup extra virgin olive oil
1 large garlic clove, crushed

About 12 black olives, Gaeta if you can get them (optional)
15 basil leaves, torn

At least 10 minutes but no more than an hour before you eat, chop the tomatoes into ½in pieces – don't remove the skin or seeds – and mix with the oil and garlic, seasoning with plenty of salt and pepper. If using, pit the olives (easiest by squashing them hard with the flat of a knife), roughly chop them and stir into the tomatoes. Let macerate at room temperature.

Put the pasta on to boil in plenty of salted boiling water. You don't want to cook the sauce, but it is a good idea to warm it gently in its bowl over the boiling water. Drain the pasta *al dente* and toss with the sauce and basil leaves. Serve immediately – it won't be piping hot and will get cold all too quickly.

ORECCHIETTE WITH BROCCOLI RABE
PUGLIA

Orecchiette are another of those semolina pastas that can be heart-stoppingly delicious fresh, or dismal dried. They are hard to find in anything other than their obnoxious dried form, that takes so long to cook inside the outside will have turned to slime. It is quite a feasible proposition to make your own, which does take more than a little time, but is a rather pleasant way to while it away.

Serves 4 as a starter, 2 as a main

About 1 cup fine semolina, or 9oz bought fresh *orecchiette*, or 7oz dried (but only if you must)
About 1lb *broccoli rabe*
2 garlic cloves, thinly sliced

6 tablespoons extra virgin olive oil
½ teaspoon hot red pepper flakes
Freshly grated Pecorino Romano, to serve (optional)

Make a semolina pasta dough with the fine semolina and ⅓ cup water – it should be firm but malleable. Knead well, let it rest for at least 20 minutes, then make the *orecchiette*.

Roll the dough into a sausage (it may help to do this in a few batches) ½in wide. Cut across to make scant ½in dumplings. Take a cheap table knife (a basic, institutional one – rounded and bluntly serrated) and make the *orecchiette* one by one. With the flat of the knife at 30° to the table, use a smearing action (away from your body) to press the dumpling out, using the rounded end of the blade. It should stretch, flatten and curl around the blade, becoming thinner in the middle than at the edges, one of which will be slightly stuck to the blade of the knife. Put your index finger gently against the centre of the little curl of pasta, hold the loose edge gently with your thumb, and pull the knife away, so as to invert the pasta over your fingertip and simultaneously detach it from the blade. It should now look like a little ear, with a slightly thick rim (the lobe), and a rough texture on the thinner centre, from where the knife pulled against the dough. A lot of words for a very small pasta, these take some practice before they come right, but after are as easy as pie. Leave them spread out on a wooden or floured surface until you're ready to cook – they're best left for half an hour or so, to become a little leathery.

Prepare the *broccoli rabe*: pick the leaves off the stem, leave any under 4in whole, whilst larger ones should have the tough midrib removed. (If the *broccoli rabe* are very young indeed – paler and tender looking – you can leave this rib in and roughly chop the larger leaves instead.) Keep the central broccoli-like florets intact.

Set a single pan of salted water on to boil, and you can cook pasta and greens together. The *broccoli rabe* will likely need a few minutes longer than the fresh pasta (but a minute or two less than dried), so put them in first. Boil for 4–5 minutes until you think they're about 5 minutes away from being done – they should be fully tender in the end, with no crunch. Add the fresh *orecchiette* now, which will need 4–5 minutes' boiling in all.

About 2 minutes before they're done, heat a frying pan over a medium heat, add the garlic and oil, and fry until the garlic is starting to colour. Add the pepper flakes, then a few seconds later the drained *broccoli rabe* and *orecchiette*. Sauté briefly, seasoning with salt and pepper, then add a few tablespoons of the pasta water. Cook together for a minute, and serve either with grated Pecorino or without.

RICOTTA TORTELLONI WITH BURNT WALNUT PESTO PUGLIA

This was the second course of a meal I ate at Oasis in Puglia, after a similar yet contrasting *antipasto* of fresh ricotta and raw walnuts. The combination of ricotta and walnuts is so good, and the difference in flavour between raw and toasted walnuts so profound, that it made perfect sense to have one after another, a combination of dishes I occasionally reproduce at home.

Serves 8 as a starter, 4 as a main

Tortelloni
Egg pasta dough made with 1½ cups
  Italian OO flour, 3 egg yolks and
  1 whole egg (page 124)
½ lb fresh ricotta (preferably sheep's milk)
2 egg yolks
1 cup freshly grated Parmesan, plus extra,
  in shavings, to serve
A few grates of nutmeg

Burnt walnut pesto
½ garlic clove, very thinly and
  evenly sliced
Sunflower or corn oil, for frying
Generous ½ cup shelled walnuts
½ teaspoon thyme leaves
½ cup extra virgin olive oil
Crunchy sea salt (such as Maldon)

You can start by making either the pasta or the sauce. For the pasta filling, beat together the ricotta, egg yolks and grated Parmesan by hand and season with salt, pepper and nutmeg (the nutmeg should be a discernible flavour, but just a hint) to taste.

Make the *tortelloni* exactly like *tortellini* (page 138), only a little larger – cut 2¾in squares of pasta, and use a heaped teaspoon of filling on each.

Make the walnut pesto. Starting from cold, fry the garlic in the vegetable oil (enough to eventually cover the walnuts) in a small pan over a medium-low heat. The garlic will sizzle for a while, then stop and turn an even golden brown. Remove with a slotted spoon and drain on paper towels. Add the walnuts to the oil, and fry until they are as dark as you can get them *without* burning, then drain. The colour of a very tan Mediterranean skin is good, as they will continue to brown more as they cool. Crush the crispy garlic with the thyme leaves in a mortar until fine, then add the walnuts and pound, but leave a little texture. Add the olive oil and stir in the crunchy sea salt to taste, seasoning also with pepper.

To assemble the dish, boil the *tortelloni* until *al dente*, a matter of minutes, then drain, and serve with the sauce sparsely drizzled over and a few scales of shaved Parmesan.

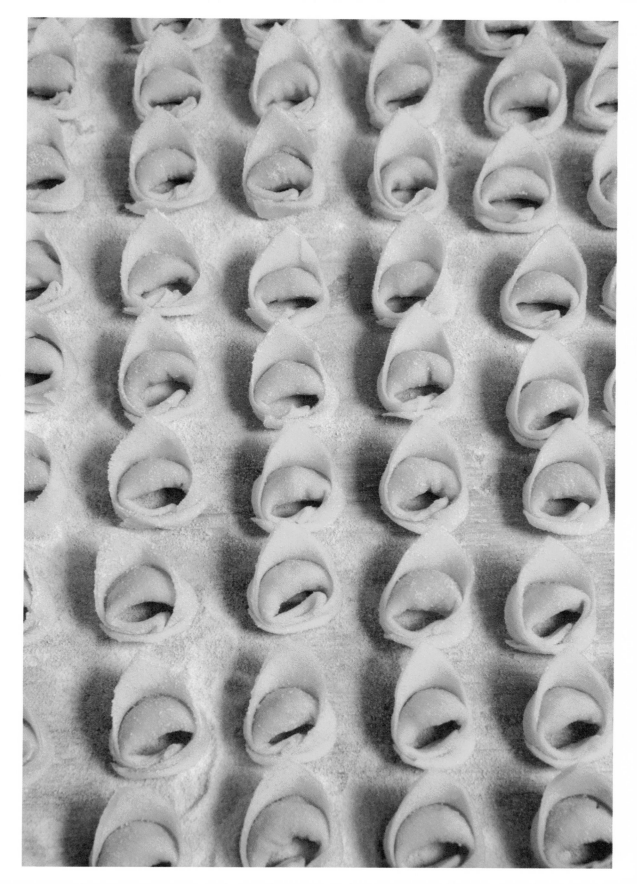

ORECCHIETTE WITH 'NDUJA
CALABRIA

Even a small amount of *'nduja* is enough to make for an extremely spicy pasta, but the heat is tempered slightly by the cream. Nonetheless it is imperative to serve a crisp yet aromatic white (Grillo or Fiano or Falanghina, say), or an ice-cold beer, to help you through.

Serves 4 braves as a starter, 2 as a main

7oz fine semolina, or 9oz bought fresh *orecchiette*, or 7oz dried (but only if you must)

1 red onion, halved and sliced with the grain

¼lb cherry tomatoes, quartered

3 tablespoons extra virgin olive oil

1¾oz *'nduja** (page 83) – or ¼lb if store-bought and not quite so strong

¼ cup white wine

⅓ cup heavy cream

1½ cups arugula, very roughly chopped

Freshly grated Pecorino Romano, to serve

'Nduja can be replaced with ¼lb crumbled Italian sausage and as much chili – dried, fresh or both – as the cook can bear.

Make the *orecchiette* as on page 154. It is a labour of love, but you will be well rewarded.

Just before you put the *orecchiette* on to boil (or just after if they are dried), fry the onion and tomatoes in the oil over a high heat for 3 minutes, until softened and slightly browned. Crumble in the *'nduja* and fry for 30 seconds, then add the wine and a small ladleful of water. Let it bubble for a few moments, then add the cream.

Allow the sauce to cook until the cream has reddened, and thickened if it looked watery, then add the drained pasta (still a little wet) and the arugula. Cook until the arugula is wilted and the pasta coated in the sauce. Serve with grated Pecorino on top.

SPAGHETTINI WITH LOBSTER, MUSSELS AND GINGER SICILY

I first had this dish at Al Merluzzo Felice in Milan – one of the loveliest Sicilian restaurants in Italy. It has a tiny dining room, and a menu of seminal dishes – many of which have been assimilated here: fish with capers and *ricotta salata* (page 260), *cannoli* (page 394), and a dish of *spaghettini* cooked *in bianco* (without tomato) with white wine, ginger, mussels, clams, shrimp, langoustines and lobster.

A version of the last can also be found, from time to time, on my menu at Bocca di Lupo, but there I have corrupted it by adding tomato and reducing the panoply of seafood to a minimum – only decadent native lobsters and humble mussels. Here it is.

Serves 4 as a starter, 2 as a main

7oz spaghettini
1 live lobster, weighing around
  1¼–1½lbs
16–20 small, plump mussels
2 tablespoons very finely chopped
  fresh ginger
1 garlic clove, finely chopped

Scant ¼ teaspoon hot red pepper flakes
⅔ cup extra virgin olive oil
⅔ cup light tomato sauce, or ½lb
  ripe cherry or baby plum tomatoes,
  quartered
5 tablespoons white wine

Prepare the lobster first: anaesthetise it for 15 minutes in the freezer, then split it down the middle. This is, as far as I know, the most humane death available, but if you're squeamish, drop it in furiously boiling water for 3 minutes (having already freezer-numbed it) before splitting. Cut it into ¾–1¼in chunks (head and all: it's full of flavour, and flesh if you're happy to bite and suck at the table), and split the claws for easy access. Remove the dead man's fingers from under the carapace if you know what these are, otherwise don't worry about them. Beard the mussels.

When you're ready to eat, put the pasta on and heat a very wide frying pan over your largest flame. Start to cook the sauce 3–4 minutes before the pasta is done. All at once, add the lobster, ginger, garlic, pepper flakes and ½ cup of the oil, and fry for a couple of minutes until the crustacean shells have turned red, and some of the garlic has started to brown. Add the tomato and mussels and fry for a minute more, then add the wine and let it bubble until all the mussels have opened. Drain the pasta, *al dente* as ever, and add to the pan with the remaining oil. Stir together over the heat for a minute, and serve straightaway.

RISOTTO / SOUP

Silence is rarely heard in my kitchen. I am convivial, and most cooking is noisy business. But soup- or risotto-making is a contemplative affair – there's little to do while the pot bubbles away, or the rice is stirred. The end result is as comforting and mellow to eat as it is to make.

Where most of my recipes are elemental – they showcase a single flavour, or contrast a few distinct ones – soups and *risotti* are alloys, a number of ingredients melded together into a pleasingly homogeneous whole. Often, the joy of such a dish is the challenge of making something from almost nothing. A handful of mushrooms and a scrap of cheese, or a crust of stale bread and a bit of cabbage, perhaps a leftover sausage or the remains of a roast become, with a little care, a dish fit for any table.

No ingredients are more important than the basics – stock, and rice for risotto. When used at all, stock should be light and flavoursome (it is better to use water than a gratuitous stock – don't use chicken broth unless you want the dish to taste of chicken). Of the three main varieties of risotto rice, *arborio* is a general-purpose one I rarely use as it can be sticky; *carnaroli* a stouter one that I prefer for meaty or rich *risotti*; and *vialone nano* a finer one, best for seafood and lighter *risotti* with distinct rice grains and a thin sauce. The *soffritto* of fried onion, garlic and other vegetables must be fully cooked before anything else is added to soup or risotto: if not fried properly first, crunchy, raw onion will end up tasting like crunchy, boiled onion. Patience throughout is key.

This may be an unorthodox statement, but for such humble dishes it is far more crucial even than the ingredients themselves to pitch the seasoning right and, for risotto, to cook the rice perfectly. These are almost impossible demands, where your indecision has a crucial role to play. The moment you can't decide whether or not to add more salt, and when you're unsure if the rice is twenty seconds over- or under-cooked, is the moment it is perfect. A far nicer dish will result if you start adding salt from the very beginning, when you sweat the onions. Then, season a touch more when you add anything – vegetables, rice, wine, water or stock. Keep the dish perfectly seasoned from start to finish, and every part will be seasoned through. By making such repeated, slight adjustments you are less likely to miss the mark and end up serving a bland dish or, worse, one too salty to eat.

Stirring is unimportant for a soup so long as it doesn't stick, and less important for a risotto than some would have us believe. Stories that a risotto must be stirred constantly, clockwise or counterclockwise depending on the inclination of the storyteller, might as well tell you to do so naked, by the light of the moon, and only if you're a virgin. It *is* important to stir risotto every few minutes, lest it catch and burn – and in the final minutes to stir it a lot (constantly and fast – a wooden spoon is indeed better than metal), when the last seasonings and butter or cheese are added, to make the sauce voluptuous and creamy. But otherwise, don't worry unduly – it'll be fine, even if your spoon isn't made of unicorn horn or your pan of sterling silver.

BONE MARROW, BAROLO AND RADICCHIO RISOTTO PIEDMONT

Barolo risotto is a Piedmontese classic. I normally think to make things simpler is to make them better, but the bitterness of the *radicchio*, and profound richness of the bone marrow, make this version (or perversion if you're a *Piemontese*) a strong favourite.

Using Barolo in a risotto, and particularly this instance where there's a lot else going on, may be excessive – it is at once a subtle and expensive choice when any decent red would work. Opening a bottle of the finest Barolo to use a little for cooking does have one big advantage though – it makes a good excuse to drink the rest.

Serves 4 as a starter, 2 as a main

½ medium onion, chopped
1 celery stalk, chopped
1 bay leaf
1 small garlic clove, chopped
5 tablespoons butter
1 head *radicchio di Treviso* (long)
  or *Chioggia* (round)
¾ cup *carnaroli* rice

⅔ cup Barolo, or other red wine
1½ cups beef stock (approx.)
1 cup freshly grated Parmesan
2oz bone marrow, diced ³⁄₁₆in (about
  half a marrow bone's worth)
2 tablespoons finely diced Parmesan
Leaves of 1 sprig flat-leaf parsley
A drop of good olive oil

Gently fry the onion, celery, bay and garlic in about 3 tablespoons of the butter with a good pinch of salt until tender – about 10 minutes over a moderate heat. Meanwhile, prepare the *radicchio*. Cut off the very tip and set aside, and shred the rest about ⅛in, discarding the woody base. Put the *radicchio* in the pan and fry until wilted, then add the rice and fry gently for a couple of minutes more. Add about ½ cup of the Barolo and cook until it has been absorbed, then start adding the stock, in small measures, waiting for each to be absorbed before pouring in the next.

Cook the risotto quite dry (not very saucy at this stage) and when you are satisfied the rice is just 2 minutes from being done, stir in the grated Parmesan, the bone marrow and remaining butter. Stir over the heat until the butter is melted and the marrow largely so and take the pan off the heat. Stir in the remaining Barolo (the risotto is so rich it needs a little raw alcohol to cut through it). At this point you can also add a spoonful more stock if need be, as the finished result should be gloopy but just pourable. Taste it one last time.

Serve on plates or in wide bowls. Garnish with a little salad of the reserved tip of *radicchio*, finely shredded and dressed with the diced Parmesan, parsley leaves and a touch of oil.

RISOTTO ALLA MILANESE / SAFFRON RISOTTO
LOMBARDY

This risotto is the Milanese classic, typically served underneath *ossobuco*. Whilst I love a good *ossobuco* (braised veal shin steak with the marrowbone in the middle), the best bit by a long shot is the marrow. So when making this risotto, I normally dispense with the veal meat, and instead serve a few marrow bones to accompany it.

A vegetarian version could easily be made, omitting the marrow and adding a little extra butter, and vegetable stock instead of meat – but why? Great vegetarian food isn't made by trying to cook without meat. It is made up of dishes that are not and were never supposed to have meat in them. Recipes you can feed to an omnivore without apology or explanation – simply good food, that happens not to have ever breathed. For me, this isn't one of them: its best feature is the subtle, underlying meatiness.

Serves 3–4 as a starter, 2 as a main

1 veal marrow bone, split (by your
   butcher) down the middle and then cut
   across into 4, to give 8 semi-cylinders
   each 2½–3in long
½ medium onion
1½ garlic cloves
5 tablespoons butter
¾ cup white wine

4 sage leaves
6 strips lemon zest, made with
   a potato peeler
¾ cup *carnaroli* rice
A good pinch of saffron strands
1½ cups chicken or veal stock
2 cups freshly grated Parmesan
A tiny bunch of flat-leaf parsley

Sort out the marrowbones before you start: separate the four end sections from the four middle ones: the marrow from the ends will go in the risotto, and we're cooking the middle sections separately, to serve with it. Scoop the marrow from the end sections and dice it finely if irregularly, about ⅛in.

Now start the risotto. Fry the onion and 1 garlic clove, both finely chopped, in 3 tablespoons of the butter until tender – 10 minutes over a moderate heat.

As soon as you get the onion on, set a second roasting pan on the heat. Bring half the wine to the boil with ⅔ cup water, the sage leaves and 4 strips of the lemon zest. Balance the four centre sections of bone cut-side up, season the exposed marrow well with salt and pepper, cover the pan tightly and bake in an oven on maximum setting for 20–30 minutes.

When the onions are tender, add the rice, fry for a minute more, then add the saffron and remaining wine and cook until absorbed. Add about a quarter of the stock first, and cook for 15–20 minutes, adding more stock in small additions and stirring often, until the rice is still crunchy – a few minutes from being done. It should be buttercup yellow, but not taste too strongly of saffron: if need be, you can add a few more strands, soaked in a thimbleful of boiling water. Taste for seasoning, and add the marrow you diced earlier. Cook together for 2–3 minutes and when you feel the rice is done, stir in the Parmesan and remaining butter to finish.

In the last moments before you serve, make the *gremolata* by chopping the remaining garlic and lemon zest as finely as you can, then adding the parsley leaves and chopping some more.

Serve the risotto and the marrow bones on separate plates, both scattered with *gremolata*.

PORCINI RISOTTO
LOMBARDY

The whole of Italy gets so excited when *porcini* are in season, you'd be hard pressed to find a town, let alone a region, where *porcini* risotto can't be had. And this excitement is with good reason, as *porcini* are such meaty, mushroomy mushrooms – fat little angels rising from the forest floor. I prefer the smaller ones, which are slightly more delicate, with an almost crunchy texture. The most humungous specimens should be avoided, as their porous underside will have become slimy and nasty, which ill-befits the king of mushrooms.

Serves 3–4 as a starter, 2 as a main

½ medium onion, chopped
1 garlic clove, chopped
5 tablespoons butter
7oz fresh, young *porcini*, diced ⅛ in

¾ cup *carnaroli* rice
½ cup white wine
1½ cups chicken or mushroom stock
1 cup freshly grated Parmesan

Fry the onion and garlic in 3 tablespoons of the butter over a moderate heat with a pinch of salt for 10 minutes until tender. Add the mushrooms and fry for a further 5–10 minutes, until the mixture looks rich and dry. Add the rice, season with more salt and a little pepper, and fry for a final 2 minutes, then pour in the wine and simmer until absorbed. Add the stock bit by bit, cooking and stirring until the rice is *al dente* and the sauce thick, but still saucy – 15 minutes, or a little longer.

Stir in the Parmesan and remaining butter, and taste for seasoning to finish.

PORCINI ARANCINI / FRIED RICE BALLS

Arancini, 'little oranges', are not necessarily so little. They are a speciality in Sicily, from where my cousin recently returned. I don't think he paid much attention to the cultural mêlée, the ancient ruins, the landscape, or the exotic produce: all he could talk about was *a-r-a-n-c-i-n-i.* He is not alone, and they are now a trend across Italy and spreading through Europe. No longer are they relegated as a means of using up otherwise inedible leftover risotto. Some cooks, myself included, will make risotto just to have *arancini...*

Makes 4 large rice balls

1 quantity *porcini* risotto (page 169), cold
¼lb fresh *porcini,* diced ⅛in
2 tablespoons butter
1 cup finely chopped Fontina cheese

1 egg
½ cup breadcrumbs (made from real bread)
Olive oil, for frying

Make the risotto as usual, but cook it a little longer than you normally would, so it isn't too runny (try to make sure the rice stays *al dente*), then spread it out on a plate to cool.

Fry the *porcini* in the butter until any liquids have evaporated, and they look quite dark and mysterious. Cool to room temperature, then mix with the Fontina to make the filling.

Mix the congealed risotto with the egg, and divide into four parts. Make each into a ball (these will be large, like tennis balls), and use your thumb to make a deep well. Fill this hole with the *porcini* and Fontina mixture, and carefully seal it in with your hands, moulding the rice back to enclose the stuffing. Roll in the breadcrumbs, making the most perfect spheres you can, and refrigerate until ready to cook and serve.

To cook the *arancini,* heat a 2–2½in depth of vegetable oil, enough to eventually cover them when they're in, to 320°F, and deep-fry them for a good 8–10 minutes, until well browned. Drain on paper towels, leaving them in a warm place for 5 minutes before serving to give the heat a chance to penetrate to the very core.

GORGONZOLA, ASPARAGUS AND HAZELNUT RISOTTO LOMBARDY

I learned a valuable lesson from Sam and Sam at Moro; don't use stock unless you want to add flavour. This risotto is a case in point – asparagus, Gorgonzola and hazelnuts are a wonderful trinity, and need only the plainest of backdrops to really sing.

Serves 3–4 as a starter, 2 as a main

½ medium onion, chopped
5 tablespoons butter
¾ cup *carnaroli* rice
½ cup white wine
1 large bunch (¾lb) thin asparagus,
   cut into ½–¾in sections with the hard
   parts of the stem discarded

¼lb Gorgonzola *dolce*
½ cup shelled hazelnuts, toasted and
   coarsely chopped

Fry the onion in 3 tablespoons of the butter over a moderate heat with a pinch of salt for 10 minutes until tender. Add the rice, fry for 2 minutes more, then pour in the wine and simmer until absorbed. You'll need about 1½ cups water for this recipe, which should be added a little at a time, waiting for it to be mostly absorbed between additions. Taste for seasoning all the time and, about 5 minutes before the end (about 10 minutes after you started adding water), add the asparagus.

When the rice is still a touch too *al dente* for you, the liquor just on the wet side, add three-quarters of the Gorgonzola (crumble it in; you can use or lose the rind as you like) and the remaining butter. Continue to stir until you are satisfied, and serve with hazelnuts and the remaining Gorgonzola scattered on top.

OYSTER AND PROSECCO RISOTTO
VENETO

This simple risotto is bursting with powerful flavours. The trick is to make sure the oysters aren't overcooked – they attain a wonderfully rich flavour when they just plump up, but overcooking makes them leathery.

Serves 4 as a starter, 2 as a main

12 oysters in their shells
²/₃ cup finely chopped shallot
1 garlic clove, finely chopped
7 tablespoons butter
3/4 cup *vialone nano* rice

²/₃ cup *prosecco* (or champagne, or any dry sparkling wine)
2 teaspoons chopped tarragon leaves (or 1 tablespoon finely chopped chives)

First shuck the oysters (page 38, or ask your fishmonger to do it for you). You should tip them out of their shells into a bowl. Be sure to save all their juices, and pour them over the oysters to keep them moist.

Fry the shallot and garlic with a little salt in half the butter over a low heat for 10 minutes until tender. Add the rice, fry for a couple of minutes, then pour in ½ cup *prosecco* and simmer until absorbed. Now add the juices from the oysters, cook for a minute, then start adding water. You'll need to add about 1½ cups water bit by bit, waiting for it to be mostly absorbed between additions. Taste for seasoning often, as the rice will absorb salt as you add it. In this dish I might use white pepper for appearance's sake, but do so sparingly.

When the rice is pretty much done (but still ever so slightly crunchy, about 10–15 minutes after starting to add liquid), and the sauce becoming thick and creamy, add the oysters and remaining butter. Stir until the butter has melted and the oysters plumped. Fish them out and quickly cut them into quarters. Take the risotto off the heat and return the quartered oysters to the rice, adding also the tarragon and remaining *prosecco*. Stir briefly, taste one last time for seasoning, and serve with a glass of chilled *prosecco*.

RISOTTO AL NERO DI SEPPIA / CUTTLEFISH INK RISOTTO VENETO

There is something dangerous and sexual about black food, as though it might be best enjoyed in a dungeon. Without colour we are blindfolded – what could the ingredients be? What do they taste like? And is that the clatter of forks and spoons, or my chains rattling again? Black food offers a means for the tame and the oppressed to develop a taste for the dark side.

Serves 6 as a starter, 3 as a main

1 quantity cuttlefish cooked in its ink
  (page 204)
½ medium onion
5 tablespoons butter

1⅓ cups *vialone nano* rice
½ cup white wine
1 tablespoon cuttlefish ink
⅓ cup chopped flat-leaf parsley

Fry the onion in 3 tablespoons of the butter with a pinch of salt over a moderate heat – 10 minutes should do – until it's tender. Increasing the heat to medium, add the rice and fry for a minute or two, then add the wine and half the ink and cook until absorbed. Now add the cuttlefish stew (let the mixture come back to the boil if the stew was cold) and a ladleful of water. Continue to add water as the rice cooks (you'll need about 2 cups in gradual additions), only adding more when the mixture becomes too thick to pour slowly, like hot roofer's tar.

When the rice is all but done, add the remaining butter and ink and half the parsley. Stir vigorously to make a thick and luscious sauce, and taste for seasoning. Serve at once with the rest of the parsley scattered on top.

SCALLOP AND GREMOLATA RISOTTO
VENETO

In essence, this risotto is similar to the one on page 173, but scallops offer a milder, sweeter flavour than the oysters, and the *gremolata* gives a little kick to the palate. Where the oyster risotto offers a 1950s glamour, this recipe is somehow more contemporary in its outlook.

Serves 4 as a starter, 2 as a main

14oz sea scallops (with their roes, if possible – about 10)
½ small onion, finely chopped
½ small head fennel, finely chopped
1½ small garlic cloves
5 tablespoons butter
¾ cup *vialone nano* rice

½ cup white wine or *prosecco*
2–2½ cups light, fennely fish stock or water
2 strips lemon zest, made with a potato peeler
¼ cup chopped flat-leaf parsley

Remove the tough bit of muscle from the side of the scallops, but keep the roes unless you're funny about them. Make sure the scallops are free of stray bits of sand. Chop the roes (not too coarsely, but not to a purée), and dice the scallops ⅛in: slice the flesh through into two or three rounds, then cut these into strips and then across into dice.

Fry the onion, fennel, and 1 chopped garlic clove in 3 tablespoons of the butter until soft – 10 minutes over a moderate heat. Add the rice and stir for a minute or so, increasing the heat to medium, then add first the wine, then gradual additions of the stock, waiting for one to be absorbed before adding the next. Stir the risotto frequently, more and more so as the rice is getting close to cooked, and taste repeatedly for seasoning.

While the rice is cooking, find a moment to make the *gremolata* by finely chopping the rest of the garlic with the lemon zest as finely as you can, then adding the parsley leaves and chopping together finely again.

When the rice is nearly cooked, just firmer than you'd like (10–15 minutes after you started adding the stock), add the scallop roes and stir for a minute or two over the heat, mashing them with the back of the spoon to turn the rice a delicate pink. You want to keep the risotto to a just pourable, porridgy consistency, so add stock judiciously at this stage. When the rice is just about cooked, still quite *al dente,* add the scallop meat and the *gremolata* along with the remaining butter. Stir for a few seconds until the cubes of flesh are half-cooked, semi-opaque. Serve, like all *risotti*, on warmed dishes.

ZUPPA COADA / BAKED PIGEON AND BREAD SOUP VENETO

This soup is an obscurity from Treviso. It is almost a lasagne, made from layers of bread and pigeon meat, doused in pigeon broth and then baked to coagulate. The resulting pudding, aromatic with cheese, cinnamon and sage, is served in a limpid pool of more of the same broth. The flavours are deep, layered and medieval – as delicious today as they ever were.

Serves 4–5 as a starter, 2–3 as a main

7 tablespoons butter or 4oz lard, plus a
  little extra for greasing the dish
2 plump pigeons, plucked and drawn
3 celery stalks, diced
1 carrot, diced
1 medium onion, diced
½ scant teaspoon ground cinnamon

⅔ cup white wine
1½ quarts dark poultry or beef stock
8 sage leaves
9 x ½in-thick slices crust-on rustic bread
  (enough for 3 layers), nicely toasted
About 2 cups grated *grana* cheese
  (Parmesan or other), plus extra to serve

In a medium saucepan, heat 5 tablespoons of the butter over a medium heat until it foams. Season the pigeons liberally with salt and pepper, and brown them on all sides. When you fear that bird or butter might get too dark, add the celery, carrot and onion and fry until very soft – about 10–15 minutes more. Add the cinnamon, wine and stock, seasoning to taste with salt and pepper. Simmer, covered, for an hour until tender.

Pluck out the birds and pick all the meat off the bones. Strain the broth, reserving both the vegetables and the stock (you should be left with around a quart, taste it for seasoning). Chop the sage leaves and mix with the cooked vegetables and picked pigeon meat.

Find an ovenproof casserole about 8–12in in diameter, and grease it. Line the bottom with some of the toasted bread, scatter with a little of the meat mixture and cheese, and cover with more bread. Continue until all the ingredients are used up, making sure the very top layer has only bread and a little cheese, and all the meat is within. Ladle about half of the broth on top, so that its level comes to the bottom of the top layer of bread. Dot with the remaining butter and bake at 320°F for an hour or until bubbling and browned. Let the dish rest for half an hour before serving in wide bowls surrounded with a pool of the remaining, heated broth, and scattered with a little more cheese on top.

Magic.

MINESTRA VERDE / GREEN VEGETABLE SOUP
LIGURIA

My mum always makes this verdant vegetable soup, enriched with a hunk of Parmesan rind, and has done since I was tiny. It is her second most potent restorative after Yiddishe-mama chicken soup. Until I went to Liguria, I assumed this was the true *minestrone alla Genovese*, but soon discovered that is a heartier and redder concoction of dried beans, pasta, zucchini and often tomato. Locals would call my mother's soup *minestra verde* ('green soup') instead and, like the more famous *Genovese*, serve it with a fresh, vibrant dollop of *pesto Genovese* in it. We often do at home too, but just as often use a sprinkling of Parmesan if pesto isn't on hand. The vegetables can be varied according to the season and your will – as long as they are green and fresh, the soup will always be lighter, tastier and healthy than any *minestrone alla Genovese* I have had so far...

Serves 6 as a starter, 3–4 as a light meal

1 medium onion, diced
1 small leek, washed and cut in ½ in rings
3 garlic cloves, thinly sliced
1 large waxy potato, peeled and diced ½ in
½ cup extra virgin olive oil, plus extra
   to serve
10 cups spinach or young chard
1 zucchini, diced about ½ in
Rind of a chunk of Parmesan
⅔ cup thin green beans, topped and
   halved (I leave the tails on)

½ cup cooked borlotti beans (optional)
In winter, 1 small or ½ large Savoy
   cabbage, 14oz or so, shredded ¼–½ in
In summer, 2 medium artichokes,
   cleaned and sliced ¼ in (page 26),
   ½ cup shelled fresh peas and 1 cup
   shelled fresh fava beans

To serve
1 quantity pesto *Genovese* (page 136)
Freshly grated Parmesan

Fry the onion, leek, garlic and potato in the oil over a medium heat for 10–15 minutes, until the onion is tender and the potato par-cooked. Stir frequently or the potato will stick. Add the spinach, zucchini, Parmesan rind, beans and cabbage (if using). Add water to cover (hot or cold, just over a quart), season to taste, and bring to a simmer. About 10 minutes after the soup has started to bubble, add the summer vegetables (if using), and simmer for 5–10 minutes more until all the vegetables are very tender, but the potato not yet cooked to the point of disintegration.

Discard the Parmesan rind, and serve the soup with a dollop of pesto in the middle of each bowl, a good grating of Parmesan, and a generous drizzle of oil. A crusty hunk of bread might not go amiss, either.

PORCINI AND CHESTNUT SOUP

This soup is my invention, but it screams AUTUMN and TUSCANY to me in equal voice. Between the chestnuts and the mushrooms, you almost have a forest in a bowl. I normally prefer the texture of small *porcini* (grilled, roasted, fried or raw), but as this soup is blended smooth, larger ones (which can become mushy when cooked) are just as good, or even better as they have a greater depth of flavour. It is an irony that ingredients which should be peasants' food (foraged mushrooms and fallen nuts) command such high prices today.

At home, I add bacon or *pancetta* and use pork stock, as porcine flavours complete the trinity. When I make this soup for the restaurant, I omit the bacon and use water, to keep the soup friendly to vegetarians, and the vegetarians friendly to me.

Serves 4 as a starter, 2 as a light meal

1oz *pancetta*, bacon or *guanciale*, cut into lardoons (optional)
⅓ cup extra virgin olive oil (or ½ cup if omitting the *pancetta*)
1 small or ½ medium onion, chopped
1 celery stalk, chopped
1 garlic clove, chopped

1 tablespoon chopped rosemary leaves
¾lb fresh *porcini*, cleaned of dirt and cut into chunks
14oz cooked, peeled chestnuts (vacuum-packed are easiest)
1 quart pork stock, or water
Rosemary oil (page 39, optional)

Fry the *pancetta* (if using) in about a quarter of the oil over a medium heat, until browned and crispy. Add the onion, celery and garlic and a good pinch of salt, and fry until soft and golden – 10–15 minutes. Add the rosemary, the *porcini* and three-quarters of the chestnuts. Fry together for 5 minutes just to par-cook the mushrooms. Cover with the stock, season well with salt and pepper, and simmer very gently for 30 minutes, until the chestnuts start to fall apart, or can be easily crushed to a paste with a spoon.

Transfer the soup to a blender. Take care when blending hot liquids: only half-fill the top, and hold the lid on with a thickly folded cloth. Blend until velvety and smooth – just let the machine run for a few minutes and do its work. Stir all but a spoonful of the remaining oil into the soup.

Cut the remaining chestnuts into quarters, and fry them in the last spoon of oil until browned and crisp outside. Serve the soup in bowls with a few sizzling pieces of chestnut in the centre of each. A drizzle of rosemary oil is nice, but not essential.

SAMPHIRE AND CLAM RISOTTO
EMILIA-ROMAGNA

The combination of seafood and greens is a Romagnolo quirk – clams and rampions, squid and broccoli – particularly with pasta or rice. It doesn't always work for me, but the seaside taste of marsh samphire is natural and complementary to the shellfish.

Samphire, *asparagi di mare*, makes a delicious risotto on its own if you add a little Parmesan, and it does, in this context at least, taste surprisingly like asparagus. It is salty and, together with briny clams, delivers a saline double-whammy. Add a very little salt at the start of cooking, to get into the rice, then resist the temptation to season again until the risotto is done – it will likely be perfect without any help.

Serves 4 as a starter, 2 as a main

½ small onion or 2 shallots, finely
  chopped
3 garlic cloves, finely chopped
7 tablespoons butter
¾ cup *vialone nano* rice

⅔ cup white wine
1lb clams
5oz samphire, washed and chopped,
  about ½ in

Fry the onion and garlic in 5 tablespoons of the butter with a pinch of salt until tender – about 10 minutes over moderate heat. Add the rice, and fry gently for 2 minutes before adding the wine. Allow it to boil away until what hasn't evaporated has been absorbed, then start to add water gradually. You will need about 10–15 minutes and 1¼ cups to obtain a thick risotto that is still undercooked. Add the clams and samphire, and continue to cook for 5 minutes, now over a slightly higher heat, continuing to add just enough water to keep the thing moving – the clams will help, releasing their own juices as they pop open.

Taste for seasoning, check the rice is cooked to your liking and stir in the remaining butter. Serve the risotto in a glorious ramshackle pile of shells, rice grains and samphire flecks. You will need many napkins to eat this dish, as it is hands on, and all the better for it.

Variation: Scallop and Samphire Risotto This dish is at least as delicious with scallops instead of clams. Follow the instructions above, omitting the clams and adding instead about 10 large scallops, roes and flesh diced finely, just before you serve.

Variation: Samphire Risotto For a plain samphire risotto, omit the clams, reduce the white wine to ½ cup, increase the samphire to 7oz and add 2 cups freshly grated Parmesan along with the butter at the end.

PAPPA POMODORO / BREAD AND TOMATO SOUP _TUSCANY_

This soup has its roots firmly in rural Tuscany, where stale bread is made into exquisite soggy soups and salads. Such bread soups are common across Italy, but somehow the Tuscans make theirs that bit more zingy and uplifting. The secret? Oodles of the best tomatoes and very little else.

Serves 4 as a starter, 2 as a light meal

1 garlic clove, thinly sliced
½ cup extra virgin olive oil, plus a little
   extra to serve
2lbs ripe, dark red tomatoes

7oz crustless rustic white bread,
   stale is best
10 large basil leaves

Fry the garlic in half the oil until it just barely starts to colour at the edges. Chop the tomatoes (skins, seeds and all) and add them to the pan with a good pinch of salt and some black pepper. Simmer over a medium heat for about 40 minutes, until very concentrated, with the oil risen to the surface. Tear the bread into bite-sized chunks (lightly toast these if it is fresh bread). Add 3½ cups water to the tomatoes and bring to the boil. Take the pan off the heat and quickly stir in the bread – stop as soon at it is immersed in the sauce, as you want sodden chunks of bread, which would quickly be pulped by too long a stirring.

Let the soup cool until just warm. Roughly chop the basil, then stir it in with the remaining oil. Put the soup in the fridge and serve cold. It should have a gloopy consistency but if too solid can be thinned with a little more water. I have seen it served with grated Parmesan or Pecorino, but personally I prefer nothing more than a touch of the fruitiest, greenest oil to finish the plate.

CANNELLINI BEAN AND ESCAROLE SOUP
CAMPANIA

This soup is simplicity itself, hot and warming enough for the autumn, and light enough for the summer. Escarole is a wondrous lettuce – bitter, sweet, fleshy, refreshing. Think iceberg crossed with frisée, and on steroids. It can be replaced with chopped romaine lettuce, which has a similar texture and sweetness even if it does lack that bitter edge.

Serves 4 as a starter, 2 as a light meal

1 garlic clove, thinly sliced
²/₃ cup extra virgin olive oil, plus extra
  to serve
A pinch of hot red pepper flakes
½ head escarole or romaine lettuce,
  cut into 1in-wide ribbons at the very
  last moment
1lb cooked cannellini beans
  (canned are fine)

2 cups of the cannellini bean cooking
  liquor (if available), or water
10 basil leaves, torn
½ cup chopped flat-leaf parsley

To serve
Freshly grilled bread
Freshly grated Parmesan

This soup takes moments to cook, so have everything ready for it, and probably start cooking after your guests are at the table. You *can* keep the soup hot for a while if you have to, but it is better as soon as it's done, while the lettuce is fresh and remembers being crisp.

Fry the garlic in half the oil until the edges turn a pale golden brown. Add the pepper flakes and let it enjoy the oil for a couple of seconds. Put in the escarole, season with salt and pepper and turn with a spoon until the edges of the lettuce leaves just start to wilt. Add the beans, their water, and the remaining oil and heat over a high flame until the soup boils for but a minute or two. Take it off the heat, add the basil and parsley, and it's ready.

Serve over the toasted bread if you like it soggy (like me), or with the bread on the side if you're English about it. In either case, a sparing hand should sprinkle the Parmesan and a slightly more generous one the oil.

RISOTTO ALLA CREMA DI SCAMPI / CREAM OF LANGOUSTINE RISOTTO CAMPANIA

In Gaeta there is a restaurant, Masaniello, where they serve the best octopus salad in the world. They also make a mean langoustine risotto – this is my guess at how.

Serves 4–6 as a starter, 2–3 as a main

1¾lbs small live langoustines
   (or 1 live lobster)
½ cup butter
1 medium onion, halved
½ head fennel, or 1 celery stalk
1 bay leaf
3 garlic cloves
1lb canned or fresh tomatoes

⅔ cup heavy cream
1¼ cups white wine
A small bunch of basil
¾ cup *vialone nano* rice
¼lb cherry tomatoes, cut in eighths
A drizzle of extra virgin olive oil
   (optional)

First prepare the langoustines. Anaesthetise them for 10 minutes in the freezer, then kill them by plunging in boiling water for 10 seconds (until they stop moving), then drain and refresh immediately in iced water so their meat stays raw. Peel the tails, reserving the heads, claws and shells for the stock. (If instead you are using a lobster, boil it for longer, 3 minutes, and take the flesh from the body, claws and knuckles, saving the shells and cutting the meat into chunks.)

Next, make a stock. Fry the shells in 5 tablespoons of the butter over a high heat for 10–15 minutes, until they smell like grilled seafood. Add half the onion and the fennel, both cut in chunks, the bay leaf, and 2 garlic cloves (bruised but whole). Fry for 3 minutes more, then add the tomatoes, the cream and wine. Simmer for 15 minutes before adding half the basil, then pulping (a stick blender works well) and pushing through a coarse sieve. You should have around 3 cups.

To make the risotto, fry the remaining onion and garlic, both finely chopped, in half the remaining butter over a moderate heat for 10 minutes until soft. Add the rice and fry for a minute or two, then half the stock. Season to taste and simmer, stirring often with a wooden spoon until the liquid is absorbed. Continue adding the liquid bit by bit until the rice is just a touch crunchy inside. Add the langoustine meat and cherry tomatoes and cook for around 4 minutes, until everything is perfectly cooked. Add the remaining basil (leaves torn) and butter and stir in. If the mixture is too stiff, add a touch more stock. Serve plain, or with a drizzle of oil.

PANCOTTO / BREAD AND VEGETABLE SOUP
PUGLIA

Pancotto just means 'cooked bread'; it is a hearty soup, more surly then *pappa pomodoro* (page 187), and more southerly. I first had it at Pane e Salute in Orsara di Puglia, a bakery with small dining room attached, where I was taken by Faith Willinger, the culinary curator of Italy. The oven burns straw instead of wood, and has done so since 1526, baking the most delicious breads in the process.

We had a rather epic meal, one of the first (and therefore best remembered) courses of which was *pancotto* served in 'little' (not very) hollowed-out loaves. Every course was delicious in an epiphanous way, but there were about twenty of them, any one large enough to fill our stomachs on its own. Each of our soups had a sausage in it – a nice surprise at the bottom – but one which can be omitted for the sake of vegetarianism, or if you subscribe to a religion that precludes the pleasures of the pig.

Serves 3–4 as a starter, 2 as a main or light meal

2 large, or 4 small Italian sausages,
  spicy or mild (page 72)
½ cup extra virgin olive oil
4 celery stalks, sliced into ⅛ in crescents
1 small onion, diced
1 carrot, diced
3 garlic cloves, sliced

A pinch of hot red pepper flakes
½ Savoy cabbage, shredded
4oz crustless, slightly stale rustic bread,
  torn into bite-sized chunks
⅓ cup chopped flat-leaf parsley
Freshly grated Caciocavallo cheese or
  Pecorino, to serve

Fry the sausages in a splash of the oil until well browned on two sides. Add the celery, onion, carrot, garlic and pepper flakes and another splash of oil along with a hefty pinch of salt. Fry for about 10 minutes, until the vegetables are tender, then add the cabbage and cover with about 1 quart water. Bring to the boil and simmer for 30 minutes, until the sausage and cabbage are tender.

Toast the bread slightly if it's still soft – don't bother if it's stale – and arrange in soup bowls. Stir the parsley and remaining oil into the soup and season with a good amount of pepper, tasting also for salt. Spoon the soup over the bread and let it sit for a few minutes before serving with grated cheese on top.

STEWS

Dreaming away as the stew-pan simmers is an excellent way to pass an afternoon. A long braise takes no effort once it's on, but you must rest with one eye open. Should your attention wander too far from the stew it may burn, or become insipid, or overseasoned. An ancient means of cooking, the principles are easy (brown the meat, add liquid and simmer), but the right texture and balance of flavours can be elusive.

Stews above all else give the cook a chance to shine. You need to work even to make a simple salad – to choose the best lettuce, to season it well, to add only just enough vinegar and not too little oil – but what really defines it is the quality of the leaves and the olive oil. With something slightly more complicated – grilled vegetables, roasted meat or fried fish, say – your efforts have yet more impact on the outcome. But the nub of the matter is still the ingredient: your job has simply been not to screw it up too much. A stew is different, though: the more work it takes to make a dish, the more the work *is* the dish. Who will notice if the onion was red or yellow, the age of the chicken, the breed of beef – and will they care? A stew is all about how dark you seared the meat, how soft you fried the vegetables, how much wine you put in, how much salt, how much you reduced the liquor and whether you timed it so the sauce thickened exactly when its contents were perfectly done. Sometimes it's all about the ingredients. And sometimes it's all about you.

So very crucial is the cook's hand in making a stew, that their personality and mood will be discernible in the finished dish, just like cinnamon or black pepper. Sharing a meal is the second-most primal act of union I can think of – and as with that first-most primal one, it feels sordid to do with those you don't want to. On the few sorry occasions I've had to cook for people I don't like, the food was somehow not so good – perhaps underseasoned, or overdone, but certainly underwhelming. When faced with such a situation again, I might disguise my distaste by grilling something quickly. I certainly wouldn't attempt a stew, where my true feelings would be as clear and abrasive as grappa.

A truly great meal is measured neither in quantity nor quality of food or wine consumed, but in the quality of time and degree of closeness achieved at the table. Bringing people together is the best reason to cook at all – and how better to do so than with a homely stew, that wears your heart so proudly on its sleeve?

TRIPE WITH POTATOES AND CLOVES
FRIULI

You either like tripe or you don't. Some dishes combine its distinctive flavour with other pungent ingredients to make a rich and layered harmony (such as *trippa alla romana*, page 215), and are a good place for the uninitiated to start. Others are plainer affairs, like this one from Trieste which, although aromatic with cloves, has a simpler taste that allows the tripe's to stand to the fore. If you already are unsure about tripe, this one isn't for you. All the more for me, then?

Serves 4 as a starter, 2 as a main

1lb cooked (white) tripe
1 small onion, chopped
1 tiny carrot, chopped
1 garlic clove, chopped
1 bay leaf
16 cloves, pounded
½ cup olive oil
2 medium potatoes, peeled and cut
 into ¾in chunks

3 tablespoons chopped flat-leaf parsley
⅔ cup white wine
1 large plum tomato, chopped,
 or a ladleful of puréed and strained fresh
 or canned tomatoes
Freshly grated Pecorino, to serve

Terracotta is a wonderful cooking medium, giving a gentle heat, as it conducts poorly. If you have a terracotta stewing pot or tagine, use it here, otherwise choose a heavy-bottomed saucepan, cast iron being the next best thing.

Cut the tripe into rough mouthfuls – 1 x 2in or so. Don't rinse it, or it will lose its flavour. Fry the onion, carrot, garlic, bay and cloves in the oil over a medium-low heat for 15 minutes until very soft. Add the potatoes, seasoning well with salt, and fry for a further 5–10 minutes until they start to turn translucent at the edges, then add the tripe and the parsley. Fry for a couple of minutes, turning until well coated in the oil, then add the wine and the tomato. Bring to a simmer, taste for seasoning (don't be shy with the pepper) and cover tightly with a lid. Cook very gently for half an hour, until the potatoes and tripe are meltingly tender but substantial enough to hold their form.

To serve this hearty stew, all that remains is to sprinkle with cheese.

HARE IN SALMÌ (IN SPICED WINE)
LOMBARDY

Cooking *in salmì* involves marinating dark meat, normally game, in red wine and spices before stewing it in its marinade. It is a technique found throughout northern Italy and much of France, and makes for deep, aromatic flavours and a fleeting insight into a hunter's life. Most typically prepared with hare, this is country-style Lombard cooking at its very best – slow, uncomplicated and delicious.

      Perhaps because there's not much to do in winter, when the days are short, or perhaps simply because it makes for a better tasting dish, this recipe has a rather lengthy timetable. Allow a minimum of twelve hours to marinate the hare (up to three days), and up to four hours to cook the stew. It is worth making more than you think as, cooked, it will keep for several days in the refrigerator, or longer frozen. You will need a big knife and board to prepare the hare, and a large bowl in which to catch the blood.

Serves 4, as 2 courses (with *pappardelle*), or as a main (with polenta)

1 good hare
4 sprigs sage, chopped
3 bay leaves
A few sprigs of thyme, tied in a bunch
2 sprigs rosemary
3 teaspoons black peppercorns, crushed
10 juniper berries, crushed
12 cloves, crushed
2½ in cinnamon stick, or 1 teaspoon
  ground cinnamon
¼ nutmeg, grated
1 large carrot, sliced
2 celery stalks, sliced into ½ in crescents
3 garlic cloves, broken but whole
2 quarts red wine (Barbera is best)
⅓ cup all-purpose flour
¼ lb lard or butter

¼ lb *pancetta*, finely chopped
1 medium onion, chopped
2oz bittersweet chocolate (to add
  roundness, optional)

To serve
4 slabs grilled polenta (page 304)
  and no cheese
or
Some wet polenta (page 303)
Freshly grated Parmesan
or
7oz dried (11oz fresh) *pappardelle*
3 tablespoons butter
¼ cup finely chopped
  flat-leaf parsley
Freshly grated Parmesan

The hare, having been hung for at least a week, should be skinned by your butcher. You may have the misfortune to have to cut off the head, tail and feet, but you'll quickly recover. The smell is slightly acrid, and there's crimson blood everywhere. You catch as much blood as you can in a bowl, and recover any that has spilled by scraping it from the board. You extract the liver, lungs and heart and put them with the blood, tightly covered, in the fridge. You wash the hare under running water for a good 5 minutes, and wipe down the chopping board. Sanity is restored. You now joint the hare, cutting it into about 16–20 chunks, and put it in a large bowl with all the herbs, all the spices, the carrot, celery and garlic. You toss it together with a tablespoon of salt and cover with the red wine. Putting this bowl in the fridge, you rest, knowing you must wait at least a day before proceeding any further.

The hare has marinated, and it is the afternoon, on the day of your grand hare dinner. You take the hare from the marinade (which you keep, including all the vegetables within), shaking off any excess liquid. Having tossed the hare in the flour with a generous dose of salt and pepper, you now fry it in a Dutch oven over a medium-high heat in half the butter or lard, turning until well browned on all sides before removing from the pan. You have left the pan on the heat and, as it starts to smoke, throw in your bowl of blood and offal, and cook (now over a high flame) until it starts to sizzle and colour. You remove the browned innards and set them aside. In the same pan, turning the heat down a touch, you add the remaining fat along with the *pancetta* and onion and fry for 10–15 minutes.

Meanwhile, chop the cooked innards finely. When the onion has softened and started to colour you add, all at once, the hare, chopped offal and marinade, and bring the dish to a simmer. Having tasted once for seasoning, you put a tight lid on the pan, and leave it for a good 2–3 hours, until the meat is almost falling off the bone. You may find yourself opening the lid a few times, but only to check the pot isn't running dry, and to inhale the heady aroma of spices and alcohol. The originally acrid, biting smell will have gradually mellowed, becoming warm and seductive like fresh pipe tobacco.

To finish the dish, you just stir in the chocolate (if you're using it at all).

To serve, you consider your options. You might serve it as it is, on slabs of freshly, darkly grilled polenta. Or you might have it with wet polenta, in which case you'd have had a pot bubbling away at the same time as the hare, as it takes almost as long to cook. In this case, you'll have put a great deal of Parmesan into the polenta, but managed to set some aside to sprinkle over the dish.

But if you're like me, you'll serve sauce and hare separately. You'll boil up some *pappardelle,* and dress these in a separate pan with the hare's cooking liquor, the extra butter, and the parsley. You'll sprinkle the pasta with Parmesan, and serve it as the first course. The hare itself you'll serve as the main, this time served with nothing to distract from it, or perhaps just a little salad.

BOLLITO MISTO
PIEDMONT

I suppose this dish, in English, should be called 'mixed boiled meats' or something, but boiling has lost its lustre, and the grandeur of *bollito misto* would not be conveyed.

A Piedmontese classic, *bollito misto* has become ubiquitous across Italy, such that there are famous restaurants specialising in it right down the axis, from Turin to Bologna to Rome to Palermo in Sicily at the excellent Casa del Brodo (whose other forte is *cassata*; their not-too-sweet rendition inspired mine on page 397). Some deliver a plated dish to your table, others bring something akin to a carvery trolley studded with wells, large and small. The bigger of these hold a meat and its own broth, the smaller each of the seven sauces served with this epic dish.

The meats used can be varied according to availability. Calf's head is a personal favourite, but not for the faint-hearted, so I've omitted it from the recipe below. If you do want to include it, boil it separately as it will spoil the broth. I normally serve *bollito misto* with only *bagnet vert* (*salsa verde*) and *mostarda* – less than the myriad you might find in Piedmont, but enough.

Serves 8 as a hearty main

Bollito misto
1 veal tongue or ½ ox tongue
8 celery stalks, 4 whole and
    4 halved across
2 medium onions, halved
2 garlic cloves
12 whole black peppercorns
2 bay leaves
1 small bunch flat-leaf parsley, tied
    with string
1lb braising beef or veal in 1 chunk –
    breast is best
1 *cotechino* sausage (18oz, page 76)*
1 capon or chicken, weighing 3½–4¼lbs,
    trussed, or boned, rolled and tied
3lbs new potatoes, peeled
    (a labour of love)
4 carrots, peeled, halved lengthways
    and then halved across

Bagnet vert (*salsa verde*)
1 garlic clove
½ teaspoon fennel seeds
¾oz bread (white, just the crumb,
    no crust)
1 tablespoon red wine vinegar
1 whole anchovy, filleted
    (or 2 anchovy fillets)
12 pickled onions and/or cornichons
2½ tablespoons salted capers, soaked in
    water until edible
1 cup flat-leaf parsley leaves
2 tablespoons raw pine nuts, preferably
    the long European ones (optional)
½ cup extra virgin olive oil

To serve
¾lb *mostarda* (page 306)

*Instructions below assume you are using a fresh *cotechino*. Store-bought ones, unless you're very lucky, will be pre-cooked, and need only be warmed through by removing from the packet and adding to the broth at the same time as the potatoes.

Wash the tongue in a few changes of fresh water for a good 15 minutes. Set a large stockpot half-filled with water over a high flame and add the 4 whole celery stalks, the onions, garlic, peppercorns, bay and parsley. Season with salt, remembering that if your *cotechino* is raw, or your tongue brined, these will add their own seasoning to the water. When the water comes to the boil add the tongue, beef breast and *cotechino*. As soon as it returns to a simmer, reduce the heat to the minimum needed for the surface to shimmer. Cook for 2–2½ hours, until the meat is just beginning to soften (test with a skewer). Taste for seasoning – the broth should be deliciously salted, as it must not only taste good on its own, but season the meats that cook in it. Add the capon and continue to poach for 30–40 minutes, by which time the slow-cooking cuts should be tender, the bird just about done.

Remove the meats and strain the broth, returning it to the pan. Skim off as much fat as you can, then return the pot to the heat. Taste again for seasoning – the broth should be quite highly salted, almost to the limit of palatability. Add the potatoes, carrots and remaining celery and simmer for 15 minutes, or until the potatoes are just cooked. Meanwhile, prepare the meats: skin the tongue and *cotechino,* and remove the trussing string from the capon. Once the vegetables are done, return the cleaned meats to the pan and turn off the heat while you prepare the *bagnet vert* (*salsa verde*).

For the *bagnet vert*, pound the garlic and fennel seeds with a good pinch each of salt and pepper. Soak the bread in the vinegar. Add the anchovy and bread to the mortar and pound to a paste. Finely chop the pickled onions or cornichons, capers and parsley and stir into the paste along with the pine nuts (if using) and the oil.

To serve the dish, lift the meats and vegetables from the broth. Carve the beef, *cotechino* and tongue into beautiful slices and the capon into joints. Lay at least one piece of each meat in a wide bowl, along with a selection of the vegetables, all half-covered in the broth. Have a bowl of *mostarda* and a bowl of *bagnet vert* at the ready, and hopefully a fine Piedmontese red.

BURIDDA / FISH STEW WITH POTATOES, BASIL AND OLIVES LIGURIA

There are perhaps as many fish stews as there are houses near the sea. *Buridda* is from the *Cinque Terre* in Liguria, the proximity of France betrayed in the name (which I am certain stems from *bourride*). I must admit I have been, at times, rather cavalier in my interpretation, by adding a variety of fish along with langoustines and shrimp. The original versions are more austere – salt cod, stockfish, cuttlefish or stonefish – but normally only one kind in the stew. This recipe is, perhaps, a halfway house between Liguria and me.

Serves 4 as a starter, 2 as a main

½ lb peeled waxy potatoes, diced ½ in
1 quart fish stock
1 lb small red mullet or bass
2 medium squid, cleaned
1 small onion, diced
1 red bell pepper, seeded and chopped
2 garlic cloves, sliced
½ head fennel, finely chopped
Scant ½ cup extra virgin olive oil,
   plus a little extra to serve

1 large or 2 medium tomatoes, chopped
1 bay leaf
1 tablespoon chopped oregano
   (optional)
½ lb clams or mussels (or small,
   shell-on shrimp)
About 15 small black olives (stone-in)
½ cup white wine
12 basil leaves, torn
Toasted bread, to serve on the side

Par-boil the diced potatoes in the fish stock, seasoned with salt to taste. Drain them when they are cooked but not overly soft, reserving the stock they cooked in. Check the fish are cleaned, scaled and gutted well, the gills removed. Leave nice little ones whole, but cut any longer than about 4in into manageable chunks about as long as they are wide. Cut the body and wings of the squid into small squares – ¼in – and cut the tentacles into pieces of comparable size. This can all be done in advance.

To make the stew, fry the onion, pepper, garlic and fennel in the oil with a good amount of salt and pepper over a medium heat for 10–15 minutes until the onions turn amber. Add the tomatoes and cook gently for a few more minutes until they start to break down. Add the bay, oregano, par-cooked potatoes, fish, clams and olives and turn to coat in the oil for a couple of minutes. Increase the flame to high, add the wine and let it boil for a minute. Add the stock and stir once. Taste for seasoning and simmer for 2–3 minutes, until all the clams have opened, then turn off the heat. Stir in the chopped squid and torn basil leaves. Let the stew sit for just a minute, to make sure the fish is cooked through and the squid not quite raw any more. Serve in wide bowls, with a drizzle of oil over toast and *buridda* alike.

MUSSELS WITH CELERY, TOMATOES AND THYME
VENETO

I spent a little over a week travelling around Lake Garda, just as spring was breaking, the snow-caps melting, the sun shining but the tourists not yet arriving from over the Dolomites. Curiously, it was in Malcesine that I had the best plate of mussels I have had in my life – despite the distance from the sea, and the abundance of freshwater fish dishes on authentically local menus.

There is therefore some claim to say this recipe is from the Veneto, but I have no idea how typical it is. I have probably cooked the dish for more people at Bocca di Lupo than ever ate it on the shore of Lake Garda – of that I am pretty much certain.

Serves 4 as a starter or light main

3 celery stalks, sliced on the bias
  into 3/4in chunks
4 garlic cloves, broken but whole
8 sprigs thyme
A good pinch of hot red pepper flakes

3/4 cup extra virgin olive oil
3/4lb cherry or baby plum tomatoes,
  halved
About 2lbs mussels, bearded
20 basil leaves

In a wide pan, fry the celery, garlic, thyme and pepper flakes in the oil very gently for 5 minutes, to infuse the flavours. When the garlic threatens to colour on its broken edges, crank up the heat to high and add the tomatoes and mussels, a good amount of pepper and a tiny amount of salt. If your pan is wide enough (the mussels no more than two or three deep), you should be able to cook it easily, just by shaking the pan for 3 or 4 minutes until all have opened. In a narrower, deeper arrangement I prefer to pick the mussels out as they pop – they are ready as soon as this has happened, and my dislike for overcooked mussels is so entrenched it extends even to the people who make them that way.

In either case, when the mussels are open, stir in the basil, taste for seasoning and serve with good bread. The liquid will be a rich, velvety broth – quite sparse as it is only the natural juices of the ingredients, hence its pure and intense flavour.

SEPPIE COL NERO / CUTTLEFISH COOKED IN ITS INK VENETO

A delicious, rich and fishy stew that will take you right back to Venice, if you've ever been. Although cheap in terms of money, cuttlefish is dear in time – it takes ages to clean, and ages again to clear up the mess you've made in the process. Have your fishmonger prepare it for you and you have got a great deal (have him leave the skin on the tentacles, and ask for big, meaty ones) – but do not go so far as to buy the pearly white frozen cuttlefish that are more easily found. They taste as bland as they look.

Serves 2 as a main

2lbs whole cuttlefish (or 3/4lb
  cleaned ones)
½ medium onion, finely chopped
1 celery stalk, finely chopped
½ head fennel, finely chopped
1 garlic clove, chopped
1 bay leaf
A small pinch of hot red pepper flakes
3 tablespoons chopped flat-leaf
  parsley

½ cup extra virgin olive oil
½ cup white wine
1lb chopped fresh or canned tomatoes
1 tablespoon cuttlefish ink

To serve
Grilled yellow polenta (page 304),
  or a wet white one (page 245)
Chopped flat-leaf parsley

Clean the cuttlefish and cut body and tentacles into rough 3/4 x 2in chunks.

Fry the onion, celery, fennel, garlic, bay, pepper flakes and parsley in the olive oil with a hefty pinch of salt over a medium heat until soft – 10–15 minutes. Add the cuttlefish and increase the heat to high until the flesh turns white. Add white wine and chopped tomatoes to cover, along with the cuttlefish ink, and bring back to a boil. Season well with salt and pepper and braise at a gentle simmer until the cuttlefish is tender, the sauce rather thick, and a reddish oil has risen to the surface – 1½–2 hours.

Serve the stew draped half-on, half-off the polenta and sprinkled with a little parsley.

CUTTLEFISH WITH PEAS
VENETO

Venetians hold many trade secrets up their sleeves. Glassblowers on Murano once held a world monopoly on their techniques, employing a team of assassins to make sure no-one who knew them could leave the island. Modern Venetians are expert in extracting money from tourists – fake Gucci bags, *carnevale* masks and irrelevant glass trinkets collect cash for the locals and dust in the purchaser's home. And Venetian chefs cook seafood with peas – but don't tell anybody, or they might have to kill you. *Canocchie* (pistol shrimp) with peas, *scampi* (langoustines) with peas, *vongole* (clams) with peas, and *seppie* (cuttlefish) with peas – all are delicious. The peas are cooked until they are soft, their sweetness complementing the sweetness of the crustacea or molluscs they accompany, and tempering the salt.

Serves 4 as a starter, 2 as a main

2lbs whole cuttlefish (or 3/4lb cleaned ones)

1/3 cup extra virgin olive oil

2 garlic cloves, thinly sliced

5 tablespoons white wine

1lb freshly shelled peas (2lbs peas in their pods, or less late in the season)

1 bunch scallions, chopped in 1in lengths

1 small bunch of flat-leaf parsley, roughly chopped

A few fronds of fennel or dill, chopped, or a few basil leaves

Grilled yellow polenta (page 304), or a hunk of bread if you prefer, to serve

Clean the cuttlefish, and cut the body into rough chunks, separating the tentacles thoroughly if large, or into little bunches if that seems more appropriate. Heat the oil over a medium flame until it releases its olivey perfume, add the garlic and then, 20 seconds later, the cuttlefish. Fry until just opaque (this will take next to no time), season with salt and pepper, then add the wine with enough water to cover. Simmer until starting to soften, but not there yet – about half an hour. You may need to top the water up as you go.

Add the peas and scallions and boil over a high heat so the liquor reduces as the vegetables cook. They'll take about 15 minutes – adjust the heat or add water so the juices, although scant and slightly thick, do not quite disappear. Add the herbs 5 minutes before the end, and serve with grilled polenta or bread.

COTECHINO WITH LENTILS AND MOSTARDA
EMILIA-ROMAGNA

Cotechino is a winter food, always eaten at New Year's celebrations with lentils to bring prosperity and good luck – perhaps because the sliced discs of sausage (and, to a lesser extent, lentils) resemble coins. *Mostarda* is a kind of sweet fruit preserve, but bitingly peppery with pure mustard oil – an astonishing sweet-hot, and one of the better things life has to offer. Here I assume a lot – that you have made your own *cotechino* or managed to buy an uncooked one, and that you might be inclined to make your own *mostarda*.

Store-bought, pre-cooked *cotechino* and jarred *mostarda* will, with good lentils, make an excellent meal. The *cotechino* might be a little more bouncy and less crumbly, a tad less porcine, and the *mostarda* taste less of the specific fruit(s) in it, but they'll be okay on their own and delicious together. If you do have the time to source or make the real McCoy, you will be doubly rewarded with a sense of accomplishment and subtle flavours.

Serves 4 as a starter, 2 as a main

Cotechino
1 uncooked *cotechino*, about 1lb
  (page 76, or buy some)
2 celery stalks
½ small onion
1 bay leaf

Lentils
1 carrot, peeled and finely diced
1 celery stalk, finely diced

½ small onion, finely diced
1 garlic clove, thinly sliced
1 bay leaf
¼ cup extra virgin olive oil
1½ cups green or brown lentils
¼ cup balsamic vinegar
3 tablespoons chopped flat-leaf parsley

To serve
Mostarda (page 306, or buy some)

Put the *cotechino* in the smallest pot it will fit in with the vegetables, cover with water, season very lightly with salt, and simmer for an hour and a half until tender.

For the lentils, fry the carrot, celery, onion, garlic and bay in the oil over a moderate heat for 5–10 minutes, until softened. Add the lentils, cover with about 2 cups water, and simmer for 40 minutes or until the lentils are done – soft but not mushy – adding more water as needed. Turn off the heat, add the vinegar and parsley, and season with salt and pepper.

Drain the *cotechino*, and discard the vegetables and stock. Skin it and slice the sausage into ½in discs. Serve on a bed of lentils with a little *mostarda* on the plate (I like to trickle a bit of the syrup over the sausage). Have more in a bowl on the table for those who need it.

PEPOSO / BEEF AND PEPPERCORN STEW
TUSCANY

Tuscan food is hardly ever spiced, with the exception of fennel seeds in sausages and *salumi*. Yet strangely, one of the most highly spiced Italian stews I know comes from the area. *Peposo* is a dish of beef, stewed with tomatoes and exceptionally massive amounts of whole and crushed peppercorns. These soften in texture and taste as they braise, creating a pleasantly warming, spicy dish.

Serves 4 as a main

⅓ cup extra virgin olive oil
1¼lbs braising beef, shin, flank or cheek, cut into 1½in chunks
1 medium onion, diced
3 garlic cloves, chopped
2 tablespoons whole black peppercorns

1 tablespoon coarsely ground black pepper
1 bay leaf
1 cup red wine
2lbs canned tomatoes, or 2½lbs fresh, chopped

Heat the oil in a heavy-bottomed Dutch oven. Season the meat well with salt, and brown well over a medium heat – about 15 minutes – turning only when the areas in contact with the pan are nice and dark. Add the onion and garlic and cook for another 10 minutes, stirring occasionally, until they are well softened. Add the whole and ground black pepper and the bay leaf and fry for 1 minute more before adding the wine and tomatoes. Taste for seasoning and bring to a simmer, then reduce the heat to its lowest and cook, lid on, for 1½ hours or until the meat is meltingly tender – taste again for salt and it's done.

It can be served straightaway, or refrigerated and reheated. Ideally serve with a crust of bread and cannellini beans. Polenta or roast potatoes are nice too, and any leftovers can be used as an invigorating sauce for *pappardelle* or *pici*.

POLPETTE / MEATBALLS IN WINE AND LEMON

Meatballs are exquisite cooked in a light, sharp sauce. I serve these tennis-ball-sized monsters, braised and glazed in white wine and lemon slices, with a fluffy mashed potato. They make for a glorious lunch at any time of the year.

Serves 4 as a main

Meatballs
1¼lbs ground veal
1¼lbs ground pork
¼lb stale bread, moistened in milk
1 large egg
2 cups freshly grated Parmesan
⅓ cup finely chopped flat-leaf parsley
1 garlic clove, grated
¼ cup heavy cream
A little grated nutmeg
1 tablespoon extra virgin olive oil

12 x pinwheel slices lemon
4 bay leaves
1¼ cups white wine

Mashed potato
About 2lbs russet potatoes, peeled
　and chunked
1 quart milk
1 bay leaf
7 tablespoons butter

Mix together the veal and pork with the bread, egg, Parmesan, parsley, garlic and cream. Season with nutmeg, salt and pepper and cook a tiny bit in a frying pan to check the seasoning. Form 8 large, perfectly spherical meatballs. Keeping your hands wet will help to keep that cold veal/pork fat off them. Rub the *polpette* with the oil, place them on a wide baking sheet, and balance a disc of lemon on top of each, like a hat. Roast at 400–425°F for 15 minutes, until browned in part. Remove from the oven and transfer them, taking care not to lose the lemon slices, into a small roasting pan which fits them snugly.

Tuck the remaining 4 slices of lemon and the bay leaves between the meatballs, and pour in the wine. Cook at 300°F for 2 hours, topping up with water if the juices run dry (the sauce should be thick and velvety by the end). Baste occasionally and the meatballs will come out glazed, and particularly gorgeous.

While the meatballs are braising, make the mash. Cover the spuds with the milk, adding the bay leaf and more salt than you might think. Simmer for 30 minutes, until the potatoes are completely soft. Drain, reserving the liquid. Rice the potatoes with the butter, then add enough milk to make a loose mash. It should be soft and supple, semi-liquid like volcanic mud. Season with extra salt if needed, but stir as little as possible. Serve the meatballs on a bed of this mash, glossy with a spoonful of their citrussy sauce.

POLENTA CON SPUNTATURE / POLENTA WITH PORK RIBS AND SAUSAGE *LAZIO*

Ginny is my maternal grandmother, and Alfred a dear friend of hers, and of mine. Walking together through Rome, from the Pantheon to Piazza Navona, we go through a tiny alley where Alfred had his first kiss, and under the window in Ginny's old flat, past which an electric guitar once fell from a druggy party being thrown by the rockers in the apartment above. Rome, which seems almost a cultural back-alley today, breathes for a moment with the life it had in the 1950s, when it was the centre of the world.

Together they lived *La Dolce Vita* in 1950s Rome. Fellini's film is based in part on Ginny's side of my family; my mum and her brother supposedly Steiner's children. The hedonism of Steiner's wife can still be seen in Ginny, full of vim and lust for life; her own paintings stud the walls in the film, while guests at a dinner party she threw, and Fellini attended, make up the extras.

Rome has since lost its life-force, but retains its status as the very definition of man-made beauty, so when I snap out of it and realise it's today, I'm hungry and surrounded by tourists, it's not all that bad. We end up at Dal Paino near Piazza Navona, always, and if I don't have a pizza I'll have *polenta con spuntature*.

Serves 4 as a main

1 rack spare ribs (a dozen ribs in a rack)	2lbs fresh tomatoes, or 1 3/4 lbs canned
4 Italian sausages (page 72)	3/4 cup white wine
1/2 cup extra virgin olive oil	3 sprigs rosemary
2 garlic cloves, sliced	1 quantity wet polenta (page 303)
A pinch of hot red pepper flakes	Grated Parmesan or Pecorino Romano

Cut up the ribs, so that each bone is separated with its fair share of meat. Brown them and the sausages in the oil in batches, in a heavy-bottomed pan over a medium heat. When the last batch is browned, add the garlic and fry until golden. Put the pepper flakes in the pan, and return the previous batches of sausages and ribs to it, along with any liquids they have leached. Add the tomatoes, wine and rosemary and braise, lid ajar, for an hour and a half or until the meats are tender, the sauce reduced, and oil rising to the surface. While the meats are braising, make the wet polenta.

Serve the polenta spread out flat on wide plates, with one sausage and two or three ribs per person, and a scattering of cheese. Perhaps I'm uncouth, but I like to use Parmesan in the polenta and Pecorino on top. Purists wouldn't mix.

CODA ALLA VACCINARA / OXTAIL WITH CELERY AND TOMATO LAZIO

Oxen were the beasts of burden around Rome for thousands of years, ploughing fields and carrying loads. *Vaccinari* slaughtered the animals on retirement, selling their hides and flesh – they served well, even in death. The beefy tradition continues in Rome, especially in Testaccio around the old meat market. Still today, the closer you are to that quarter, the more tails and offal are used in cooking: choice cuts travelled far with the wealthy, tough and wobbly ones stayed with the market workers. The latter got the better deal.

This stew can be made in two ways – light and almost brothy as below, or rich and tomatoey. The thick version is decidedly inferior, but the sauce it makes is delicious on tubular pasta – *rigatoni* or *tortiglioni*. The thinner is served with a spoon and crust of bread instead, the two utensils you'll need to enjoy the broth to the full.

Serves 4 as a main

About 2lbs oxtail, cut into its joints
¼lb lard (or ⅓ cup olive oil, plus 3oz diced *prosciutto* fat)
1 head celery, 2 stalks diced and the rest halved
1 medium onion, finely chopped
1 garlic clove, chopped

⅓ cup chopped flat-leaf parsley
2 bay leaves
¾in piece cinnamon stick and/or 6 cloves
1½ cups white wine
1lb fresh or ¾lb canned tomatoes, chopped

Season the oxtail liberally with salt and pepper and brown it very well in the fat, then remove. In the same pan, sweat the diced celery with the onion, garlic, parsley, bay and cinnamon for about 10 minutes, until soft.

Return the meat to the pan, add the wine and tomato and enough water to cover, seasoning generously with salt and pepper. Simmer for about 3 hours, covered (I find this easiest in a slow oven, about 275°F, but it's up to you), until the meat is very tender indeed. The sauce should be thin, almost like a rich broth – top up with water as and when required, and taste it for seasoning, especially towards the end of cooking. Up to this point the dish may be made in advance – hours or days if refrigerated.

To finish, skim the pan pretty scrupulously, add the halved celery sticks and simmer for 10–15 minutes until they are tender, but still vibrant green. Serve in wide bowls with plenty of the sauce, and be sure to gnaw the gelatinous cartilage from the cut ends of bone.

TRIPPA ALLA ROMANA / TRIPE WITH TOMATO, MINT AND PECORINO LAZIO

This dish is manna to the tripophile, and a good introduction for the uninitiated, the pervasive aroma of tripe balanced by equally strong flavours – tomato, bay, *guanciale*, Pecorino and *mentuccia* (pennyroyal, a mint halfway between oregano and spearmint, which can be used together as a substitute). It is my favourite lunch, and my strongest memory of Rome.

Serves 4–6 as a starter, 2–3 as a main

¼lb *guanciale*, skin off, or *pancetta*
2lbs cooked (white) beef tripe
½ carrot, roughly diced
1 celery stalk, roughly diced
1 small onion, roughly chopped
⅓ cup extra virgin olive oil
2 garlic cloves, sliced
1 large bay leaf
1 teaspoon freshly ground black pepper
A small pinch of hot red pepper flakes

1¾lbs chopped canned tomatoes
⅔ cup white wine

To serve
4 sprigs *mentuccia* (pennyroyal),
    or 2 sprigs each of oregano and mint,
    leaves chopped
2 cups freshly grated Pecorino Romano

Cut the *guanciale* into chunky, ½ x ¾in lardoons as long as the *guanciale* is thick, and hack the tripe into roughly rectangular mouthfuls, about 1 x 2in.

Fry the *guanciale* at a high temperature in a dry pan until partly crispy (still succulent within) – do not be alarmed by the smoke, even if your detector is. Add the vegetables and the oil along with the garlic, bay, black pepper and a good pinch of salt and fry for 10 minutes until tender, now over a medium heat. When the vegetables are tender add the tripe and the pepper flakes, stir for a minute, then add the tomatoes and wine. Cook at a gentle boil until the sauce is very thick indeed and the oil risen to the surface – half an hour or more.

Serve with the chopped *mentuccia* and grated Pecorino on top along with an extra sprinkle of pepper. A crust of bread and a rustic red will make the meal complete.

VEAL SPEZZATINO WITH ARTICHOKES
LAZIO

A *spezzatino* is a scarce stew, one cooked with a minimum of liquid, that evaporates during cooking to give a sparse, intense sauce – ideal for mopping with bread. Italians use pale veal for this dish, but rose veal (*vitellone* in Italy) is excellent and may even be served to those who won't eat veal on ethical grounds, if you check with them first. I put artichokes in this *spezzatino* – but that should come as no surprise, as I seem to put them in everything.

Serves 4–5 as a main

13/4 lbs stewing veal, flank, shoulder
  or shin
3 tablespoons all-purpose flour
2 tablespoons butter
3 tablespoons extra virgin olive oil
1 medium onion, finely chopped

1 garlic clove, finely chopped
2 bay leaves or sprigs rosemary
1 cup white wine
Juice of 1 lemon
6 medium or 4 large artichokes
3 tablespoons chopped flat-leaf parsley

Cut the veal into about 1in chunks, season with salt and pepper and toss with the flour. Heat the butter and oil in a pan wide enough to accommodate the meat (you can always do it in batches if it helps), and brown it well on all sides – about 15 minutes of very occasional turning. Add the onion, garlic and bay or rosemary and fry gently for 5–10 minutes more. Add the white wine and lemon, cover with a tight-fitting lid and reduce the heat to minimum. Braise the veal for 45 minutes, until it is just starting to tenderise.

Meanwhile, clean the artichokes (page 26), and cut each into 8 wedges, eliminating any choke. Add the artichokes to the veal, taking the opportunity to introduce a splash of water if the pan has run dry. Taste for seasoning, replace the lid, and cook gently for half an hour more, until meat and artichokes are tender. Remove the lid, and check the sauce is as thick as heavy cream. If split or non-existent, add a splash of water and shake the pan to emulsify; if a bit thin increase the heat for a minute. Stir in the parsley.

Serve with mashed or roast potatoes (pages 211 and 308) or salad (page 333) and bread.

LAMB AND FAVA BEAN SPEZZATINO
MOLISE

All young meats make for an excellent *spezzatino*. Lamb is the strongest tasting, and perhaps the most suitable in early summer when fava beans too are at their peak.

Serves 4 as a main

1 shoulder of lamb
3 tablespoons all-purpose flour
Scant ½ cup extra virgin olive oil
1 bunch scallions, cut in ¾in lengths
2 garlic cloves, thinly sliced
A small pinch of hot red pepper flakes

4 anchovy fillets, chopped
4 sprigs rosemary
2 cups white wine
1lb peeled fava beans
   (6lbs in their shells, or 1½lbs shelled,
   blanched for a minute, then peeled)

Cut the meat from the bone and dice it roughly. Toss it with the flour, salt and pepper, and brown lightly in the oil, in batches if need be.

Add the scallions, garlic, pepper flakes and anchovies to the browned lamb and fry for 5 minutes, until the greens of the onions are dark and glossy. Add the rosemary and the wine and simmer, lid on, for an hour or even an hour and a half, until the lamb is tender. Remove the lid and sort out the sauce: taste for seasoning, and add a splash of water if it looks too scant, which is likely, remembering it will still need to cook for just a few minutes more. Add the fava beans and simmer (lid back on) for 5 minutes until they are just cooked. I wouldn't serve this with anything but a fork and spoon.

OCTOPUS WITH PEAS
MOLISE

Octopus is rubbery? No, or at least it needn't be. Look for double-sucker octopus – large beasts, with twin rows of suckers on each tentacle. They quickly cook to tenderness (best left with a little bite), before the skin or muscle starts to disintegrate. The most extraordinary of marine creatures, octopus are beautiful and intelligent. If they didn't taste so good, I'd leave them be, alive in the sea. But there is something about their flavour that is addictive, especially with the sweetness of peas. The oily, purple and green composition of this dish appears as gorgeous as it does sinister. It is one of the best things I have ever eaten, and I hope you might agree.

Serves 8 as a starter, 4 as a main

1 large octopus, about 3–4lbs
2/3 cup extra virgin olive oil
2lbs freshly shelled peas (3–5lbs peas
  in their pods)
2 bunches scallions, chopped in
  1in lengths

4 garlic cloves, thinly sliced
½ cup roughly chopped flat-leaf parsley
½ cup roughly chopped basil

Submerge the octopus three times in a pan of boiling water, allowing the water to return to the boil each time before taking the octopus out and hanging it up for 5 minutes between dips to drip-dry and cool. Throw out most of the water, leaving just enough in the pan to cover the octopus. Simmer for 35 minutes, or until it looks like it's thinking of becoming edible.

Fish the octopus out and separate the tentacles, cutting them into bite-sized chunks (leave the skin on). Cut the body sac into strips. Return the octopus to the liquid in the pan, adding at the same time the oil, peas, scallions and garlic. Boil over a high flame until the liquid is reduced and sugary from the peas and onions, the peas tender, and the octopus delicious but pleasantly firm – about 10–15 minutes.

Some 5 minutes before the end, season with salt and pepper and add the parsley. The basil goes in just before you serve, with a crust of bread.

GUINEA HEN 'CACCIATORE' IN WINE AND VINEGAR ABRUZZO

Cooking *cacciatore*, 'hunter's style', always means braising in wine, but may be interpreted in any number of ways. Some add tomato, or mushroom, or olives or red wine. I keep it simple, with a mixture of white wine and vinegar for a piquant balance of flavour and meltingly tender meat. Farmed rabbit or chicken work very well, but guinea hen is my favourite – that little bit more succulent and flavoursome. It is especially delicious with roast potatoes (page 308).

Serves 3–4 as a main

1 guinea hen	3 celery stalks, diced
½ cup extra virgin olive oil	3 garlic cloves, sliced
1 medium onion, diced	A large sprig of rosemary, leaves removed
1 carrot, diced	⅓ cup white wine vinegar
2 bay leaves	¾ cup white wine
3 tablespoons all-purpose flour	

Joint the guinea hen into four, separating the wings at the first joint and leaving the breast on the bone. Cut each joint into three (leave the drumsticks whole and halve the thighs; cut the breasts across to make three pieces, one with the first joint of the wing attached).

Cut the remaining parts of the carcass (spine and wings) into chunks and brown in 1 tablespoon of the olive oil. Add half of each of the onion and carrot and fry for a couple of minutes, then add the bay leaves and cover with about a quart of water. Simmer until you have a nice stock, reduced to about 1 cup.

Season the pieces of guinea hen with salt and pepper, then toss in the flour. Heat a pan wide enough to accommodate the meat in a single layer over a medium heat, add the remaining oil and then the meat. Brown well on all sides, trying not to move it except to turn – this will take 10–15 minutes. When golden and smelling delicious, add the celery, garlic and rosemary along with the remaining onion and carrot. Season again, then shake the pan to settle the vegetables between the meat. Fry for 5–10 minutes or until tender. Add the vinegar, wine and strained stock. When this comes to the boil, reduce the heat to a gentle simmer and taste for seasoning. Cook for about an hour, until the liquor is as thick as heavy cream and the leg meat tender; shaking the pan every so often will help to emulsify the sauce. This dish can be served straightaway, or made in advance and reheated over a gentle flame with a dash of water.

CLAMS AND BEANS
CAMPANIA

This dish is based on a pasta they enjoy in Campania – short *ditali* cooked with clams and beans. I prefer it without pasta: it makes for a lighter meal, the summer flavours of clams, beans, tomato and basil singing out like a shrill trumpet calling me south.

Serves 4 as a starter, 2 as a main

About 1lb manila clams or other bivalves – surf clams, cockles or mussels
3/4lb cherry or baby plum tomatoes, halved
2 garlic cloves, thinly sliced
A pinch of hot red pepper flakes

1/3 cup extra virgin olive oil
1/3 cup white wine
About 2 cups cooked, drained cannellini beans
3 tablespoons chopped flat-leaf parsley
8 basil leaves, torn

Heat a very wide pan over a very high heat until it smokes. Combine the clams, tomatoes, garlic, pepper flakes and oil in a bowl (if your pan's not going to be wide enough to hold them all in more or less a single layer, omit the clams for now and add them after the tomatoes have fried for a couple of minutes). When you think the pan shouldn't possibly get any hotter, add the bowlful of ingredients all at once.

Cook, shaking the pan from time to time until a few of the clams pop open. Season with pepper and a tiny bit of salt and add the wine. Let it bubble for a minute, then add the cannellini beans and parsley. Boil until the beans are hot through, and the last of the clams have popped open – not very long. Stir in the basil and serve immediately.

DUCK IN CHOCOLATE AND MARSALA
SICILY

From the brutal to the refined, Sicily has it all. This rich, complex stew is food that must surely have graced royal tables. Sweet with pine nuts and raisins, it demonstrates the Arab influence on Sicily. It could even be served with couscous, a popular pasta on the island.

Serves 4 as a main

1 duck, jointed and cut into 8 pieces
1 tablespoon extra virgin olive oil
1 medium onion, finely chopped
2 garlic cloves, finely chopped
1in cinnamon stick
½ teaspoon hot red pepper flakes
2 bay leaves
1 teaspoon fennel seeds, crushed
½ cup raisins

¼ cup pine nuts (preferably long ones)
1 cup dry Marsala (or medium sherry, *oloroso*, for example)
⅓ cup wine vinegar (red or white)
2oz bittersweet chocolate, broken into pieces
3 tablespoons chopped flat-leaf parsley, to serve

Season the duck with salt and pepper, and brown it in the oil in batches, in a stewing pan over a medium heat – it will take 5–10 minutes on each side. Start it skin-side down, as the copious fat that it releases will help the process. Remove the duck and pour off all the fat.

Add the onion, garlic, cinnamon, pepper flakes and bay to the pan and fry with a pinch of salt for about 10–15 minutes over a low flame, until amber and soft – the grease left clinging to the pan will be enough to fry in. Add the fennel seeds, raisins and pine nuts and fry for 2 minutes more, then return the duck to the pot and add the Marsala and vinegar. Cover with a lid and braise very gently until the sauce is thick and the duck tender – about an hour, or a little less. Skim off any excess fat, stir in the chocolate, taste for seasoning, and serve sprinkled with parsley, and perhaps a few extra pepper flakes, if you like it hot.

The flavours are so complex I struggle to find suitable accompaniments other than simple sautéed spinach with a little garlic and chili, or a bed of fluffy couscous.

FOCACCIA MARITATA / FOCACCIA WITH SPLEEN, LUNGS AND RICOTTA SICILY

Sicilian cuisine must be the most varied of any region in Italy. Its important position in the Mediterranean has seen it host a myriad of peoples – notably the Arabs, but also Phoenicians, Greeks, Romans, Vandals, Ligurians, Catalonians, French... This dish dates from the end of the Middle Ages, when the Jewish community in Palermo was strong. Baking breads (Sicilian *focaccia*, a soft round bun, is not unlike the leavened discs of bread so popular in the Middle East) and running slaughterhouses, they sold sandwiches stuffed with ricotta or offal as a cheap snack.

In 1492 Ferdinand II expelled the Jews from Spain, and Sicily and Naples, also under his rule. They could convert (and prove it by eating pork), leave or die. Most left. The Christians took over the bread-and-offal business, mixing the meat and cheese fillings (not kosher), and cooking the meats in lard in which they also soaked the bread (definitely not kosher, but delicious). The current sandwich recipe hasn't much changed since then, although it has become a source of Sicilian pride – they even make *pasta reale* (decorative marzipan) in its image. This is brutal cooking, the meat first boiled and then stewed in lard, with a strongly ferrous taste from the spleen. I suppose whether it is delicious or not depends on your perspective.

Serves 8 as a light meal

1 beef lung (half of a pair)
1 beef spleen
10oz lard

8 soft, round *focacce* – burger buns
   or small Turkish *pide* are similar
1lb ricotta, fresh or smoked
2 lemons

Set a pan of salted water on to boil. Add the lung, and weight it down with another pan or a few plates, and boil for an hour. Add the spleen and boil for half an hour more, then turn off the heat and let them cool in the water. Slice thinly.

Melt the lard in a wide pan (a wok is great) with a ladleful or two of the murky water the meat cooked in. Add the sliced meats and simmer over a medium heat for 10–15 minutes.

Cut the buns open, and moisten both halves with a little of the lardy juices. Put in a slice of the ricotta, and pile up with the meats, fished from the fat. Season with salt, pepper and a squeeze of lemon and close the sandwich. Eat now – this is fast food.

GRILLED / PAN-FRIED

Open,
Close,
Open, close.

Life is sweet as a scallop, moseying across the sea floor, I just open, close, open and close my mouth and swim along, propelled by my silent chatter.

Open, close, open.

What's that? It's hard to focus so many eyes. It looks like a diver. Hello diver!

Close, open.

Well, now I'm hitching a lift in the diver's bag. Isn't this fun? Look at the bubbles! Where do they come from? What are they made of? They look like silver – how lovely... Bloody hell, we're getting close to the light. I'm being lifted into a giant bubble, as big as the sea.

      Brrrrr! Now I'm on a bed of ice. I'm not sure I like this, I think I'll keep my mouth shut – don't want to attract attention.

Close, close, close.

Ooh – that tickles! What's that thing you're poking into my shell? No, no! Let me stay closed. Closed, I say!

      Pop! Oh, it's only you, Jacob. I couldn't see you with my shell closed. Would you mind? I've had some sand stuck in my mantle for weeks! Aahh, that's better – cheers! Just a little salt please, a little more, and a smidge of olive oil – the posh one, mind – rub it in – ooh, that smells lush. Make sure the grill is smoking, will you? Put me on the hottest spot – that's it! Don't move me – wait,

      Wait.

      Hey – HEY – I'm brown on this side – could you just turn me over quickly? Thanks mate – I owe you one... Oi! Don't move me again – I've told you before – I was just getting comfy. Leave me alone.

      Okay, I think I'm done now. That didn't take long, did it? Be a good fella and eat me quickly, will you? Just a squeeze of lemon, a few more drops of that nice oil. Come on Jacob, open your mouth...

Open,
Close.
Yum!

GRILLED FISHES ON AN OPEN FIRE

Take some paper from a drawer,
Just one piece, not any more,
To make a fish.

Put the paper on a dish.
Make a wish.
Cut out the fish.

Color in its yellow gills
Cover it with polka pills
Cook the fish.

Serve it on a serving dish
It's delish.
Eat the fish.

My grandfather, John Becker, wrote this poem, 'How to Make a Fish'. The best way to cook a fish is as simple and as beautiful as his words – just grill it. Which is not to say that to grill fish simply is a simple feat – you need an understanding of fire, temperature, timing and the fish at hand. Here are some notes to help you on the way.

Buy the fish All fish should be bright, firm, the flesh translucent, the scales shiny, the eyes clear and they should smell of the sea – not overly fishy. Allow ½ lb filleted fish, ¾ lb fish steaks, or ⅔–1lb whole fish per person.

Oily fish like garfish, mackerel, sardines and skipjack are cheap and delicious, so long as they are not overcooked. They can make a grill flare up if put too close together.

Small fish (no more than 2in thick) are all easily grilled whole: try John Dory, bream, small to medium bass, red mullet, medium grey mullet or red snapper, and flat fish like sole and sand dabs or small specimens of brill or turbot. They should be cooked carefully, so the skin is crisp – browned and slightly charred but not burned – and the flesh just detaches from the bones.

Large fish (thicker than around 2in) are difficult to cook whole, requiring close control of the fire. Rather than filleting, I prefer to tranche them (cut across to make bone-in steaks), as they stay juicier this way. Very large fish like tuna and swordfish are never sold whole. They are amazingly common in the markets, given how rare they are in the seas. In Italy, they are usually cut very thin (¼ in), so they can be cooked through quickly without drying out. I prefer my steaks juicy and pink inside, so I cut them ½–¾ in thick.

Prepare the fish Make sure it has been properly gutted and scaled – the skin of grilled fish is the best bit, unless covered in scales. It is best to scale fish before gutting or cutting it – rub it with a blunt knife under running water, against the grain of the scales.

A good 10 minutes or so before you cook the fish, season it well with salt (1½ teaspoons fine salt per 2lbs) inside as well as on the skin. Leave it at room temperature to warm a little – it will be easier to cook perfectly if not fridge-cold. Brush it with a touch of oil before you grill – just to prevent sticking. Too much oil will make the grill flare up.

Prepare the fire Burn charcoal, or semi-dry fruitwood, olive wood, or old grape vines, and let the fire burn down to embers before you start.

Use a grill with thick bars if you can. Let these get hot above the fire before you grill, then clean them with a wire brush. Now wipe them with a wet cloth (or the cut side of half an onion, held on a fork, which is efficient and smells delicious), and rub with a little oil just before you put the fish on. Judge the height between the fire and the grill – little fish need less time to cook – the fire must be hotter, or the bars lower, to crisp the skin faster.

Don't think it's a half measure to use a griddle pan indoors – they are practical, easy and effective. I use a very big one in my restaurant, as I don't have space for a wood grill. My fish is delicious, or so I have been told.

Grill the fish Place them on the grill. Make sure they go down in the right spot, as you mustn't move them until they are ready to turn. Peek underneath every so often to check on the skin – lift a corner gently with a fork or palette knife. You're looking for it to blister, going a golden brown, perhaps blackened where the skin has bubbled.

Grill the fish only once on each side. It will need about 1 minute per side for each ½in of total thickness (at the thickest point), assuming the grill is reasonably hot – a little more for the first side, a little less for the second.

Turn the fish over when the first side is ready, gently starting to lift from the dorsal side. If it has grilled enough, the skin should come away from the bars easily, without ripping. Cook the second side for slightly less time than the first – the residual heat on the cooked upper side will continue to cook the fish.

There are three ways to check for doneness: peek inside the cavity of the whole fish, and if the traces of blood on the spine look cooked, it's done; use the tip of a knife to peek inside steaks or check the flesh of whole fish can detach from the bone; or judge it done when you have a vague feeling that it might be ready.

> Serve it on a serving dish
> > It's delish.
> > > Eat the fish.

STEAK WITH PARSLEY AND GARLIC

It is easy to grill a steak. The challenge lies in finding the best meat – dark purply red and veined with fat. I'm a big fan of rib-eye and sirloin, which have just the right balance of tenderness and flavour. Italians are masters of well-done meat, slicing it thin so it can be cooked through without drying out, but I still prefer a juicy red steak.

Per person

1 steak (perhaps rib-eye, perhaps not), about ½ in thick
1 tablespoon finely chopped flat-leaf parsley

¼ garlic clove, grated or crushed
1 tablespoon extra virgin olive oil

I let the steak come to room temperature before cooking it, and mix together the parsley, garlic and oil to make a thick dressing as I wait.

I season the steak well, then cook it on a really hot grill (griddle pan or barbecue) for just a couple of minutes on each side – I like it medium-rare, which is most un-Italian of me. After putting it on, I don't move it until it is ready to turn, and then I brush the grilled side with half the parsley mixture.

When I take the steak off the grill (again, not moving it until it's ready), I turn it over on to a warm plate, and brush this second side in the same manner. I let it rest somewhere warm, and serve it with a salad, or grilled *radicchio di Treviso* (page 299).

PORCINI AND POLENTA (WITH LARDO)
LOMBARDY

Porcini are about as rustic as you can get, and about as sophisticated as you can get. Together with golden charred slabs of polenta, they make for the barbecue to end all barbecues with no further adornment.

If you are a meat eater, and you happen across some *lardo,* there is nothing better to do with it than use it here. Draped over the hot mushrooms, the silky white ribbons of aromatic fat will melt, becoming translucent and adding only goodness to the already porcine mushrooms.

Serves 4 as a starter, 2 as a main

3/4 lb smallish *porcini*
1 tablespoon thyme or rosemary leaves
1 garlic clove

7 tablespoons extra virgin olive oil
4 slices polenta, for grilling (page 304)
8 thin slices *lardo* or *guanciale* (optional)

Prepare the *porcini.* Pare any dark or gritty parts from the stems, and cut the mushrooms in half (or in 3/4 in-thick slices if their caps are larger than 2½ or 3in). Finely chop the thyme or rosemary, then pound it to a fine paste with the garlic and plenty of salt and pepper. Add 4 tablespoons of the oil.

Brush the polenta with the remaining oil and grill it on a barbecue or griddle pan. In either case, the bars should be smoking hot (leave them over a medium fire for a long time). The polenta should grill for a good 3–4 minutes on each side for nice marks, good flavour, and no sticking. See page 304 for more on this.

Have the *porcini* brushed or delicately rubbed with the herb oil by the time you turn the polenta, for this is when they should go alongside it on the grill, cut-side down at first. The mushrooms should be turned after about 2 minutes, when they are only lightly browned – a little crunch in the finished dish is nice, more satisfying than a sodden, overcooked slab of fungus. Serve the mushrooms and polenta nestled together, draped with the *lardo* if using. Give it a few seconds to start to melt, then serve to your lucky guests.

GRILLED SAUSAGES WITH POLENTA AND/OR TREVISO

Both creamy, charred polenta and bittersweet *treviso* are the perfect accompaniments to salty, aromatic and, above all, piggy sausages. My love of sausage is that of the forbidden fruit – nobody enjoys pork as much as a fallen Jew.

Serves 4 as a starter, 2 as a main

4 plump Italian sausages (about 1¼lbs, page 72)
Possibly 4 slabs polenta for grilling (page 304) and/or 2 heads *treviso*, halved lengthways

3–4 tablespoons olive oil
3 tablespoons balsamic vinegar (only if using *treviso*)

Heat a barbecue or griddle pan until smoking, but only over a medium heat (greyed embers or a medium flame). Clean the grill bars – first with a wire brush, then with a wet cloth or the cut side of half an onion, and finally wipe them with oil. Oil the polenta and/or *treviso*. Put the polenta on at the same time as the sausages – the *treviso* goes on a little later. Be prepared to cook (and serve) in batches, if your grill hasn't enough room.

Grill the sausages for 2 minutes on each of two sides, to partially set them and to give some colour. Take them from the grill and cut lengthways, through the middle of one of the two browned sides, to almost separate them in two halves – leaving them joined by a hinge of skin, like butterfly wings. Score across through the skin a couple of times, if you don't want them to curl up as they cook more.

Put the sausages back on the grill, cut-side down. Now is the time to put the *treviso* on the grill (cut-side down too), or to turn the polenta, taking care to leave the crispy charred skin on the polenta, rather than on the grill (it helps if the polenta was well oiled, and also if you lift it carefully with a metal spatula, starting from the side closest to you). Grill the sausages for 2–3 minutes again on each side, until well browned, turning the *treviso* when you turn the sausages.

Serve straight off the grill, the *treviso* drizzled with the vinegar.

RED MULLET WITH LEMON
VENETO

Red mullet is a beautiful, bottom-dwelling fish. Despite the slightly irritating bones, it has to be one of the finest fish in existence, with delicate flesh and ruby skin that has a distinctive taste of grilled shrimp when fried. Look for bright pink fish with flashes of yellow. As the flavour is so subtle, they must be dry-scaled (i.e. not under running water) or the taste will leach out and end up down the drain. They are unfortunately not available in the States, but red snapper or bass will do nicely, or any smallish saltwater, especially pink-skinned fish.

Serves 4 as a starter, 2 as a main

**4 tiny (5oz) or 2 small-medium (8–10oz)
  red snapper or bass (smaller = nicer)**
4 bay leaves
1 tablespoon all-purpose flour

5 tablespoons butter
A wedge of lemon
½ cup white wine

Season the fish with salt and pepper, stuff a bay leaf or two in the belly and flour them very lightly. Fry them briefly (choose a pan that can go in the oven) over a high heat in the butter – a minute or two on each side, just to colour the skin – and fry the wedge of lemon with them. Add the wine, shake the pan for a moment or two to bring the sauce together as the alcohol starts to boil away, then put the pan in a preheated, very hot oven (on maximum) for just a minute or two for small fish, 6–7 minutes for large ones, until done.

They are now ready to serve with their delicate sauce. Traditionally, this is thickened with egg yolks before the fish go in the oven, but I prefer it without – light and delicate, like the queen of fishes it accompanies.

GRILLED SQUID OR SCALLOPS WITH GREMOLATA LIGURIA

Blazing inferno, hell to us, is the best place for seafood to end up. The simple, pearly white muscles of fish, crustacea, scallops and small cephalopods, being dead, feel no pain – but the flesh reacts deliciously with searing hot metal over open flames. The sugars that once fuelled these creatures in the deep blue sea caramelise, accentuating the natural sweetness that so complements their faint ocean taste. Whether or not there is a heaven for seafood, beautifully grilled it will transport you there, if only for a moment.

Serves 4 as a starter, 2 as a main

4 medium squid, or about 1lb sea scallops (16–20 of them)
½ garlic clove
2 strips lemon zest, made with a potato peeler

¼ cup chopped flat-leaf parsley
7 tablespoons extra virgin olive oil
A bunch of arugula
Lemon wedges, to serve

Clean the squid. Remove and wash the insides, peel the skin from the body but leave the wings attached, and sever the tentacles just in front of the eyes. Or prepare the scallops. Cut off the tough white ligament on the side of the muscle, but leave the coral attached if it came, and you like it. Do not wash them, but wipe away any sand.

Make the *gremolata* by chopping the garlic and lemon zest incredibly finely, then adding the parsley and chopping finely again.

Before you start to cook, heat a barbecue or griddle pan until smoking hot. Season the seafood with salt and pepper and rub with 3 tablespoons of the oil. Grill the scallops or squid very quickly: put them on the searing bars, and don't move them for 90 seconds, until caramelised and browned, then turn them over for another minute and a half. Scallops should be cooked medium-rare, translucent in the centre. Squid should just turn opaque all the way through. The tentacles can be tricky to cook where they join together: open them like a flower and cook with the base down on the grill first before turning.

Serve sprinkled with the *gremolata*, arugula on the side, and the remaining 4 tablespoons of oil drizzled over. Leave your guests to decide how much lemon to squeeze for themselves, as no two people can ever agree on this.

EEL (OR MACKEREL OR SARDINES) AND WHITE POLENTA VENETO

Eel is controversial – over-fished yet unloved. White polenta is also hit and miss – bland to many, delicate to me. Together, they are delicious: oily, fatty, intense fish, with the Italian equivalent of grits. If you can't stomach an endangered fish, or just can't stomach eel, try mackerel or sardines.

Serves 4 as a starter, 2 as a main

2/3 cup white polenta (or grits)
2 tablespoons butter
1 medium eel (skin-on, filleted – your fishmonger may manage to do this with
    less drama than you), or 2 mackerel (butterflied), or 8 sardines (whole)
1 tablespoon extra virgin olive oil

Cook the polenta at the gentlest of simmers in a quart of water, having stirred it in at a steady stream when the water came to the boil. Given the small quantity, you may need to top the water up once or twice as the polenta cooks – it will take 90 minutes to reach the custardy texture you're aiming for. Stir in the butter and season with salt to finish.

Portion the fish, score the skin across a few times to keep it flat, season with salt and rub with the oil. Grill it on a hot griddle pan or barbecue skin-side down until almost cooked. For mackerel or sardines this will be a mere 3 minutes – at least 6 or 7 for eel, which is fatty and needs time to render and crisp. Turn the fish over for a final minute or two and serve draped over a puddle of the polenta.

Variation Eel is just as good deep-fried. Dust the fillets in a mixture of all-purpose flour, cornstarch and semolina flour, along with a dozen, 1/8 in-thick pinwheel slices of orange. Deep-fry the eel first, in oil at 350–375°F for 2–3 minutes until golden, then add the floured orange slices for a final minute. Drain the lot, sprinkle with salt and serve on a bed of runny white polenta, or mâche and orange salad (page 296). A few fried shrimp would be lovely in the mix too.

LANGOUSTINES WITH PEAS (AND MORELS)
VENETO

Peas and seafood couldn't be a more Venetian combination if they tried (see page 205). With langoustines, they make for a particularly joyous plate – pastel pinks and whites are gorgeous with pea green, the sweet taste of each accentuating that of the other.

Peas start to come as morels start to go, and there is a brief window of opportunity to eat them together in late spring. Their combination is not particularly Venetian, but is particularly wonderful, and worth exploring if you haven't before.

Serves 4 as a starter, 2 as a main

1¼lbs live langoustines or shelled
  large shrimp
5oz fresh morels (optional)

¼ cup extra virgin olive oil
1 quantity peas with scallions
  and basil (page 300)

The cruelty of killing beautiful and lively langoustines can by mitigated by putting them in the freezer first for 10 minutes, which numbs them so they'll hardly feel a thing. It also slows them down, so you need be less nimble to avoid their flailing claws. Cut them in half down the middle. If using shelled shrimp, leave them whole.

Rinse the morels, if using, by briefly dunking them in cold water, draining and blotting them dry immediately. Cut off soily stems, and halve any big mushrooms. Fry the morels for 2 minutes in the oil first, over a medium heat in a hottish pan.

If not using morels, get the pan smoking hot and then add the oil.

In either case, now add the langoustines, make sure the heat is high, and sauté for 2 minutes until they are more or less cooked (less is better than more). Add the peas and cook for a minute more, until the last stubborn langoustines have only just turned opaque. Serve straightaway.

TAGLIATA / STEAK FOR TWO
TUSCANY

Bistecca alla Fiorentina is *the* Tuscan steak – cut from the sirloin of young *Chianina* animals, seasoned with nothing (not even salt or pepper), and grilled rare over a semi-enclosed wood fire. It is perhaps unsurprising that the English love it when you learn that it was originally created for their palate. Tuscans may have acquired a taste for rare meat, but other Italians find it disturbing.

That said, this recipe is not for *Fiorentina*: it would be cruel to require you to buy a Tuscan grill, or to ask you to source *Chianina* beef; and it would be wrong to call anything else a *Fiorentina*. Instead, here is a recipe for *tagliata* ('sliced' steak). It is found today all over Italy, and consists of a steak cooked the 'English' way (pink – the only time you'll see this in Italy), sliced, and served plain, or with some sort of a sauce. Here I dress a steak for two with rosemary, Parmesan and balsamic vinegar, and it is a dish fit for kings.

1 massive sirloin steak on the bone
  (2lbs, 1–1½ in thick, from the T-bone
  or rib end as you prefer)
2 garlic cloves and 2 sprigs rosemary
  (only if you have a day for marinating)
1 tablespoon extra virgin olive oil

A big handful of arugula leaves,
  to serve
1 quantity rosemary oil (page 39)
A few shavings of Parmesan,
  made with a potato peeler
1–2 tablespoons balsamic vinegar

Two pounds of meat (or a bit less, accounting for the bone) is a massive amount of meat for two – but that's the beauty of it. If you obtain this thick, red slab the day before you plan to cook it, smash the garlic cloves and the rosemary, rub the meat in the olive oil and marinate it with these aromatics overnight.

An hour before you cook, pull the steak out of the fridge to come to room temperature. Season with salt and pepper and rub with the oil (unless you oiled it yesterday). Have ready a moderately hot barbecue or griddle pan – just smoking, over a medium-high heat – and grill the steak. Don't move it too much – just cook for 5 minutes on each side (for rare), plus an extra one for each increment you want it cooked more (i.e. 6 minutes each side for medium-rare, 7 for medium, etc). Also grill the fatty edge for a couple of minutes to make it nice for fatophiles. Leave it to rest somewhere warm for a couple of minutes.

Cut the meat off the bone, and slice it thinly (⅛ in). Serve on a large plate with the bone (to gnaw on, and for drama) and the arugula. Drizzle the meat with the rosemary oil and sprinkle with a little extra salt. Scatter the Parmesan shavings over meat and salad, and drizzle both with the vinegar. Serve straightaway – it will get cold quickly.

GUINEA HEN IN PANZANELLA (BREAD SALAD)
TUSCANY

Tuscan (saltless) bread tastes so boring they have come up with some rather ingenious ways to make it palatable. *Panzanella* – a sodden bread salad – is just one of those, and is one of my favourite things to eat (page 311). Elsewhere in Italy it can be less than stimulating (just bread moistened with water and vinegar), but Tuscans understand the dullness of their loaf, and know to add tomatoes, capers, onions and herbs. The version below is further enhanced with pine nuts and raisins, and a whole guinea hen tossed through, to make for a mad and rustic bowlful.

Serves 2–3 as a main

1 guinea hen (or a medium chicken)
¼ cup pine nuts (preferably long ones)
½ cup extra virgin olive oil
1 bunch scallions, cut in ¾in lengths
2 garlic cloves, thinly sliced
½ cup raisins, soaked for an hour in water

½ lb very ripe and very good tomatoes
5 tablespoons salted capers, soaked until
   tolerably salty and squeezed dry
¼ cup red wine vinegar
4 slab-like slices rustic bread, ¾in thick
2 big handfuls salad leaves, baby or torn

Spatchcock the guinea hen. Use shears or a knife to cut out the spine (snip down either side of it) and open the bird out like a book. Press it down hard on the board to flatten.

Make the *panzanella* before you cook the bird. In a pan, fry the pine nuts in 3 tablespoons of the oil until they turn a pale gold. Add the scallions and garlic and cook gently for 5 minutes until tender, then add the drained raisins and a splash of their water and simmer until they puff up. Tip this mixture into a salad bowl, chop the tomatoes and add them along with the capers, 4 tablespoons more oil and the vinegar. Season to taste, that is to say, heavily. Toast the bread on a heating barbecue or griddle pan, then tear it into mouthful-sized chunks and toss them into the bowl too.

When the grill is smoking, season the guinea hen with salt and pepper on both sides, and rub with the last spoonful of oil. Grill, skin-side down, for about 8 minutes until well browned and crisp. Turn it over for another 8 minutes on the skeletal side. Turn it again and cook for a final 4 minutes on the skin side, maybe more, maybe less. Check it's cooked, then leave to rest for a minute or so. Joint the bird into eight equal pieces and toss with the salad leaves into the *panzanella*.

SCOTTADITO DI AGNELLO / FINGER-BURNING LAMB CHOPS LE MARCHE

Scottadito ('finger-burning') lamb or kid goat chops are popular throughout south-central Italy. Cut often from extremely young animals, they have the skin, fat and belly flap attached – lots of calories and lots of flavour. They are cut thinly and grilled over an exceedingly hot fire, so they char a little, the fat crisping up. The meat cooks through so quickly it becomes well done without drying out. You have to love fat to enjoy them as much as I do.

To make them at home, I recommend lighting a barbecue in late spring or early summer, when the lambs are young and plentiful, and it is warm enough to cook outside and thus avoid smoking yourself out of house and home. Just get some nice, thinly cut, fatty lamb chops (or kid goat chops if you can find them – they have a more delicate taste), season well with salt and pepper, and grill over a very hot flame. They will flare up, they will char at the edges, and they will be delicious with just a little bitter salad.

PLUCK WITH ARTICHOKES
LAZIO

Pluck has fallen out of fashion. As some cuts of offal have become popular (liver and sweetbreads), so others have never recovered from their post-war decline – who eats lungs any more? Pluck (*coratella* – what a lovely word) is the whole lot, everything that comes when you pull (pluck) out the wind-pipe – heart, lungs, liver and sweetbread. That from young animals – calves, lambs and kid goats – is utterly delicious. The tissues are still tender, with only a delicate hint of their future flavours.

Kid is my favourite – esoteric and delicate – while lamb pluck is equally tasty. If you can't get either, try an assortment of lamb's offal (heart, kidneys and liver, perhaps also sweetbreads, about 1¼lbs in all), or pieces of calf's liver, kidney and sweetbread.

The quantity given here is quite large, and must be cooked either in an enormously wide pan, or in batches. You can halve the quantities if you have something else to do with the pluck (eat it yourself or feed it to a cat or dog). It is even cheap enough to discard – but the waste seems wrong, especially with the sentimentally precious flesh of a young animal.

Serves 6 as a starter, 3 as a main

1 kid or lamb's pluck
6 medium artichokes, cleaned and choke
  removed (page 26)
1 bunch scallions
12 sage leaves

7 tablespoons butter
1 garlic clove, thinly sliced
½ cup white wine or dry Marsala
¼ cup chopped flat-leaf parsley

Cut the good bits of the pluck (anything identifiable) from the trachea (ridged wind-pipe), which you should discard. Thinly slice (about ⅛in) all the bits of pluck you've kept. Stand the artichokes stem-side up on a board and slice them ⅛–¼in thick. Cut the scallions into ¾in lengths.

Fry the sage in the butter in your widest pan over a high heat until the butter just starts to brown. Add the artichokes and fry for a couple of minutes, then add the scallions and garlic and fry for 2 minutes more.

If your pan is very wide indeed, and there is room for the pluck to nestle in with the artichokes in a single layer, add it now, when some of the artichokes are becoming tender. Season with salt and pepper, and fry this mixture for 2–3 minutes, stirring only once or twice until the meat is almost all cooked and just starting to brown in a couple of places.

If even your widest pan is on the small side, cook the vegetables for a few minutes longer over a now reduced heat until they're all pretty much tender, but still have a little bite. Take them out and set them aside. Quickly put the pan back on, now over a high flame. When it smokes, add the sliced pluck, season with salt and pepper, and fry briskly until partly browned and almost cooked. At this point, return the artichokes to the pan.

In either case, add the wine, and let the sauce bubble until thick, the offal just cooked through. Taste for seasoning, stir in the parsley, and serve with bread and a light yet aromatic white – Frascati or something.

Variation: Chicken Livers If you're squeamish about pluck (and you shouldn't be), or you don't have a helpful butcher, 1¼lbs chicken livers can be cooked in exactly the same way and are just as delicious. Serve with delicate mashed potatoes (page 211) instead.

SCALOPPINE / VEAL CUTLETS WITH ARTICHOKES AND MARSALA LAZIO

Scaloppine are usually served with *either* artichokes *or* Marsala *or* lemon. Less is generally more (or 'enough is too much' as my grandfather John used to say), but here more is just that – and better for it. The flavours of veal, artichoke and Marsala are heaven together. But the artichokes, themselves bitter, somehow accentuate the sweetness of anything they accompany – and even dry Marsala (*secco*) will seem sickly. The lemon mitigates this otherwise out-of-place sweetness, and renders the combination delectable.

Serves 4 as a starter, 2 as a main

14oz veal cutlets
3 tablespoons all-purpose flour
4 medium artichokes, cleaned
  (page 26)
3 tablespoons extra virgin olive oil

3 tablespoons butter (plus a little extra,
  optional)
3 tablespoons chopped flat-leaf parsley
½ cup dry Marsala
1 lemon, halved

Take a look at the cutlets. Sandwich them between two sheets of parchment paper and beat them out to ⅟₁₆in if they're any thicker than that. Season them with salt and pepper and dust very lightly with the flour. Remove any choke from the artichokes and slice them thinly, or into wedges if you prefer (as pictured).

Get a frying pan very hot indeed. Add the oil and fry the cutlets, two at a time, so they brown outside but remain a little undercooked within – 20–30 seconds on each side if your flame is fierce. Remove them from the pan and add the butter, followed swiftly by the artichokes. Fry them for a few minutes over a now medium heat until almost tender – 3 minutes may suffice.

Return the cutlets, add the parsley and then the Marsala along with a squeeze of lemon. Cook for a minute or two, shaking the pan to emulsify the sauce and gradually adding more lemon to taste. A little extra butter added at this stage is an indulgence that's nice for the palate if not the heart. When the sauce is thick and velvety the meat and artichokes will be done, and it will be time to serve. This is delicious with mashed potatoes (page 211).

CHICKEN CUTLETS WITH LEMON

Veal cutlets with lemon is an absolute classic of a dish, which my mum refused to have at the table during the BSE scare of the late 1980s. She worried that by eating the meat we'd all turn into mad cows. (I may have made comments then that I regret today – sorry, Mum!) She cooked the dish with chicken instead, and it remains a family favourite.

Serves 2 as a main

2 skinless chicken breast halves	**3 tablespoons butter**
3 tablespoons all-purpose flour	**Juice of 2 lemons**
3 tablespoons olive oil	**3 tablespoons chopped flat-leaf parsley**

Cut the chicken into thin cutlets – either lengthways (quicker, if you're good with a sharp knife – hold it parallel to the board so the cutlets come out as wide as the breast), or by slicing it on the bias into ½in medallions which you can then beat out flat (slightly slower, and more onerous or more fun depending on your perspective). Season them with salt and pepper and dust very lightly with the flour.

Heat the oil until smoking hot in a wide pan over a high flame. Fry the chicken quickly in batches, giving it less than a minute on each side – it needn't be fully cooked through yet, but should take a little colour. When the last batch is done, return the rest to the pan along with any resting juices, the butter, the lemon juice, the parsley and about ¼ cup water. Shake the pan while the sauce boils to emulsify it. When it is thick, luscious and velvety, the chicken will be done too. If it splits, you can always add a touch more water and shake the pan over the heat again. Season to taste, and serve with mashed potatoes (page 211).

GRILLED TUNA WITH ONIONS AND OREGANO
SICILY

Salmoriglio, the sweet-and-sour oregano dressing in this recipe, must share its roots with *salmorejo* – a chilled bread and tomato soup from Andalucía in Spain. *Agrodolce* (sweet and sour) is a combination found throughout Italy as a relic of medieval and Moorish cuisines. In Sicily, the sweetness is often exaggerated with riches – sugar, raisins, apricots, chocolate – left by her exotic past. In this dish, the sweetness is provided by humble onions instead, making for a simple sauce that accentuates the delicate, oily flavour of tuna fish.

Tuna is heavily over-fished – line-caught Mediterranean or Atlantic yellowfin tuna is the lesser evil. Skipjack tuna is a good choice too, flavoursome and comparatively abundant. Swordfish, often served in the same way, is even more at risk. We have only ourselves to blame, and any decision to eat such fish should be a conscious one.

The steaks can be cut wide and thin (¼in if you like your fish well done and authentic) or thick (3/4in for Californian rare). I cut mine medium (3/8–5/8in) for a moist, blushing pink, medium steak. Leave the dark red 'blood-line' on, as this has a strong and wonderful flavour.

Serves 4 as a starter, 2 as a main

2 tuna steaks, 7oz each
1 large white onion
⅓ cup extra virgin olive oil
¼ cup wine vinegar (red or white) or
  lemon juice
3 tablespoons chopped oregano leaves

1 teaspoon or so superfine sugar
  (optional)

To serve
A few salad leaves
Lemon wedges

Chop the onion finely and fry over a low heat in 3 tablespoons of the oil with a pinch of salt until completely softened, but not coloured – about 10–15 minutes. Add the vinegar and oregano and taste for seasoning – a teaspoon of sugar may be added if the onions have not added enough sweetness themselves, and a dash of water to make it saucy.

Halve the steaks if serving four as a starter. Heat a griddle pan or barbecue until blazing hot, season the fish with salt and pepper, rub with the remaining oil and grill for 1 minute on each side. Serve on a scarce bed of salad leaves with the dressing spooned on top and the lemon on the side.

CATFISH ALLA PALERMITANA (WITH CAPERS AND RICOTTA SALAD) SICILY

I first had this dish in Milan, at Al Merluzzo Felice – and it was a revelation. The pairing of cheese and fish is unusual, and a delicious pairing doubly so. At this, my favourite Sicilian restaurant (despite its northerly location), they prepared it with swordfish, or perhaps it was *palombo* (smoothhound). It would be magnificent, when you find this book lurking on some shelf in the future, if these fish were plentiful again. But until that time let's use catfish, which is excellent, cheap and abundant – at least, for now.

Serves 4 as a starter, 2 as a main

2 catfish fillets, 7oz each
¼ cup salted capers, soaked until
   tolerably salty
1 egg
⅓ cup breadcrumbs (made from real
   bread)
Oil, for frying (best a mixture of
   good olive oil and sunflower oil)
A small bunch of wild arugula leaves

¼lb white endive, sliced across
   into ½in rounds, or a few leaves
   of *castelfranco*, torn
1 teaspoon extra virgin olive oil,
   for dressing
¼ lemon
3oz *ricotta salata* (pressed and
   salted ricotta)

The fillets should be butterflied until ½–¾in thick. Halve them if serving twice as many as a starter.

Season the catfish lightly with salt and pepper. Take two-thirds of the capers, chop them roughly and press them firmly into the flesh. Beat the egg in a shallow bowl, and make a bed of breadcrumbs on a second dish. Delicately coat each fillet in the egg, trying not to dislodge too many capers, then move it on to the breadcrumbs. Turn the fish over, and press down firmly. Turn a couple of times more, pressing well to secure the coating.

Heat ¼in oil in a frying pan large enough to accommodate the fish with some room to spare, over a medium flame. Add the fillets and fry for 3 minutes on each side, turning once only. You want the crumb to turn a deep golden brown, and the fish to be just cooked through but still just a little translucent in the middle. Transfer to paper towels to drain.

Arrange the mixed salad leaves around dinner plates, or one platter. Drizzle with the oil and a few drops of lemon. Put the catfish in the centre of the dish, and coarsely grate the *ricotta salata* over the top. Sprinkle with the remaining capers, and serve immediately.

ROASTS

San Lorenzo (Saint Lawrence) was burned to death on a gridiron. That he asked his executioners to turn him when he was grilled to perfection on one side led to his adoption as the patron saint of cooks. Would that our ingredients were so communicative! The stress of roasting meat the English way – gloriously bloody all the way through, a glistening chestnut-brown on the outside – can be too much to bear (let alone the disappointment when it all goes wrong). But take heart, there is another way.

In Italy most joints, if roasted at all, are cooked slowly in a pan kept humid with wine or stock until the meat is tender and moist all the way through. One might consider this to be baking, not roasting, but what's the difference? Baking may be the word we use for applying heat to breads and cakes, and perhaps there's less sizzling involved, or perhaps it's just less nerve-racking. But it isn't to be scorned.

In the old days, roasting meant cooking with direct exposure to a flame – a practice still common in much of Italy, at the *rosticcerie* (spit-roasters) that pepper the streets, especially on market-day. Lamb legs and shoulders, hunks of pork, whole suckling pigs, kid goats, rabbits, chickens, pigeons and quail – all cook oh-so-slowly, the skin blistering and browning, and the meat effectively braising within its protective shell. Eating them is always a delight, like eating a pot-roast, where all the gravy is inside the meat.

At home some Italians have a little *spiedo*, a spit-turner, that might be gas-fuelled, or have space for coal embers within it, or sit by the side of an open fire – like my grandmother's does. These roast and baste and turn ever so gently, but we can do without, as indeed most Italians do today. Their way with an oven, by and large, is to cook meat or fish gently, and to cook it all the way through. Fish might be protected in broth, or a thick armour of salt, or a coating of breadcrumbs, while meat will almost always be slow-roasted. Flavours have longer to infuse and intensify, liquids to reduce, flesh to brown, fat to blister outside and melt within.

Consider the chapter ahead an invitation to cook food in this most lovely way. It is a recipe for stress-free cooking and happy eating – good for everyone concerned. Five minutes more, five minutes less, slightly cooler or hotter – it doesn't really matter. Come what may, the result will be delicious.

LITTLE BIRDS WITH POLENTA
ALTO ADIGE

Italians hunt recklessly. They even have to have laws that prohibit hunting in olive groves during picking season – fruit and little birds ripen at the same time, and hunters often interpret any rustling of the boughs as a sure indicator of prey, even when humans are the probable cause. Of course, the law is there to be broken. A friend of my uncle Cami went for a walk through an old olive grove in November. As he bent to examine some object of interest on the ground, he apparently jostled some grasses in an animal manner and was promptly shot in the arse by an enthusiastic hunter. Incensed and in agony, he half-turned and swore effusively. The hunter peppered him again with birdshot, before it occurred to him that man might be more likely to curse than beast.

Around Italy, but especially in the north, you might see spits of tiny birds – blackbird, fieldfare, lapwing, ortolan, skylark, snipe, sparrow, starling, thrush and woodcock, and even protected species such as goldfinch, robin and tit – slowly turning over a fire. You may find the idea of eating such tiny birds distasteful, but the spirit of the thing is to cook whatever wildfowl has been hunted. So, for the American equivalent, either take out your gun or nip to the butcher and bag yourself perhaps some pigeon, quail, pheasant and mallard. Try to have a selection of birds, dark and light-fleshed, small and tiny – the joy of the dish is a variety, the seasonings subtle and simple to allow the taste of the meat to come to the fore.

Stuff the birds, each with a large pat of butter, a sage leaf, a sprig of thyme and a crushed juniper berry. Season them outside with salt and pepper.

If you plan to cook them on an open fire, truss them tightly. Thread them on to a spit and roast in front of a wood fire that has not yet died down to embers for about 20–30 minutes (less time for smaller birds and hotter fires), until browned. Use a tray underneath to catch the butter as it melts, and baste the birds with this from time to time.

If cooking in an oven, brown the birds first in a hot pan over a high heat – allow a good 5 minutes, and try to sear them on all sides. Roast them in the same pan in a hot oven, as hot as it will go. Tiny birds, teal and woodcock, will need just 5 minutes inside, plus 5 to rest. Small ones, like quail or pigeon, will take 7–8 minutes, plus as long again to rest. Mallard and pheasant will take a little longer – say 12–15 minutes in the oven and 10 to rest. Put smaller birds into the oven while larger ones are resting – as a rule of thumb, they are ready to rest when the butter within has melted. All should, to my taste, be served pink.

Keep the drippings, and spoon over the birds which, having rested, should be served on a steaming golden bed of wet polenta (page 303).

BAKED SEA SNAILS WITH PARSLEY AND GARLIC VENETO

Sea snails are, to my mind, superior to their land cousins. Their flavour is cleaner – still rich, but tasting pleasantly of the sea – where the earthy flavour of land snails can sometimes be a bit much. On the east coast of Italy you can find *garusoli*, spiky murex snails (also known as *bulli* or *murici*), by far the most delicious and spectacular edible snail. Their elaborate shells hint at the elegant flavour contained within: sometimes you *can* judge a book by its cover. They are popular in Le Marche and the Veneto, and are also esteemed in Spain (where they are known as *cañadillas*, or *cargols de punxes* in Catalonia), regions where seafoods are elevated above all others. You can use other sea snails instead, but keep an eye out for beautiful *garusoli* in Mediterranean markets – one of those local delights not shouted about enough.

Serves 4 as a starter

2lbs spiky murex snails, or other sea snails
  (choose not-too-big ones)
2 celery stalks
2 bay leaves
3 garlic cloves

⅓ cup chopped flat-leaf parsley
2 anchovy fillets (optional)
3 tablespoons butter, softened
⅓ cup extra virgin olive oil
2–4lbs coarse sea salt

Put the snails, celery and bay in a large pot and cover amply with water. Season very lightly with salt, bring to the boil and cook for an hour and a half, until the snails are tender to a toothpick. Drain the snails and, when cool enough to handle, use a toothpick or tweezers to remove the operculum, the horny disc the snails use to close themselves in their shells.

Finely chop the garlic, parsley and anchovy (if using). Mix with the butter and oil, adding salt and pepper to taste.

Spread the salt out on an ovenproof dish – a stainless steel platter is ideal, as you will serve the dish directly at the table. You'll need just over ½in thickness of salt, whose sole purpose is to provide a bed on which to stand the snail shells. Arrange the snails (in their shells) such that the opening faces directly upwards, providing a cup to hold the sauce. Spoon a little of the garlicky sauce into each (this can be done in advance).

Bake the snails for 10 minutes in a 350°F oven, until they start to sizzle. Serve immediately, while they're still bubbling, with an implement for their extraction.

BAKED SCALLOPS WITH BUTTER AND THYME
VENETO

I have always preferred king scallops (*cappesante*) to their queens (*canestrelli*). I normally grill the kings, but find the little queens overcook long before they take on any colour. Baked on their shells, however, queen scallops are a delight – they need only moments in the oven, retaining the taste of the sea. And they are so very tiny you can work your way through a daunting platter the size of a table, and still be hungry for more.

Serves 4 as a starter, 2 as a main

12 large sea scallops, or 48 bay scallops, either size on the half-shell if possible
2 teaspoons finely chopped thyme leaves
1 teaspoon finely grated lemon zest

3 tablespoons softened butter
¼ cup extra virgin olive oil
Lemon wedges, to serve

Check that the scallops are well cleaned or, if you bought them live, open the shells, leaving the scallops on the rounded half. Remove the mantle of each, so only the muscle remains, as well as the coral if you like it.

Mix together the remaining ingredients and spoon some on to each scallop. Season with just a little salt and pepper. Bake in a very hot oven (as hot as it will go) until the butter is sizzling and the scallop barely cooked – 2 minutes for bay scallops, 4 for sea scallops. Serve hot with a delicate squeeze of lemon.

SEA BREAM BAKED IN SALT
LIGURIA

There is a glamour to this dish, but it also presents a challenge: how to tell when the fish is done? As it is encased in an impenetrable armour of salt, this is a hard one – careful timing is the solution. I find it easier to get right with smaller fish, which are quicker to cook, so the thickest part will be done before the tail end dries out. Sea bass is the usual fish of choice for this treatment, but I prefer sea bream for flavour, and its thinner profile lends itself particularly well to the task. Large fish (big bass, salmon or sea trout) can also be cooked this way, but require a more practised hand.

Serves 2 as a main

2 sea bream or sea bass, weighing
  1–1½lbs each
4lbs coarse sea salt
About 2lbs fine sea salt
½ cup extra virgin olive oil

To serve
3 tablespoons extra virgin olive oil
A simple salad dressed with lemon and oil
Lemon wedges

Gut the bream. Though not strictly necessary, I scale them too – even though the skin isn't for eating (it will be inedibly salty), I don't like serving skin with scales on at the table. Mix the coarse and fine sea salts together and moisten with just enough water to make it clump together – about 1½ cups. Preheat the oven to 400°F.

Spread a layer of the salt about ½in thick in a baking sheet large enough to accommodate both fish with room to spare. Oil the fish liberally (or the salt will stick) – they should have a thick, glossy sheen all over. Lay them on the salt, and embalm each fish with more – aim for an even ½in jacket all around, leaving only the head and tail exposed, and the salt thin against the dorsal fin and belly-line, so it will be easier to remove later. I leave the head open, to allow me to check if the fish is cooked, and to improve the presentation. Bake the fish for 16 minutes: you can double-check it is done by looking at the little holes just in front of the eye – if they're bubbling gently, you're there.

Take the fish from the oven and let rest for 2–10 minutes before removing the salt. Chip away around the silhouette of the fish, and the rest, a domed shell of salt over the flank of the bream, will lift off easily. Using a cloth to help you hold the fish without burning your fingers, lift the bream up from its bed of salt and dust off any sticking salt grains. Lay each fish on a serving plate and pull off the skin from its upper side and pour the oil over the exposed flesh. With a little salad on the plate, and a wedge of lemon, it will be sublime.

SQUAB PIGEON STUFFED WITH SQUASH AND CHESTNUTS EMILIA-ROMAGNA

This is an extravagant and somewhat involved dish – boning whole birds without breaking the skin isn't everyone's idea of fun. But the result – a whole and perfect meal contained within the skin of a small, delectable bird – is worth the effort for a special occasion. Take the opportunity to use a better balsamic vinegar than might normally grace the table – it would be a shame to spoil all your labour with a substandard dressing.

Serves 4 as a main

1 very small butternut squash
¼ cup extra virgin olive oil
7oz cooked and peeled chestnuts
   (vacuum-packed for ease)
7 tablespoons butter
6 sprigs thyme

4 whole squab pigeons
1 head *castelfranco* (or round *radicchio*),
   leaves torn
½ head *treviso tardivo* leaves (or a bunch
   of arugula)
Balsamic vinegar (the best)

Peel the butternut squash, and cut into sections about 3in long by ¾in wide. Remove any seeds. Toss with 2 tablespoons of the oil, salt and pepper, and roast in a 400°F oven until tender and slightly browned – up to an hour.

Separate the chestnuts, and put them in a small ovenproof dish with half the butter, 4 sprigs thyme, salt, pepper and a splash of water. Cover tightly and bake in the same oven until tender – about half an hour.

Meanwhile, prepare the squab. This is the only difficult part of the dish, and the aim is to remove the carcass bones, leaving the skin of the birds intact, with only the leg and first wing bones remaining.

Sever the wings at the first joint (elbow). Now use a small knife to cut between the breast and the wish-bone on both sides. Extend the cut down to separate the wing-bone from the carcass. Make a small, horizontal cut to separate the skin from the top of the wish bone. Put down the knife – it's hands only from here on in. Use your thumbs to separate the breast from the breast bone, then work around to separate the muscles, skin and tendons from the carcass. Always apply inwards pressure – pressing into the bone will help remove all the muscle, and prevent tears in the skin. Dislocate the legs at the hip joint, and use your thumbs and fingers working your way from the breast around to the back bone. Finally, when you near the Pope's nose, just pull the skeleton out from the flesh.

Stuff each bird with a couple of pieces of squash, 3–4 chestnuts, and a few thyme leaves. If you've done a good job of boning them, a single wooden toothpick will close up the hole at the wing end of the bird.

Season the birds with plenty of salt and a little pepper, then brown them in the remaining butter evenly on all sides. Roast them in a 400°F oven for about 6–8 minutes (until they just begin to feel firmish at the thickest part of the breast), and leave to rest for another 5–10 minutes in a warm place. The flesh needs to be medium-rare, and the stuffing just warm.

Toss the salad leaves with the remaining oil, salt and pepper. Arrange on a plate, and nest the birds on top (toothpicks removed). Drizzle with the balsamic vinegar – perhaps 3 tablespoons for the 4 birds – and serve.

ROAST SUCKLING PIG
LAZIO

A simply roasted suckling pig with a few roast potatoes, or a salad, or some bitter greens, is one of the finer things in life. It requires a capacious oven, to say the least, but little else.

Allow 1¼–1¾lbs pig per person. In a domestic oven, you might have to settle for half a pig (I prefer the fore end – fattier and juicier) or a very tiny piglet indeed. If space permits, a largish suckling pig (22–26lbs) offers to me the best compromise between size and yield – very tiny ones are very delicious, but have little meat. Piglets over 30lbs start to taste suspiciously like their parents, and girls taste better than boys (this I know for a fact with pigs, humans seem to vary in their appetites for each other). Measure the oven first, and make sure your piglet supplier knows where their baby is going to end up. Remove head or trotters only if you have to, to fit it in.

I consider myself an amateur enthusiast, but when it comes to piglets I claim a certain expertise, cooking up to four each day at the restaurant. I take a pig and cut through the sternum, the cartilage which joins the two halves of the ribcage. I remove the kidneys and liver (as these would overcook) – but I save them for my breakfast the next day. Laying the pig on its back, I open out the ribcage like a book, pressing down to dislocate the ribs from the spine. If things are looking tight, I sever the head (making sure the jowls stay on the carcass) and trotters to better fit the pig in the oven – but I prefer to leave them on, as they agitate squeamish guests and excite adventurous ones. I season the pig inside and out with fine salt and lightly oil the skin. I set the pig skin-side up in a roasting pan.

With my oven on maximum, I roast the pig until the skin bubbles and crisps – around 40 minutes. I reduce the temperature to 300°F, and bake until the meat is meltingly tender – another 2–2½ hours. For very small pigs (13lbs or less) this might be 20 minutes less – test it by poking the ass with your finger – if the meat feels soft and giving beneath, it's ready. I let the pig rest for 20 minutes in a warm place – both to allow it to release some of its juices, which make for the best bread moppings known to man, and to let it cool a little, the flavour being more appreciable when the flesh isn't scalding hot.

I carve it into large chunks on the bone, which vary greatly in content. Some will prefer the leg (leaner), others the loin sections (very fatty, as they have the belly attached), or the shoulder (somewhere in-between). I serve it with nothing more than escarole salad (page 333) and bread.

Leftovers I reheat over the next day or two. It is hard to get the skin crispy again in the oven (it will go soggy overnight), so I pan-fry the chunks skin-side down until the skin bubbles and crisps, then turn them over and heat in a moderate oven for 10 minutes, until warm through. The suckling pig is just as good second time round, so get a piglet as large as you can cook in your oven and enjoy it more than once.

Variation: Suckling Pig with Grapes (pictured) I once had a leg of pork at Autotreno in Bologna (page 90), which was slow-roasted for hours with white wine and bay. Some large grapes had been thrown in for the final moments, and it was delicious. So in summer, autumn and early winter, when I roast a whole pig, as often as not I complicate matters slightly. When the pig is done, I take it from the oven and remove it from its pan. I pour off the fat, but leave the juices in the pan, to which I add at least a bottle of white wine. I cook it on the stovetop until the alcoholic smell is gone and the pan deglazed, then I add large white or flame grapes, cut into tiny bunches (say 8–10 grapes per person), and as many bay leaves as guests, and return the pan to the oven for 5 minutes while I portion the pig. In this case, I serve the pig with its sauce and the grapes, but nothing else – not even a leaf of salad.

DUCK COOKED LIKE A PIG
LE MARCHE / UMBRIA

In central Italy pigs of all sizes are boned, stuffed with their livers and aromatic hillside herbs (sage, fennel and bay), rolled and roasted. Small suckling pigs might be the centrepiece of a feasting table, whilst larger ones can be found in a fine delicatessen, to be sliced thinly for sandwiches. A whole pig is just too much for a domestic family meal.

A duck, however, is the perfect size, and with its rich, fatty skin can be cooked in much the same way as a little pig, even if the taste is different – in which case it is called *anatra in porchetta*, or duck 'cooked like a pig'. Mute ducks are particularly favoured – both for the qualities of their tender and flavoursome flesh, and for their silence as they waddle round the yard. Geese may be treated in the same way, when you have more at the table.

Serves 4 as a main

1 whole duck
1 big handful wild fennel, or the green
   tops of 2 fennel bulbs, or 1 tablespoon
   fennel seeds
4 garlic cloves
12 sage leaves

2 sprigs rosemary, plus another
   optional 2 for basting
2 bay leaves
¼lb *pancetta*, *prosciutto* or salt pork,
   diced
1 small glass red wine

Chop together the fennel, garlic, sage, rosemary and bay. If your duck came with its offal (gizzard, heart and liver), chop this too and mix with the *pancetta* and the chopped herbs. Stuff this mixture into the duck and secure the cavity shut with wooden toothpicks. Season the duck with salt and pepper. This can be done a day ahead, or just before cooking.

The duck would be best cooked on a spit, but this is not practical in my kitchen, and I'm guessing not in yours. Preheat the oven to 350°F, and roast the duck on a rack for 40 minutes until starting to brown, with a roasting pan underneath to catch the fat.

Reduce the temperature to 300°F, and cook for another 2–2½ hours: the duck will be meltingly tender, effectively having stewed in its own skin. Baste it every 20 minutes throughout the cooking time with the red wine, perhaps mixed with some of the duck's juices. My grandmother uses rosemary sprigs to do this, like a paintbrush, swearing it aromatises the meat. How much of a difference this makes, I cannot say, but brushes are always elusive in the kitchen, whereas I am always sure to have fresh rosemary within reach.

Eat it like a pig.

BAKED SALT COD OR POLLACK WITH PEPPERS, TOMATOES AND OLIVES LAZIO

Salt cod has many advantages over fresh: its texture is firmer, yet it holds moisture better and is less prone to drying out. The flavour, saline, rich, and intense, is somehow even fresher than that of fresh cod. Historically, its extremely long (indefinite) shelf-life made it an important food for those far from the sea, or when catches were poor. This ability to store is just as useful, if less life-and-death important, to the modern cook – you can have fresh-tasting fish on the shelf at any time, as long as you remember to soak it a day in advance. Once soaked, salt cod has a similar shelf-life to fresh fish – i.e. not very long.

All this being said in favour of salt cod, I rarely use it myself. Cod is a resource that has been raped by man (and this is not too strong a word for our actions), so I use pollack instead – possibly even tastier, but also cheaper and guilt-free. I pin-bone fillets for easy use later on, and pack them in twice their weight of coarse sea salt. Soaked, I normally use the fish two ways – fried (page 94), or with the punchy flavours of the recipe below.

Serves 4 as a starter, 2 as a main

1lb salt cod or pollack fillet, soaked for 24 hours in 2 changes of water
1 red onion, sliced
½ cup extra virgin olive oil
2 medium red bell peppers, or 1 very large, seeded and cut into chunks
2 garlic cloves, sliced

2 bay leaves
1lb plum tomatoes, cut into chunks, or cherry tomatoes, halved
8 small black olives, Gaeta or similar, stones in
3 tablespoons chopped flat-leaf parsley

Remove the skin and any pin-bones from the salt fish, and cut into chunky strips about ¾ x 1 x 5in. Fry the onion in the oil with a pinch of salt over a high heat until starting to soften, about 5 minutes, then add the peppers, garlic and bay and fry over a medium heat for a further 10–15 minutes until very soft and jammy. Add the tomatoes, turn the heat to high again, and cook for 10 minutes more, until much of their water has evaporated. Add the olives and take off the heat, seasoning well with pepper and adjusting the salt to taste.

Preheat the oven to 350–400°F. Lay the strips of fish in an ovenproof dish, and spoon the sauce over the top. Chunky bits (olives and peppers) sitting on top of the fish might burn, so nestle these in-between. Make sure all the fish is at least stained red with the oil, and bake it for 15–20 minutes, until the dish is just bubbling in the centre. Sprinkle with the parsley and let rest for 5 minutes before serving; it is better if the fish is not too cooked, retaining a little of the translucency and moisture it had when it was raw.

PARMIGIANA DI MELANZANE
CAMPANIA

This dish is my mum's favourite, and one of mine. The flavours should be fresh and vibrant, but at the same time deep and complex. It is rarely executed well – you must be quite particular, slicing the eggplant thinly and cooking the sauce down until thick. A gung-ho approach – cutting slabs of eggplant and exaggerating the mozzarella – will destroy it, creating a watery mess. I normally say cook with confidence and you can't fail, but the borderline between confidence and arrogance is a fine one, easily crossed here.

Serves 6 as a main

4 large eggplants, about 3lbs
Sunflower oil, for frying
All-purpose flour, for dusting
4 cups freshly grated Parmesan
½lb mozzarella, chopped, drained
20–25 leaves basil, coarsely shredded

Tomato sauce
2lbs tomatoes, fresh or canned
1 small onion
5 garlic cloves
½ dried chili (optional)
¼ cup extra virgin olive oil

Slice the eggplant lengthways ⅛in thick. Salt them for an hour or two, then rinse, squeeze dry and blot before you cook (sodden eggplant can be the nemesis of the dish).

Leontina, my old nanny (and my mum's before), showed me the simplest tomato sauce I know. Just put the tomatoes (halved if fresh, squashed if canned), onion (peeled and halved), garlic (peeled but whole) and chili (if using) in a pan with salt and pepper, and simmer gently for 45 minutes or until good and thick. Blend to a purée, then stir in the olive oil.

Heat 3/16in oil in your widest frying pan until smoking hot. Dust the sliced eggplant in flour, and fry, turning once, to colour both sides golden brown. Drain them well.

Take a baking dish, about 6 x 10in, and spread a spoonful of the sauce on the bottom, then a single layer of eggplant. Spread a little more sauce over, then Parmesan, mozzarella and basil. If the sauce and eggplant were well seasoned, you won't need any more salt. Repeat until all is used up, about five or six layers. Top the last layer of eggplant with the last of the sauce and both cheeses but no basil, which would burn.

Bake in a preheated 425°F oven for about 35–40 minutes. The dish is done when golden brown on top and starting to bubble in the middle. Let rest for at least 15 minutes before serving, and save any leftovers, as the dish also keeps well once cooked.

FISH IN ACQUA PAZZA ('CRAZY WATER')
CAMPANIA

Some make the mistake of following a recipe to cook this dish of fish baked in a chunky broth, but my *acqua pazza* is a more crazed and spontaneous affair. I make it in those creative moments when I throw everything I can lay my hands on into a pot. The last time I had one of these cooking fits, I was in Sperlonga (where there is something in the air) and, having picked the last flakes of fish from the bone, I grabbed the little notepad my grandmother keeps her *Posso* scores on (an addictive and emotional card game, rules on page 454). I risked her anger at desecrating this precious document by jotting down the recipe I had just cooked. Follow it at your peril…

Serves 2 as a main

2 lovely fish, 1lb or so each, scaled and
   gutted – bream, mullet, bass or grouper
2 celery stalks, sliced on the bias
A handful of black olives (stone-in)
1 red onion, cut in segments lengthways
1 garlic clove, thinly sliced
2 promising tomatoes, chunked, or
   16 cherry/baby plum tomatoes, halved

3 bay leaves
A handful of chopped flat-leaf parsley
A handful of basil leaves
½ cup extra virgin olive oil
½ glass white wine
A few potatoes, peeled, chunked
   and par-boiled (optional)

Slash the fish a few times (three or four on each side, diagonally), season well with salt (rub it into the cuts) and set aside. Put everything, bar the fish, in a pot. Add water to come to half the depth of the vegetables (about a glass), season well with salt and pepper and place over a high flame. As soon as it boils, turn off the heat.

You now have two options. If you are hungry, pour the hot vegetable stew into a roasting pan. Put the fish on top, and nestle them into their flavoursome bed. Spoon a little of the juice over them, put them straight into a 425°F oven, and bake until just cooked, when the flesh flakes easily from the bone – around 15 minutes. Or, if dinner is a while off, wait for the vegetables to cool. Arrange them and the fish in the roasting pan in the same way, but leave to marinate together for an hour or two before cooking in the oven: just as though you're in a hurry, as above, but for a little longer – 20–25 minutes.

Serve quickly and without fuss. The dish makes its own accompaniment.

POT-ROAST ESCAROLE STUFFED WITH PINE NUTS, RAISINS AND ANCHOVY CAMPANIA

I lost a chef, Angelo, who went transatlantic for love – the best of reasons. Just before he left he started manically cooking dishes from home, in order to leave us some pearls of wisdom by which to remember him. The shiniest of these was his stuffed escarole – a slow-cooked lettuce filled with copious quantities of anchovy, garlic, pine nuts and raisins. The taste – sweet, salty and slightly fishy – must date from Roman times, and the dish has become a firm favourite – not least for the farcical appearance of a trussed head of lettuce.

Serves 4 as a starter, 2 as a main

1 very large head escarole
4 anchovy fillets
¼ cup pine nuts (preferably long ones)
½ cup raisins

4 garlic cloves, chopped
½ cup chopped flat-leaf parsley
1 teaspoon black peppercorns, crushed
⅓ cup extra virgin olive oil

The escarole is as full and bouncy as an afro wig. Put it flat on a table, and open it out like a sunflower. Tuck the anchovy fillets in around the centre and pile the pine nuts, half the raisins, three-quarters of the garlic and three-quarters of the parsley loosely in the centre, covering all the younger, yellow leaves at the lettuce's heart. Scatter with the pepper, and a little salt around the outer leaves. Bring them together to enclose the filling tightly: they will come to a point, like a spring cabbage or the ace of spades. Take a long piece of cotton twine and make a lasso. Use it to fasten the leaves together at the tip, then spiral the string very tightly (the escarole will shrink as it cooks) to the base of the lettuce and back again and tie shut at the end.

To cook the escarole, heat the oil in a heavy-bottomed Dutch oven that's as close a fit as you have (an old-fashioned oval enamel one would be great) over a medium heat. Brown the escarole on all sides – it will take a good 10 minutes. Add the remaining garlic for the last couple of minutes, so it can brown too without burning. Tuck the last raisins between the escarole and the sides of the pot and add water to come to about 3/4in depth. Cover with a lid and cook for 40 minutes.

When the escarole looks soft all the way through, remove the lid and add the remaining parsley. Cook over a high heat until the sauce is thick and velvety. Remove the trussing strings and slit the escarole lengthways to show its filling. Serve with its sauce poured over and good bread to mop it up.

BAKED ZUCCHINI FLOWERS WITH RICOTTA AND OLIVES PUGLIA

Zucchini flowers are most commonly fried in batter (either empty or filled), or strewn over *pizza bianca* by those who know what's good for them. Few would think to bake them. Delicately stuffed and lightly roasted they keep best their gorgeous appearance, and are one way (there aren't many) to make even the evangelically health-conscious happy.

Serves 4 as a starter, 2 as a main

12 zucchini flowers (male if possible
  – cheaper and at least as good)
3/4 lb sheep's milk ricotta
1/4 cup freshly grated Parmesan
5 black olives, pitted and chopped

1/4 lb small tomatoes, seeded and
  finely diced
6 basil leaves, chopped
1/4 cup extra virgin olive oil

Stir together the ricotta, Parmesan, olives, tomatoes and basil with half the oil, and season very lightly with salt and pepper. Remove the stamens from the flowers, trying not to break the petals (or not to break them too badly). Gently spoon some of the cheese mixture into each flower, and loosely twist the petals to hold the filling in.

Arrange the flowers on a metal baking dish, drizzle with the remaining oil and bake in a 375°F oven for 5–8 minutes until the petals are wilted, and the filling just warmed through. Serve straightaway.

ROAST LOBSTER WITH BREADCRUMBS
SARDINIA

Lobster benefits in general from the simplest of preparations – boiling or grilling. Grilled lobster, one of the wonders of the world, is best achieved over an open fire, and so requires clement weather – a rare occurrence where I live. Roasting lobster is much easier, but can dry the flesh out. The Sardinians have resolved this problem with breadcrumbs, which protect the meat and soak up the sweet juices that run from the cooking flesh.

Serves 4 as a starter, 2 as a main

2 live lobsters, 1¼–1½lbs each
1 cup fresh breadcrumbs
1 garlic clove, chopped
⅓ cup extra virgin olive oil
1 anchovy fillet, finely chopped
A pinch of hot red pepper flakes

¼ cup finely chopped flat-leaf parsley
⅓ cup dry Marsala

To serve
Lemon wedges
A simple salad

Fry the breadcrumbs and garlic in 3 tablespoons of the oil until very lightly browned (stir continuously lest it burn). Add the anchovy and pepper flakes for the last 30 seconds, then take off the heat and add two-thirds of the parsley, and the Marsala to moisten the mixture.

Kill the lobsters. Numb them for 10 minutes in the freezer, then split them in half down the middle (head end first – all you need is a large, sharp knife and brave face). Open them out like butterflies (cut-side up) on a large baking sheet. Leaving all the tasty gunk in the head, cover the lobsters (heads and tails) with breadcrumbs, spreading them evenly and pressing down lightly. Drizzle with the remaining oil and bake in an oven preheated to maximum. The lobsters will be done in a matter of 12–14 minutes, by which time the breadcrumbs should have browned on top in all but the feeblest of ovens. They needn't be dark, but if they look too blond use the grill cautiously for a minute or so.

Serve the lobsters sprinkled with the remaining parsley, a lemon wedge or two and just a little lightly dressed salad.

ROAST LAMB LEG OR SHOULDER WITH ROSEMARY AND HONEY SARDINIA

My grandmother has an old, blackened clockwork spit-turner we use by an open fire every time we are at her apartment in Sperlonga. It is most effective, making a little tinkling sound when it runs out of oomph, the spit starting to turn more slowly and threatening to burn the meat. It has just enough strength to turn a leg of lamb.

A leg serves 5–8, a shoulder 4–6

1 leg or shoulder of lamb on the bone
4 sprigs rosemary
4 garlic cloves, peeled and halved

¼ cup aromatic honey – chestnut
**   or wild thyme**
1 tablespoon white wine

Remove the leaves from half the rosemary. Make eight incisions in the lamb with the tip of a knife and stuff each with a bit of garlic and a few rosemary leaves. Rub the lamb with plenty of salt and pepper, and about a quarter of the honey. Thin the rest of the honey with the wine, to baste the meat with later.

To cook like my grandmother (and this works only with a leg), force a sturdy spit of decent weight through the lamb, running lengthways parallel to the bone, and making sure the weight is evenly distributed for the spit to turn. Secure the lamb with a couple of metal spikes that screw on to the spit. Roast the lamb next to an open fruitwood fire, about 8in from the flames. Adjust the distance according to the ferocity of the fire so the lamb browns deeply without burning as it cooks. Baste the lamb with the thinned honey, using the remaining rosemary sprigs as a paintbrush, and catch the drippings with a metal tray.

To cook in an oven, roast in a roasting pan for 30 minutes at 400°F until browned. It would be a shame not to roast a few potatoes around the lamb, which should go in at the same time. Turn the oven down to 320°F (shoulder), 350°F (leg), and baste the meat regularly with the winey honey until done. Shoulder of lamb will be done 2½ hours after reducing the heat, when the meat feels soft and can just be pulled away from the bone.

In my opinion, legs (of lamb at least) are better judged by the senses than by time.* Whether cooked over a wood fire or in a domestic oven, to check a leg for doneness insert a metal skewer or thin blade into the thickest part of the meat, and test its temperature by putting its tip against your lower lip: cool = undercooked; lukewarm = rare; just warm = medium-rare; quite warm = medium; uncomfortable = medium-well done; painful = well done. Let the lamb rest for 15 minutes covered loosely with foil before serving.

*Timings are necessarily inaccurate: lamb legs of the same weight vary in shape, they start from differing ambient temperatures, fires burn up and burn down, and ovens are as different as the people who use them. That said, for indicative purposes only, a spit-roast leg by an open fire will take about 1½ hours for a 4¼lb leg, plus 30 minutes for each additional 18oz. In an oven, after the initial 30 minutes at 400°F, allow 40 minutes at 320°F for a 4¼lb leg, plus an extra 20 minutes per additional 18oz. But even in a reliable oven I never time my roasts...

SARDINES 'BECCAFICO', WITH A SWEET AND SOUR STUFFING SICILY

You can cook duck like a pig (page 277), beans like little birds (page 310) and sardines like garden warblers (*beccafichi*, 'fig-peckers'). If you don't already know how to cook such a small songbird, here's how. Or at any rate it is the Palermitan version, as made for me by my chef Alberto. By presenting me with small, divine plates, he has a nasty habit of reminding me how many more delicious things he knows how to cook than I do. At least I get to eat them.

Serves 4 as a starter, 2 as a main

1 3/4 lbs fresh sardines
1 2/3 cups breadcrumbs (made from real bread)
1/4 cup extra virgin olive oil
5 tablespoons pine nuts (preferably long ones)
1/3 cup raisins, soaked in cold water until plumped, then drained

4 salted anchovy fillets, chopped
1/3 cup chopped flat-leaf parsley
3 tablespoons superfine sugar
Finely grated zest of 1 orange
Juice of 2 oranges
12–15 bay leaves

Scale the sardines by rubbing them with your thumb under running water, and fillet them. This is easily done: pinch off the head at the nape of the neck, breaking the spine, and pull it out forwards in line with the fish to draw out the entrails. Use your thumb to separate the flesh from both sides of the spine, working towards the tail. The skeleton can now be easily pulled away. Clean any dark matter from the stomach cavity, leaving a pair of beautiful, pink-tinged fillets joined along the dorsal edge.

Fry the breadcrumbs in the oil over a medium heat, stirring often until about half are golden. Take the pan off the heat and add the pine nuts, raisins, anchovies, parsley, sugar, orange zest and juice. Stir well (fingers are best), season with salt and pepper and taste for a fine balance of sweet, sour and salt (if need be, add a dash of white wine vinegar or lemon juice for balance). The stuffing should be moist, but still crumbly and crunchy.

Lay the sardines out on a board, skin-side down, and spread a thin layer of the breadcrumb filling to cover the flesh. One-by-one, roll them up so the tail stays on the outside. Arrange them in a baking dish, quite snug to each other, and tuck the bay leaves in between. Bake at 350°F for 15 minutes, until just cooked through. Serve them warm.

SIDES

I'm setting out on a trip down the length of Italy, from top to toe. I am impatient for sunshine and tomatoes, but I'll have to wait. Food in the north – notably Piedmont, Lombardy and the Veneto – is warming and elaborate. The radishes, turnips, cardoons, cabbages, beets and squashes served alongside hearty *salumi* and gamey stews offer more comfort than excitement; butter and cream are more common than oil. The people are wealthy and the food rich – am I in Italy at all?

A little further south, Liguria is tiny, and perfumed with basil. The Bolognese are justly proud of their yellow potatoes, which they export around the world. They boil cabbage and dress it with green olive oil, so sweet it is revelatory. In the summer Tuscans are crazy for red things – every permutation of tomatoes and peppers; for the autumn and winter months the earthiness of mushrooms and truffles dominates. Borlotti and cannellini beans, popular all over the country, are stars here too, and the pungent yet delicate aroma of sage is everywhere. This is the Italy that the world loves so dearly and invades annually – it's time for me to leave.

I've reached the area I know best, Lazio, where I've holidayed almost every year of my life. Signature varieties of greens define the cuisine – *broccoli romaneschi*, with their mind-bending geometry of chartreuse minarets; *zucchine romane*, mottled and pale-green zucchini ridged like a star; *lattuga romana*, the sweet and crunchy romaine or *romano* lettuce that is now ubiquitous worldwide. Baby bunched chard is delicate and ferrous, ever-so-slightly bitter and absolutely wonderful, *mammole* artichokes are almost spherical and blushing violet, and *puntarelle* are just brilliant. Here vegetables are treated simply – boiled until tender and served cold with oil and lemon, or then pan-fried with garlic and chili.

Heading further south still, it's all about the soil: humble pulses (dried chickpeas and fava beans), and greens that are as uncompromising as the earth (peppery, astringent *broccoli rabe* and bitter, bitter black-green endives). Chili is used freely, especially in Calabria, and is loved with the same passion it is loathed in the north. By the time I reach Sicily, I seem to have left Europe behind. Here the tomatoes are good even in winter, served raw or stuffed with breadcrumbs, or in *caponata*, with its endless run of flavours in every spoonful. Honey, sugar, onions and raisins are used in abundance – life is sweet. The sharp tang of vinegar, lemon and orange keeps it all from becoming sickly, and spices lend an other-worldliness. Couscous is common, served alongside fish and meat stews. Am I in Africa? Everything oozes exoticism. It's almost too much. Time to head home.

MÂCHE AND ORANGE SALAD
VENETO

I remember my first platter of tiny, crisp soft-shelled crabs (*moleche*, page 89) at Da Fiore in Venice. They were arranged around a bed of mâche just like the one below, in a ring, like a paper chain of golden crabs worshipping the mountain of delicate salad. My family, food idolaters all, were arranged around the table in the same way. We certainly did worship the wondrous plate in front of us.

Serves 2 as a starter, 4 as a side

4 cups mâche
1 blood orange, in season, or 1 smallish
   normal orange

½ garlic clove
1 teaspoon chopped thyme leaves
¼ cup extra virgin olive oil

Clean the mâche: wash it, and pinch off the root, leaving the leaves connected at the base. Taste a bit – it's delicious – but if it's still at all gritty, wash it again.

Cut a quarter from the orange, lengthways from tip to navel. Halve this quarter into two long segments and, leaving the skin on, slice these across to make incredibly fine (⅛ in) little triangular wedges.

Rub a salad bowl with the garlic, which can then be discarded. Add the thyme, the juice of the remaining three-quarters of the orange and the oil, and season to taste with salt and pepper. Toss into this the lettuce and little bits of orange. Serve immediately – mâche is quick to wilt.

GRILLED RADICCHIO
VENETO

You can read a man by his shoes, and you can tell a Venetian town by its lettuce. From Chioggia round *radicchio,* from Castelfranco yellow, from Treviso long, from Verona pink or round. If it has a *radicchio* named after it, it is clearly a place of importance, and worth a visit. Treviso and Verona doubly so, as each has two varietals. Treviso has an early type – torpedo-shaped and fleshy – and a more beautiful late one (*treviso tardivo*), shaped like a cockerel's tail, which is better for salads, but not so good for grilling. Any of the closed-head types can be used for this recipe.

Grilling brings out the sweetness of the lettuce, while the bitterness of charring harmonises with the bitterness of the lettuce. I use a dribble of balsamic to balance the dish, boosting the sugar and adding a hint of acidity.

Serves 4 as a starter or side

2 large heads *radicchio di Treviso* or round *radicchio*, halved lengthways

1 tablespoon olive oil
3 tablespoons balsamic vinegar

Heat a barbecue or griddle pan until smoking hot before you start. Season the halved *radicchio* on the cut side with salt and pepper, and rub with the olive oil. Grill over a medium heat for a good 4–5 minutes, cut-side down, until it is hot through (the closed leaves will keep the steam in and help the *radicchio* to cook). Turn it over, press down a little, and grill for another 3–4 minutes, such that both sides are well marked by the grill, and the *radicchio* is hot and tender all the way through.

Serve the *radicchio* cut-side up and splayed slightly with your fingers to display their beautiful, geometric form. Drizzle with balsamic vinegar. Serve as a starter, or an excellent side to anything grilled, or to roasted meats.

PEAS WITH SCALLIONS AND BASIL
VENETO

Venetians love their peas, as everyone should. Cook them in late spring or early summer when local peas are young and sweet and you'll be tempted to go wild with them too.

In this recipe, they are cooked with scallions, and just a little water. You are looking for a luscious, sugary sauce, which the scallions and peas will provide themselves – all you have to do is let the water boil away. This particular recipe is equally at home with fish, seafood and white meats.

Serves 4 as a side

1 bunch scallions
1lb freshly shelled spring peas
2 garlic cloves, thinly sliced

7 tablespoons extra virgin olive oil
1/3 cup chopped flat-leaf parsley
12 basil leaves

Cut the scallions into 3/4–1in lengths. Put the scallions (green and all) into a small saucepan with the peas, garlic and oil. Add water so the liquid comes to just below the level of the vegetables and season with salt and pepper.

Boil at high heat for a good 10 minutes, or until the peas are completely tender (but still green) and the sauce thickish, reduced, sweet and velvety. Add the parsley 2 minutes before the end, and the basil (torn or roughly chopped) when you take the pan from the heat. Serve hot or at room temperature.

WET POLENTA WITH PARMESAN
LOMBARDY

Polenta, the golden yellow savoury porridge, was long the poor food of the north of Italy. Its use was so prevalent in winter that in the eighteenth century it was almost the only food in the area. An epidemic of pellagra ensued, with dramatic skin lesions and psychotic and emotional disturbances, caused by a lack of niacin in the diet. Polenta, blamed for the illness, was outlawed. The ensuing winters of malnutrition and famine killed more than the pellagra itself.

Today good polenta is a luxury – not for its cost, but the time taken to prepare it. Instant polenta is bland in taste and texture. The real deal – high-quality grain, stone-ground – takes well over an hour to cook, about as long as the stews that might accompany it (pages 196 and 212). The result – creamy but coarse, with a complex and earthy flavour – is worth the investment.

My mum remembers going to feasts in remote villages around Rome, where the polenta would be poured out to cover an enormous, scrubbed wooden table at which the entire community would sit. With the butt of her spoon, she would draw a circle in the polenta to represent her plate. Stewed little birds or meat or sausages would be piled on to this disc, the meat eaten first and the plate after. I just slop a spoonful of polenta on a normal plate and am done with it.

Serves 4 as a side

1 quart water
1 teaspoon fine sea salt
1⅓ cups coarse yellow polenta

2 cups freshly grated Parmesan
3 tablespoons butter

Bring the water to the boil with the salt in a large saucepan. Add the polenta in a steady stream, stirring vigorously with a wooden spoon or whisk to avoid lumps. Simmer for 90 minutes, stirring often (not quite constantly, unless you're mad) with a wooden spoon, until thick and luscious (fine polenta may cook in half the time, but I prefer the coarse). You should *almost* be able to stand a spoon in it, but add water if you actually *can* at any point in the cooking. Beware sticking and spluttering (volcano-like polenta, like any porridge, has a tendency to project its lava a great distance if cooked too fast). When you're happy with the texture, add the cheese and butter and stir in.

Leftover polenta can be grilled (overleaf), baked with a sauce, or reheated by stirring over a low flame with a little water.

GRILLED POLENTA
LOMBARDY

Grilled polenta seems lighter than wet, the charring offering contrast to the taste and texture of the cornmeal. It is undoubtedly more summery, and to my mind the ideal partner to oily fish, and grilled meats.

Serves 4 as a side

1 quantity wet polenta, cooked without cheese or butter, and a little drier than you might like
3 tablespoons extra virgin olive oil

Use a wide roasting pan, to make a layer about ½ in thick, or a small, brick-shaped mould (a plastic container), to make a tall block of polenta. In either case grease it well with half the oil so it doesn't stick. Pour in the polenta, and shake the container to level it. Let cool completely (it can be refrigerated for a few days) until set firm, then cut into slabs (any size you like, really). Rub these slabs on both sides with the remaining oil.

Heat a griddle pan, or barbecue (best if it has thick bars), until smoking hot over a medium heat. Rub the bars with oil or fat to season them and lay the slab of polenta on to grill. It takes some time for the grill to mark the polenta properly, and form a crust thick enough to lift from the grill with the polenta (it is all too easy to lift the polenta and leave a half-baked crust stuck to the grill). About 5–6 minutes on the first side should do the job: do not move the polenta during this time, except to peek under a corner if you really have to. Lift it with a metal spatula, slid under in the direction of the bars, flip over, and do the same for the second side.

MOSTARDA DI FRUTTA
LOMBARDY

Mostarda takes its name not from mustard, but from *mosto* – the sour grape must it was originally made from, and still is in some areas. That said, it is today a mustardy confection of candied fruits, delightfully sweet and peppery at the same time. It is the ultimate accompaniment to boiled meats and sausages (see *bollito misto* on page 198 and *cotechino* on page 207). Start making the *mostarda* a month or two before you eat, when the ingredient you wish to candy is in season. The process is a slow one. The fruit is poached in a light syrup, quite watery, or it will harden. Gradually, over a few weeks, the syrup is reduced, slowly replacing the water in the fruit with sugar. It is important to keep an eagle eye on it, as burning a batch, or boiling it until it solidifies, will ruin quite a lot of fruit and a great deal of work. Test the boiling syrup in small amounts on a chilled spoon or plate – if it crystallises when cool, your work will be ruined unless you quickly add some water. It should never get as thick as honey, even when cold, nor may it ever be allowed to caramelise.

Mostarda will keep for a very long time in the fridge, but is not easily jarred at home as it shouldn't be heated once the mustard oil is in. I prefer to use only one kind of fruit – or vegetable – in each batch, for an intense and distinct flavour.

Makes just over 4lbs

2lbs pears, apples, quinces, clementines, kumquats or watermelon peels – or vegetables like pumpkin or fennel

2 ½lbs white sugar
3/4 cup light corn syrup
1 teaspoon essential oil of mustard

Peel and halve pears, apples or quinces. If you want them to be very tender in the end, boil them for 5 minutes in water before you start. For firmer fruit, start to candy them from raw.

Blanch citrus fruits for 1 minute to soften the skin, then prick them all over with a sharp skewer, penetrating the pith but not the flesh. Blanch three more times for 5 minutes in three changes of water to reduce their bitterness, which will be partially restored as it is concentrated over the coming weeks.

Vegetables should be prepared as though for roasting. Cut pumpkin into seeded segments (peeled or not, up to you), fennel halved or quartered. These, or chunks of watermelon skin, should be boiled in water until completely tender, then drained.

Mix the sugar and corn syrup with about 2 quarts of water, bring to the boil and add the fruit. Boil for 10 minutes, then turn off the heat, weight the fruit down and wait for a day or, at most, two. The next day, carefully remove the fruit from the syrup. Bring the syrup to a rolling boil for 10–15 minutes, to evaporate some of the water, then return the fruit to the pan. Let it come back to the boil, switch off the heat and wait another day, before repeating the process.

One day you'll notice that the syrup that is boiling away has started to thicken, and has some body when you taste it. As soon as this happens, return the fruit to the pan, bring the pot back to the boil and turn the heat off immediately. A day or two later, the syrup will likely be runny again, having drawn more water from the fruit. You are working gradually towards an equilibrium, where the syrup is reduced enough to be satisfyingly thick *when cool*, and the sugars are as concentrated in the fruit as in their surroundings.

The day you are satisfied that the fruit is candied and the syrup thick enough, procure some essential oil of mustard. This may not be easy to find, and should be handled like TNT: rubber gloves must be worn, wear some glasses too, and don't smell the bottle directly. This may sound over-cautious – but it is a dangerous and irritant substance before dilution in the *mostarda*. I use around 1 teaspoon of this oil for the above quantity, but be guided by taste as it can vary in potency. Add the mustard oil to the cooled *mostarda*, and taste only when well mixed or you might damage your tongue. Make it slightly hotter than you'd like it today, as the heat will mellow as it penetrates the fruit over the next few weeks. By then, it should be hot and spicy, but still edible and enjoyably so. Keep refrigerated until it's all gone.

ROAST POTATOES WITH...
EMILIA-ROMAGNA

I prefer slightly yellow, waxy and sweet potatoes for roasting. Fluffy white ones for mash and *gnocchi*, yellow ones (Yukon gold) for the oven. I find roast potatoes alone a bit boring, and like to cook them with something seasonable: ramps (leaves only) in the spring, fresh red onions in summer, *porcini* in autumn and chestnuts or stored red onions in winter.

I preheat the oven to 400°F, peel the potatoes and cut them into rough chunks. I season the potatoes in a bowl with salt, pepper and fresh rosemary leaves. I mix them with my hands, and lick a finger to taste for seasoning, then toss with a glug of good oil. I spread them on a baking sheet, which they almost fill in a single layer, and roast for 50 minutes until done, adding something extra, as follows.

I use about a quarter the potatoes' weight of ramps leaves, half the weight of cooked peeled chestnuts or raw *porcini*, or an equal weight of red onions – or a combination thereof. The red onions I peel, quarter, and put in at the same time as the potatoes, seasoned, oiled and roasted amongst them. The chestnuts (cooked, peeled and whole) or *porcini* (young, cleaned and halved or quartered) I add 10–15 minutes before the potatoes are done. Ramps leaves I roughly chop and stir in when I take the potatoes from the oven, to wilt in the residual heat.

HOT BOILED VEGETABLE WITH LEMON AND OIL
EMILIA-ROMAGNA

The brutal simplicity of boiled vegetables, served steaming hot and doused in oil, is in stark contrast to chilled ones (page 314), which seem somehow more elegant. Boiling your greens is an uncomplicated way to treat them, and allows their earthy flavours to come to the fore. The starchy sweetness of a pumpkin, the bitter-sweetness of zucchini or the fresh and green sweetness of a good cabbage – all will startle you in their purity.

Serves 4 as a side

1 dense-fleshed pumpkin
  (*delica* or kabocha), peeled,
  seeded and cut into chunks
or
6 medium-large zucchini, halved
  lengthways and then across
or
½ Savoy cabbage, roughly
  shredded into ¾–1½ in strips

To serve
Fruity olive oil
Lemon wedges

Have a pan of well-salted water already boiling. Put the vegetables on to boil, and cook until soft – about 12 minutes for pumpkin, 8–10 for zucchini or 5–6 for cabbage.

Drain in a colander and then blot dry on a clean kitchen towel. Use a second towel to press down on the zucchini, which may be watery. Transfer to a serving dish and drench with the oil, and send to the table immediately with lemon wedges on the side.

TOMATO AND PURSLANE SALAD TUSCANY

I love the fleshy, refreshing leaves of purslane, and love even more its Italian name, *porcellana comune* – it does indeed resemble celadon porcelain. In high season, when tomatoes are blood-red and sugary, in many ways at their peak, they are almost too sweet to eat on their own (page 330). A little red onion, a splash of vinegar and a few leaves of *porcellana* will make them into the finest of salads. Choose tomatoes that smell as green at the pointy end as their stems, the only sure indicator of flavour.

Serves 4 as a starter or side

Generous 1lb delicious tomatoes
½ small red onion
1 teaspoon red wine vinegar (optional)

¼ cup extra virgin olive oil
4oz purslane leaves and tips

Quarter the tomatoes and slice the red onion very thinly across the grain. Macerate these with the vinegar, oil and plenty of salt and pepper for 5 minutes, then toss in the leaves and serve, with a crust of bread on hand to mop the bowl afterwards.

BEANS WITH SAGE AND TOMATO TUSCANY

Tuscans cook little birds (*uccelletti*) with just a hint of tomato and sage. When they cook cannellini beans the same way, they call them '*all'uccelletto*' (cooked 'like little birds'), and serve them with *bistecca alla Fiorentina* (see steak for two, page 249) or sausages (page 72).

Serves 4 as a side

2 garlic cloves, thinly sliced
½ cup extra virgin olive oil
12 sage leaves, roughly chopped
A tiny pinch of hot red pepper flakes

About 5 cups cooked cannellini beans,
plus a little of their liquor
Scant ½ cup light tomato sauce or puréed
and strained fresh or canned tomatoes

Fry the garlic in the oil until it looks like it's thinking of colouring, but hasn't quite started to. Add the sage and pepper flakes, then quickly follow with the beans, a small ladleful of their liquor, and the tomato sauce. Season to taste and boil for a few minutes, until the sauce is thick enough to coat the beans.

PANZANELLA / BREAD AND TOMATO SALAD
TUSCANY

My favourite part of a salad is the crust of bread I use when it's finished, to mop up the little puddle of dressing at the bottom of the bowl, with a few wilted fragments of leaf in it. *Panzanella* is juice-mopping *ad absurdum*. It gives all at the table the opportunity to enjoy what has always been *my* furtive treat. More egalitarian, and no less fun.

Serves 4 as a side

6 slab-like slices rustic bread, crusts
 removed, fresh or stale
1lb very ripe and very good tomatoes
¼ cup salted capers, soaked until
 tolerably salty and squeezed dry

3 scallions, thinly sliced
6 basil leaves, torn
3 tablespoons red wine vinegar
7 tablespoons extra virgin olive oil

Tear the bread into mouthful-sized chunks, and lightly toast it. Cut two-thirds of the tomatoes into 3/4in chunks, and either chop the rest finely or purée them in a food processor. Toss the bread with both lots of tomatoes, the capers, scallions, basil, vinegar, and the olive oil. Leave it to steep for 15 minutes, then taste for seasoning.

Variation: *Panzanella* with Anchovies This salad makes a delicious starter, especially with anchovy fillets draped over. Take 6 whole salted anchovies, and fillet them under running water – or take 12 fillets from a can. Dress them with a little olive oil (if preparing them in advance, a few slivers of garlic and lemon zest only add to the pleasure) and serve them draped over the salad.

STEWED BORLOTTI BEANS WITH TOMATO AND BASIL TUSCANY

Borlotti beans are always good, and exceptional when fresh – pulses are not only a wintry food, nor the sole dominion of better-than-thou vegans and earth mamas. Dishes like this one, packed with light and zingy flavours, are a reminder: the earthiest of vegetables is in fact a summer fruit. This plate is good enough to turn even me into a veggie hippie (though only for a moment).

Serves 4 as a side

1lb freshly shelled borlotti beans – around 2lbs in their shells (or 10oz dried, soaked overnight)
½lb cherry or baby plum tomatoes, halved

2 garlic cloves, thinly sliced
12 basil leaves, torn
⅓ cup extra virgin olive oil

Simmer the borlotti beans in 1 quart of water (2 quarts if using dried) until tender (1 hour for fresh, 2 for dried). They are done when they are soft and creamy all the way through – no crunch at all, but not disintegrating. Their liquor should just reach the top of the beans when still boiling (it might drop when taken off the heat, no longer buoyed up by the bubbles). Pour off any in excess of this, or add a dash of water if need be.

Add the tomatoes and garlic, and salt and pepper to taste. Simmer for 5 minutes more, until the tomatoes soften and colour the sauce ruddy. Stir in the basil and oil, and serve hot or at room temperature. Or add a little water and eat as a soup.

CHILLED CHARD OR SPINACH WITH LEMON AND OIL LAZIO

The ferrous, green taste of chard or spinach is best savoured cold. To appreciate it as the Italians do, you need to forget all you ever learned – both the English way of stewing until brown, and the French 'just-wilted' approach. Italians like their greens cooked until completely tender, but not quite a mush, at which time their full depth of flavour becomes apparent. Water needs to be good and salty, and you must be careful with your timings, tasting the cooking vegetables often to drain them at that precious moment when stalk is meltingly soft, but before the leaves turn to a pulp.

Serves 4 as a side

1¼lbs spinach leaves (best from
  1¾lbs bunched) – not too young
or
1¾lbs baby chard, stems
  no thicker than a pencil
or
1¾lbs broad-stemmed young Swiss chard

To serve
⅓ cup of the best extra virgin olive oil
  you can get
4 lemon wedges

Spinach should just be washed, and root-end removed if bunched. Cut off the roots and wash baby chard in the same way. Swiss chard should be separated – stem from leaf – before washing. To wash the greens, fill the sink with cold water and stir the leaves around with your hands. Lift the leaves out and drain in a colander (so sand will stay at the bottom of the sink).

Have ready a pot of very well salted, boiling water and boil the greens. Spinach will take 3 minutes, and baby chard with thin stems 5 – both until the stalks are completely tender, but the leaves not even beginning to disintegrate. To cook Swiss chard, cut the stems into 2in lengths and boil them first. When they are cooked but crunchy (about 6 minutes), add the leaves and boil for 6 minutes more until everything – stem and leaf – is tender. Drain, refresh in iced water, and drain again immediately.

Squeeze the greens as hard as you can. If you have strength in your fingers, do this between your hands; or roll them in a kitchen towel and twist to wring it out. Spread the dried greens out on a platter with your fingers, to make a flat, uneven layer. Sprinkle with salt and pepper and drizzle with the oil. I like to serve the lemon on the side, both so your guests can judge their own, and so any leftovers can be kept without being browned by the acid.

BOILED ROMANESCO BROCCOLI
LAZIO

Romanesco broccoli is one of the most amazing vegetables in the world. Composed as a fractal, each of its spiralling minarets is covered with more spiralling minarets, *ad infinitum*, and it is possible to get as lost in its pea-green beauty as in dancing flames of a winter's night. It is, to the inquisitive mind, an edible acid trip.

      The flavour is also delectable, light and subtle, like refined cauliflower. Being a Roman vegetable it must be well cooked, just shy of disintegration, at which point it will soak up olive oil like a sponge, becoming rich, buttery and indulgent. It can be served hot or at room temperature, and is particularly delicious with light meats and grilled fishes.

Serves 4 as a side

1 big head Romanesco broccoli
About ½ cup extra virgin olive oil
3 tablespoons chopped flat-leaf parsley

A few shavings of Parmesan or Pecorino Romano, made with a potato peeler

It is vital that vegetables are cooked in water so salty it seasons them as they cook – this obviously salts them, but also helps to preserve their flavour – so put on a big pot of well-salted water and bring it to a boil.

Prepare the broccoli. Snap off any large or bruised leaves from the outside, but leave attached the small ones whose tips are intact, and are no longer than the head of broccoli they encircle – they are decorative and delicious. Trim off the end of the stem, to the base of these little leaves. If I'm going to serve the broccoli hot, I like to keep it whole, and cut a cross in the base of the stem; if I plan to eat it at room temperature, I cut it into rough florets.

Boil until completely tender, around 12 minutes: it is ready when the sharply geometrical shape starts to look a little softer or out-of-focus, just before it starts to break up. Lift the broccoli from the water and let it steam dry for a few minutes, then put on a plate and douse with the oil.

If you're serving it at room temperature, leave it to chill before garnishing, otherwise carry on while it's still hot. Taste for seasoning (it should need only pepper), scatter with the parsley and cheese, and serve.

ZUCCHINE TRIFOLATE / ZUCCHINI WITH PARSLEY LAZIO

The best zucchini are long, not too large, and pale-jade-green-skinned. These are delicate and sweet in flavour, without any hint of bitterness. Choose zucchini that feel heavy – these will be young and dense, with only embryonic seeds within. My favourite variety is *romano*, also called *romanesche*, which is deeply ridged (stellate in cross-section) and utterly delicious. If you ever see decent-sized zucchini (not the baby ones – these offer style over substance) available with the flowers still on, buy them – this is a sure sign of youth and freshness, and the flowers can be cooked with their fruits.

Pan-fried zucchini, in my opinion, should be partly browned for the wonderful depth of flavour that you normally have to grill for. As they can only be cooked for a few minutes before turning to a mush, I have developed a rather idiosyncratic technique for the perfect zucchini, which is described below.

Serves 4 as a side

1¼lbs zucchini
¼ cup extra virgin olive oil
2 garlic cloves, thinly sliced

A tiny pinch of hot red pepper flakes
A small bunch of flat-leaf parsley, finely chopped

Slice the zucchini thinly (⅛in), discarding tops and tails.

Heat a very wide pan (black iron or stainless steel will work better than non-stick), large enough to accommodate the zucchini in a layer two to three slices deep, over a high heat until smoking profusely (if black) or just very, very hot (if stainless and too clean to smoke). Put in all the zucchini, give the pan a shake to settle them, and leave for 30 seconds until they are starting to brown. The purpose of this is to cook the zucchini in a pan so hot it would scorch the oil.

Drizzle on the oil and sprinkle with salt and, still without stirring them, let the zucchini cook for another 30 seconds – they will brown further in the oil. Now add the garlic and pepper flakes along with some black pepper (all of which have not yet seen the pan for fear of burning), and give a single toss, so the bottom zucchini are more or less on top, the garlic and pepper flakes now underneath. Leave to cook for 15 seconds, give the pan a little shake, and cook for 15 seconds more, until the zucchini at the bottom and the garlic have taken a little colour. Sprinkle with the parsley and toss the zucchini in the pan a few times to mix, then take off the heat. Leave them in the pan for a minute to finish cooking in the residual heat and serve, hot or at room temperature.

DEEP-FRIED ZUCCHINI
LAZIO

Better than fries!

Serves 4 as a side

1¼lbs zucchini
Vegetable oil, for frying

½ cup all-purpose flour
⅓ cup cornstarch

Trim both ends of the zucchini, cut them in half across, then in half lengthways. If they are large, and the seeds look like a cucumber's, scoop them out; leave in the core if it looks dense and white instead. Cut the zucchini into batons about ¼in wide, and soak these in a little cold water as salty as the sea. A few ice cubes won't hurt – the colder the water is, the better. Leave them to soak for at least half an hour, but not so long as overnight.

Heat a good depth of the oil to 375°F – at least 2in in a decently wide pan, but for safety's sake no more than a third its depth. Pick the zucchini from the water and let them drip dry, but make sure they're still moist so the coating sticks. Toss them in a mixture of the flour and cornstarch. Let them sit in the mixture for a minute, then pick them out and shake them off, and fry for 3 minutes until golden. Drain well, sprinkle with salt and serve.

PUNTARELLE WITH ANCHOVY
LAZIO

Puntarelle, a weird variety of chicory that grows like a head of asparagus spears, defines Roman cuisine for me. It is *the* typical winter salad, served with a punchy anchovy dressing. Bitter, acidic, fishy, salty, these are bold flavours that exemplify the Roman attitude to taste – make it taste good, and make it taste strong.

In Rome, every fruit and vegetable stall has a wizened grandmother sitting on a stool at the back, cleaning artichokes, shelling beans and cutting vegetables for *minestra* (soup). She also prepares *puntarelle* with the aid of a grid of tightly strung wires she can push them through to make julienne strips that will coil up like beautiful pale green bedsprings when soaked in cold water. I often just cut the spears in half, lengthways – an attractive preparation, and much easier. The *puntarelle* must be eaten on the day they are prepared, as they quickly turn brown and, when oxidised, taste like the bottom of a pond.

Serves 3 as a side, or just me

1 head *puntarelle*
1oz anchovy fillets, preferably filleted
  at home from 2 ½oz salted whole
  anchovies

3 tablespoons lemon juice
⅓ cup extra virgin olive oil
1 scant teaspoon crushed black pepper
½ garlic clove, crushed to a paste

Prepare the *puntarelle*. Discard the very outer leaves if they look mangy. Pull off all the long inner leaves too – keep these, but strip off the green fronds and keep only the white stalks. Within, you'll find a cluster of green spears, looking for all the world like the spires of the Emerald City. Cut or snap them off at their bases.

To prepare the leaf-stalks, cut them into about 3in lengths. Put each one flat on a board and cut through horizontally to the board – separating the leaf rib into two ribbons helps it to curl. Cut these lengthways into ⅛in strips, which you should put into iced water as you go.

To prepare the central spears like a Roman, slice them lengthways into 3/32in slices, then cut these into 3/32in-wide batons. Do not discard any less-than-perfect trimmings, as they all taste good. To do it the lazy way, just cut the spears in half, lengthways. Soak with the prepared leaf-stalks in iced water for at least 30 minutes, no more than 8 hours, before dressing.

To make the dressing, finely chop the anchovy fillets and mix with the lemon juice, oil, pepper and garlic. Toss the well-drained *puntarelle* in this. Salt will not be necessary, as anchovies have their own. This may be the greatest dish known to man. Serve it immediately.

FAGIOLI CON LE COTICHE / BORLOTTI BEANS AND PIG SKIN LAZIO

Fagioli con le cotiche is a stalwart of the Roman *trattoria* – nourishing, cheap and tasty. The skin adds body and flavour: fresh skin is okay, that from a *prosciutto* is better, while that from a smoked ham (*speck* or similar) is best of all.

Serves 4 as a side

A good piece of skin, from a pig,
   prosciutto or *speck*, about 8 x 8in
3 tablespoons dried oregano
½ teaspoon ground black pepper
½ small onion, chopped
1 celery stalk, chopped

1 garlic clove, chopped
1 bay leaf
⅓ cup extra virgin olive oil
¾lb dried borlotti beans, soaked
   overnight in water

Lay the skin outside-down on a board, and sprinkle the fat side with the oregano and pepper. Roll it tightly like a cigar, and tie securely with string. In a large saucepan, fry the onion, celery, garlic and bay in the oil over a medium heat until tender, 5–10 minutes. Add the roll of skin and about 2 quarts of water. Simmer for an hour or so (you can omit this first boiling if using fresh, rather than cured skin), then add the drained beans and simmer for 2 hours more, when the beans are tender, and their liquor reduced until level with them.

Pick out the skin, remove the string, and cut the long roll across at 3/16in intervals to make little spirals. Return these to the beans, season with salt, boil until the liquid is thick if it isn't already, and serve hot. These beans will keep for days in the fridge, but will likely need additional salt, as they soak it up over time like a sponge.

VIGNAROLA / STEWED SPRING VEGETABLES
LAZIO

I never realise how depressed I've been over winter until spring arrives. The days lengthen, the sun warms, and spring is as much in my step as it is in the air. The winter vegetables, whose decline from comforting to boring I never noticed at the time, are elbowed out of the way by vibrant greens – artichokes, asparagus, peas and fava beans. I may be a couple of months older than I was back in February, but I feel ten years younger.

Named after the grape vines (*vigne*), *vignarola* is a pot of all the vegetables traditionally grown between them, to maximise the yield of the land and deter pests and weeds. Potatoes and cabbages store only so long, and endives bolt, so a sense of desperation must have turned into colossal relief when a family could eat their first *vignarola* of the year. They would likely have enriched it with their last few scraps of *pancetta* or *guanciale* – as indeed can you, even if I prefer to keep mine clean.

Serves 4 as a starter or side

1 bunch scallions

2 large or 4 small artichokes, cleaned (page 26) and cut into ½ in wedges

7 tablespoons extra virgin olive oil

½ lb freshly shelled peas (1lb in their pods)

½ lb freshly shelled young fava beans (1¾ lbs in their shells)

1 bunch asparagus, cut in 1in lengths (optional, not traditional)

1 head romaine (*romano*) lettuce, or 2 Little Gems, coarsely shredded

1 tablespoon chopped fresh mint (optional)

¼ cup chopped flat-leaf parsley (optional)

Cut the scallions into 1in lengths. Fry them with the artichokes in the oil for a few minutes over a medium heat, until hot through. Add the peas, fava beans and asparagus, if using, and fry for a minute more – then add water to come about ½ in *below* the top of the vegetables, ⅔ cup or so.

Season with salt and pepper and boil furiously for 10–15 minutes until all the vegetables are meltingly tender, the water reduced to a scant but velvety sauce. Add the lettuce 5 minutes before the end, and stir the herbs in when the pan comes off the heat, if using. Serve with bread (for mopping), as a starter, or to accompany light meats or fish.

TOMATOES
CAMPANIA

It is hard to imagine Italian cuisine without tomatoes, although they were introduced only in the sixteenth century. The Aztecs prized the precious golden seeds, discarding the flesh. The Italians often squeeze out the watery seeds to keep only the red flesh. The French remove the tough skin before farting around with the fruit within. Nature, as ever, got it right: the whole fruit is wonderfully balanced, so I use it all, the skin providing green flavours, the flesh a sweet richness, and the seeds their sauciness and acidity.

Early tomatoes (varieties like *Camone* and *Marmandino* in Italy) are best eaten tinged with green; they are fresh, delightfully acidic, and taste like tomato stalks smell (green, a little like a freshly mown lawn), surely the best aroma in the world.

In summer, look for ripe, deep red tomatoes that still have enough acidity to balance their sweetness – the gnarly, deeply grooved ugly ones, or massive beefsteak tomatoes. These should be as ripe as they can be: at this time of year, softness wins over crunch, sweetness over greenness.

From midsummer through to autumn, and into winter where sun permits (Sicily, for example), *datterino* or little baby plum tomatoes are the best option. Their thick skin and intense flavour makes them brilliant – a welcome reminder of the taste of sunshine.

All year round, rely on touch (is the tomato firm, or giving? in a nice way?), sight (any intense colour, blood-red, forest green, or nearly black is a sign of quality), and smell (if the base smells green, like the stem, it is both delicious and ripe), in your search for good eating.

When you have found the perfect tomato, don't mess with it – your work is done. Cut into chunks, seasoned with salt and pepper and doused with a green, fruity olive oil, there is nothing more you can do to improve what nature perfected for you.

ESCAROLE SALAD
CAMPANIA

Almost any lettuce, green, crisp and refreshing, is a wonderful thing. That said, a good number of salad leaves are particularly great and particularly Italian. But were I to choose one, it would have to be escarole. Fleshy but light, crunchy and still forgiving, bitter and sweet at the same time, it is all I could wish for in a salad.

Serves 4–8 as a side, or after a main

1 head escarole
½ garlic clove (optional)

2 tablespoons lemon juice
½ cup extra virgin olive oil

The escarole is best washed whole, by immersing it upside-down in a sinkful of water and moving it around a little, then shaking dry. Remove any damaged outer leaves, then separate all the rest from the stem and tear into generous pieces.

My grandmother rubs a wooden salad bowl with the garlic, then discards the clove. My mum makes the dressing in advance, and leaves the garlic to steep in it for half an hour or more before discarding it. I sometimes make the salad without any garlic at all. In any case, dress the escarole moments before you serve, seasoning with salt and pepper. The sodden bits of salad left at the bottom are best eaten with a crust of bread, also used to mop the bowl.

WILD ASPARAGUS AND MORELS
CAMPANIA

Our sense of taste is a product of our history. We have grown up – as individuals and as a society – eating foods that grew themselves in the same place, and at the same time of year. It has taken millennia for our cuisines to evolve, to find ways that seem right of combining the crops. And as you grew up, as I did, we tasted these combinations together – so lamb, and sheep's cheeses, are great with fava beans; tomatoes are good with scallions; *porcini* with chestnuts and game.

Walking through an Italian forest in May, and treading carefully to avoid the little blue anemones, purple violets and pink cyclamen, you might find the first mushrooms of the year, morels, growing alongside the purple-green, fine fronds of wild asparagus. It should not be surprising, therefore, that they taste so damned delectable together.

Serves 4 as a side

½ lb fresh morels
1 lb wild asparagus or very fine
  (thin) cultivated asparagus (pictured)

1 garlic clove
⅓ cup extra virgin olive oil

Clean the morels: trim off any dirty bases, and rinse them if they look gritty. Fresh morels will seem dry and firm – discard any wet, flaccid ones that are past their prime. Cut the asparagus into 1½ in lengths, discarding the tough part of the stem. Thinly slice the garlic and fry gently in the oil, but don't let it colour. Add the morels, season with salt and pepper, and fry for 2 minutes. Add the asparagus and fry for a minute more, then add a ladleful of water and sauté over a high heat until the water has evaporated, leaving the glistening mushrooms and asparagus tender, but still with a little bite.

Variation: Asparagus with Morels and Eggs To make a delicious starter, add a pat of butter at the same time as the water. Fry 4 eggs (hen's, duck's or gull's), leaving the yolks completely runny, and serve these draped over the asparagus and morels. A few scales of Parmesan shaved on top, although not entirely necessary, won't go amiss.

BROCCOLI RABE WITH GARLIC AND CHILI
PUGLIA

Broccoli rabe, sometimes sold as turnip tops, are the heads of young rape picked before the flowers have opened into the sunshine yellow that enlivens so much countryside these days. They have a green taste, slightly peppery and delightfully bitter, and are at the heart of Pugliese cookery. Neapolitans, being difficult, will insist that the *friarielli* they are so proud of are a different beast, although I can't taste the difference. Romans have no such conceit about their *broccoletti*, also very much the same thing.

Broccoli rabe are always boiled until quite soft, then normally pan-fried, but also used in soups or to top pizzas. They have a natural affinity with Italian sausages – as a side, in soups, on pizzas or even in pasta.

Serves 4 as a side

13/4 lbs *broccoli rabe*
2 garlic cloves, thinly sliced

⅓ cup extra virgin olive oil
A good pinch of hot red pepper flakes

Broccoli rabe at the start of the season will be young, and likely have tender stems (test them with a fingernail, or snap a leaf stem: if it has no strings, it's young). Cut the leaves and stalks of young *broccoli rabe* into 2–4in lengths, but keep the broccoli-like central shoot intact, and discard any parts of the central stalk much wider than ½in.

More mature plants must have all but the smallest leaves stripped from the tough leaf-stalk (which should be discarded), still keeping the tender florets and tiniest leaves intact.

Boil the *broccoli rabe* in well-salted water until tender (from 4 minutes if young to 10 minutes if mature). If you boil the *broccoli rabe* just before you eat, they can be lifted straight from the water, given a little shake, and put directly into the frying pan in the next step. Otherwise drain them and spread out to steam dry until ready to use.

Fry the garlic in the oil until it starts to brown. Add the pepper flakes, let it fry for a few seconds, then add the *broccoli rabe*, seasoning with salt and pepper. If they were fully drained before adding to the pan, add a splash of water to moisten them once coated in the oil. Pan-fry until hot through, the water absorbed by the leaves – just a few minutes.

DRIED FAVA BEANS AND CHICORY
PUGLIA

The Pugliese are expert with vegetables, growing and cooking them with equal, natural flair. The bitter chicory (*cicoria* or *catalogna*) that makes this dish is hard to find outside Italy – it looks like giant, dark green dandelion, with leaves half a metre long. But you can use dandelion leaves, bought or foraged, which taste pretty much the same and just as good – or the dark green leaves of *puntarelle*, which seem identical in every way. In any case, the result will be bitter, delicious, peasanty and wholesome.

Serves 4 as a side

½lb dried fava beans, in their shells
  or out
½ cup extra virgin olive oil
¾lb *cicoria* – or dandelion leaves

1 garlic clove, thinly sliced
A pinch of hot red pepper flakes –
  make it a big one

If the fava beans are in their shells, soak them in water overnight, then simmer them in plenty of water for 3–5 hours until very soft, the water evaporating for the most part (keep it topped up so they never boil dry), such that when you beat them with a wooden spoon they make a chunky purée. If you happen to have a pressure cooker, it will save literally hours of watching the pot run dry. Shelled fava beans, which don't need soaking, may be cooked in 2 quarts of water for just 2 hours until soft, and beaten in the same way. Season with 2 tablespoons of the oil, and some salt and pepper.

The chicory, cut into 2–4in lengths and washed, should be boiled in well-salted water until soft (8 minutes or so), then drained, refreshed and squeezed dry. Fry the garlic in half the remaining oil until browned, add the pepper flakes, then the chicory, and sauté over a low flame for 5 minutes. Add the fava beans and stir over the heat until warmed through. Serve drizzled with the last of the oil.

Variation: Fava Bean and Chicory Soup To eat as a delicious soup, add water to the desired consistency in the final throes of cooking, and serve drizzled with even more oil.

CAPONATA
SICILY

Food is an emotive subject, especially for Italians. Everyone has their own way of doing things, whilst everyone else's is not *worse* but *wrong*. I made the mistake, when Bocca di Lupo first opened, of asking our Sicilian waiters (we had four at the time) what they thought of my *caponata*. They all detested it.

'You can't put celery in *caponata* – it's disgusting – but at least the vegetables are nice and chunky.'

'You idiot, the vegetables should be small and combined – but I like that you serve anchovies on top, like my mother.'

'You *never* put anchovies in *caponata* – Luca's mother is a whore! And where are the pine nuts?'

'Pine nuts? Imbecile! Jacob *ha fatto il bravo* without pine nuts, and of course it has to have celery... Oh, but you're right, this *is* gross – there aren't any peppers!'

I think, in fact, they came close to killing each other that day over a plate of *caponata*. Voices grew loud, chests puffed out, and body language became threatening. I felt like crying, but put an end to the argument by saying:

'This is the way *I* make *caponata*. And everyone else is wrong...'

Serves 4–6 as a starter or side, 2–3 as a main

2 large eggplants, cut in 1¼in chunks
Vegetable oil, for frying
2 medium onions, sliced across the grain
⅓ cup extra virgin olive oil
1 head celery, cut in 1¼in chunks
3 tablespoons salted capers, soaked until tolerably salty

2 garlic cloves, thinly sliced
1½lbs plum tomatoes, quartered
½ cup superfine sugar
⅓ cup red wine vinegar
3 tablespoons chopped flat-leaf parsley
3 anchovy fillets, halved lengthways into 6 strips (optional)

Sprinkle the eggplant with salt (just enough to season the eggplant, no more, no less) and let it sit for 10 minutes. Heat about ¼in depth of vegetable oil to about 375°F in a wide pan and fry the eggplant until golden brown. Drain well and let it blot on paper towels.

Fry the onions in the olive oil in a wide pan over a medium heat until starting to soften – 5–10 minutes. A pinch of salt early on will help them along. Add the celery, capers and garlic and fry for a further 10–15 minutes, until the onions are completely soft, the celery still crunchy and vivid green. Spread this cooked vegetable mixture out in a roasting pan, no more than ¾in deep. Arrange the eggplant on top, and finish with the quartered tomatoes, cut-sides up. Sprinkle with salt and pepper, as well as the sugar and the vinegar. Cook in a 310°F oven for an hour and a half, until the watery juices have evaporated to a thick syrup, and the tomatoes are halfway to being dried. Taste the liquor a few times during cooking: there should be a robust balance of sweet, sour and salt.

Take the *caponata* from the oven and let it cool – it should be served only slightly warm, or at room temperature. Toss the vegetables together before serving scattered with parsley, the anchovy fillets draped over if you want them.

Because of its acidity, *caponata* made in this way can keep for at least a week in the fridge.

EGGPLANT WITH MINT AND BREADCRUMBS
CALABRIA

Eggplant is not everyone's favourite thing, and admittedly it can be quite repugnant if not cooked properly. But careful grilling or fierce frying renders the flesh soft as butter, the flavour delicate and smoky. I challenge anyone to try this dish, where it is marinated in a piquant dressing of vinegar and mint, and not love it.

Serves 4 as a starter or side

2 large eggplants
²/₃ cup extra virgin olive oil
¹/₃ cup breadcrumbs (made from
   real bread)

½ garlic clove, crushed to a paste
A good pinch of hot red pepper flakes
¼ cup finely shredded mint
¼ cup red wine vinegar

Slice the eggplant across into ⅛ in rounds, season them with a little salt, and rub with 7 tablespoons of the oil. Heat a barbecue or griddle pan over a medium heat until smoking, and grill the eggplant for about 3 minutes on each side – until it has charred grill-marks, and is tender all the way through.

Rub the breadcrumbs with half the remaining olive oil and bake them in a 320°F oven until golden brown. Make a dressing of the remaining oil, the garlic, pepper flakes, mint and vinegar and season it with salt and pepper. Drizzle this over the fried eggplant, and let marinate for 5 minutes. Serve scattered with the breadcrumbs, to give a little crunch and absorb any errant juices.

BLOOD ORANGE, RED ONION AND OREGANO SALAD SICILY

I have had a love affair with blood oranges for as long as I can remember. Their colour is so miraculous, flesh so sweet, and flavour so orangey that they seem too good to be true. As one of the few fruits or vegetables that has not yet been farmed globally, they remain seasonal, available only in winter. This adds to the excitement, a rare thing when the nights are long and the sun cold.

This salad can be made at any time of year, with any decent oranges, but is of course best with blood oranges, and best in season. All the flavours – orange, raw onion, fresh oregano and fruity oil – are fresh and zingy. They make for a plate that is as enticing to the palate as it is to the eye.

Serves 4 as a starter or side

**6 small, very dark blood oranges,
  or 4 medium ones**
½ small red onion

¼ cup extra virgin olive oil
1 tablespoon oregano leaves

Cut the skin and pith from the oranges, then slice them across into ⅛in pinwheel rounds. Slice the onion very thinly across the grain, and soak for 5 minutes in iced water to crisp it and render it a touch milder. Arrange the orange slices flat on a plate and scatter with the drained red onion. Season well with salt and pepper, drizzle with the oil and dot the oregano leaves on top.

Variation: Oranges with Pecorino In Sicily, this salad is sometimes served with a few slices of peppercorn Pecorino as a starter or a side dish, the cheese best if fresh or medium, rather than very mature.

Variation: Oranges with *Bottarga* Scatter the salad with 2–3oz very thinly sliced mullet *bottarga* for a refined and luxurious *antipasto*.

DESSERTS / COOKIES

O my poor belly! You have suffered so, stuffed like a teddy bear, and yet I can't refuse pudding...
As a child I used to say that I had two stomachs, which was why I might be too full to finish the sprouts but still have room for a slice of cake. And then another...

Those who refuse dessert do themselves a disservice. Either they won't make room for it on grounds of vanity, or they are masochists who deny themselves the simple pleasures. To convince them to indulge would be an act of charity.

The undisputed capitals of Italian desserts are Naples and Sicily. Both places benefited from foreign expertise bequeathed by turbulent histories: in Naples, the French leaving behind the techniques of fine *viennoiserie* and *pâtisserie*, and in Sicily, the Arab legacy includes a love of sugar, spice, citrus and soft cheese. The rest of Italy has grown up in isolation, each region producing a few delicious and typical puddings, but as limited in range, compared to these sugary strongholds, as a puddle is to the sea.

Sweet food, by and large, presents a challenge – how far can we push artifice? And, how can we preserve in something as artificial as a jelly, pudding or cake the flavour and freshness of a fruit? The art of a pastry cook is to take the same basic combination of flour, sugar, egg and milk (or cream or butter or cheese) and concoct from this minimalist palette a million confections. By adding only experience, and perhaps a little fruit or chocolate or nut, alchemy is performed.

The exacting methods needed to make the most ethereal sponge, the lightest dough, the most indulgent pudding, call for a certain temperament. Before we dive into the recipes, might I query whether you are the nurturing type? Have you a sweet tooth? And do you have the patience to watch a yeast dough slowly rise? I ask only because it is easy to buy cookies and cakes, and you have to be a certain sort of person to enjoy their manufacture. If you are that person, then we are cut from the same cloth – and we are the lucky ones. Our desserts will bring a smile to every guest's lips, they have the power to make friends and will end wars.

PEARS BAKED IN RED WINE AND CLOVES
VENETO

At a little *trattoria* in Treviso (Toni Del Spin, where I first had *zuppa coada,* page 177), at the end of a resplendent meal, the waiter suggested baked pears for dessert. When a pair of small, wrinkled fruit arrived, unadorned on their plate, I was reassured by the perfume that he had recommended well.

Pears cooked in red wine sounds rather ordinary and uninteresting. But these are baked, with their skins on, in large quantities of wine, sugar and cloves until the syrup is thick, the fruit condensed and very aromatic. Served cold, they are as perfect a conclusion to a meal as one could wish for.

Serves 4

2lbs firmish pears
3½ cups superfine sugar

50 whole cloves
1½ quarts red wine

Use a baking pan – one with deep sides – into which the pears will fit in a single, snug layer. Sprinkle with the sugar and cloves, then add the red wine, such that it rinses any sugar from the surface of the pears, and comes just level with their tops. Bake in a 350°F oven, with the heat coming mostly from below if your oven allows. Bake for around 2½–3 hours, turning only two or three times until the syrup is thick and the pears wrinkled – perhaps a few have split, and are slightly browned on top.

Let cool, then serve at room temperature. I think these are perfect on their own, but if you yearn for an accompaniment, try mascarpone cream (page 359).

BONET
PIEDMONT

Bonet is *the* typical dessert of Piedmont. I first ate it at Trattoria Valenza, in Turin, where a little wedge of the pudding, like a dense crème caramel but black with chocolate, thick with *amaretti*, and heady with coffee and rum, marked the happy ending to one of the most magical meals I can remember. I was quick to try a few recipes, but found them too subtle, too light, too delicate. Normally a delicate hand improves a dish, and never more so than when making sweets. *Bonet* is the exception to the rule, and I discovered that the more of everything I added – more chocolate, more *amaretti*, more caramel, more rum, more chocolate again – the better it became. Developing the recipe was like Paddington Bear making his dumplings, only I made a beauty, and he a monster.

Serves 8–10

1⅓ cups superfine sugar

2 cups milk

¾ cup unsweetened cocoa powder

2oz bittersweet chocolate, chopped

1 double espresso (¼ cup)

1 teaspoon vanilla extract

2 large eggs

3 large egg yolks

¼ cup rum

7oz *amaretti* cookies

Most people make caramel by adding water to sugar, because they live in fear of it. A life lived in fear is a life half lived, and you can make a brilliant caramel, even more reliably, without water. Take a scrupulously clean pan – it is best if the walls meet the base in a gently rounded corner, and both are thick. Put the sugar in it and place over a high heat. Stir with a metal spoon, not too vigorously, and watch as the sugar first heats, then start to clump together, then melts into a pale amber caramel. This is not yet what you are looking for, so leave the pan on the heat until the colour turns a deep chestnut brown, and starts to smoke a little faster. Take it off the heat and leave it in the pan – it will continue to cook.

The moment you fear the caramel might soon become too bitter pour it into a 7–8in *bundt* pan (*kugelhopf*, or decorative doughnut-shaped mould, or use a simple loaf pan). Wearing gloves for protection, carefully rotate the mould to coat the sides thickly, and spoon it up the central projection of the pan. Keep on turning and spooning until the caramel has set.

Bring the milk to a boil. Beat together all the remaining ingredients except the *amaretti* to make a thick paste, then add the boiling milk, very gradually at first, beating all the time to avoid lumps. Crumble the *amaretti* in your hands and beat them into the mixture.

For a lighter pudding, with a cakey base, pour this mixture straight into the caramel-lined mould. If, like me, you are aiming for a more substantial, evenly-textured dessert, let the mixture stand in the mixing bowl for 15–20 minutes so the *amaretti* are thoroughly soused, and whisk again until they no longer rise to the surface, then pour into the mould. In either case, stand the pan on top of a submerged kitchen towel (to steady it) in a water bath of preheated water that comes to the level of the top of the *bonet* (not to the top of the pan). Cover the mould with foil to protect the surface from the hot air of the 320°F oven in which it is to be baked for 45 minutes or until just set in the middle. Lift the mould from the water bath, let cool, then refrigerate until ready to turn out and serve.

It is best to wait overnight before unmoulding for as much caramel sauce as possible to develop – it slowly dissolves in the pudding's moisture to make the syrup – as it is this that makes the pudding so very delectable.

PANDORO CON ZABAIONE
PIEDMONT

I love a good *pandoro,* so much more so than its big brother, the *panettone.* I find the candied fruits of the latter detract from the featherlight, golden sweet yeast dough that is surely the epitome of the baker's art. And good *pandoro* is easy to find: it keeps well, and Italian delicatessens are literally stuffed to the rafters in winter. Simply dunked in cold milk it makes for my favourite breakfast. Served with steaming *zabaione* it is almost as good.

Serves 4 (twice)

1 *pandoro* (or large *panettone*)
6 large egg yolks
3/4 cup superfine sugar
2/3 cup dry Marsala

For the next day
4 glasses cold milk

Pandoro, at least from a shop, always comes in a big cellophane bag with a sachet of vanilla confectioners' sugar. Before going any further, dump the icing sugar into the bag, twist the opening shut and shake vigorously to dust the cake with the sugar. Cut four star-shaped slices from the top of the *pandoro* by slicing across at 3/4in intervals. You will have about half left over – wrap this in the bag to keep it from drying out before tomorrow.

For the *zabaione,* mix together the egg yolks, sugar and Marsala in a metal bowl and whisk over boiling water – it doesn't matter if it touches the water or not – until hot, thick and fluffy. This will take a little time, and a strong arm.

Quickly warm the slices of *pandoro* in a 350°F oven (it just takes a minute) and serve with the *zabaione* poured on top.

The next morning, for breakfast, serve the leftover *pandoro* sliced into wedges and dusted with a little extra confectioners' sugar, with the milk on hand for dunking. This will at once bring back memories of dinner the night before, and bode well for the day that is to come.

ROSE CAKE
LOMBARDY

The earliest cakes were yeast cakes, like hot cross buns and *babkas*, likely none-too-sweet until the Arabs brought us sugar in the thirteenth century. This cake, shaped like a bunch of opening rosebuds, was invented not long after, for the wedding of Isabella d'Este to Marquis Gonzaga of Mantua in 1490. The shape, a bouquet of roses, represented beauty and kindness – Gonzaga's court chefs had created it for the young bride.

The airiness and beauty that are supposed to define this cake are not easily achieved – it should be as light as the cloud of flowers it represents, and as indulgent as it can be. The secret is a fine brioche dough, the flour well worked, the dough supple, and the butter integrated. It may take a while to get a feel for working with such a fickle pastry, but once your fingers have learned the knack it's as easy as pie.

It should also be noted that such refinement takes time – allow an hour to make the dough (including 40 minutes to get the yeast going), then 6 hours' rising in the fridge (while you're at work or overnight), and then a further 3–4 hours to rise again after the cake has been formed. Achieving the shape is actually the easy part…

Serves 8–12

Brioche dough, step 1
1 cup bread flour
2 large eggs
2 tablespoons dried yeast, or ¼ cup fresh

Brioche dough, step 2
4 cups bread flour
Generous ¼ cup superfine sugar
1 tablespoon fine salt
1 tablespoon runny honey
5 large eggs

Brioche dough, step 3
1 cup unsalted butter, fridge cold,
   diced ½–¾in

Butter spread
10 tablespoons unsalted butter
¾ cup superfine sugar

First make the brioche. Combine the ingredients of step 1 to a thick paste, and leave in a warm place for 40 minutes or until it triples in bulk.

To this add all the ingredients of step 2. Knead in a bowl (the mixture is sticky) for a good 10 minutes until very smooth, and very glossy indeed. Doing this by hand achieves a superior result, but only if you have the persistence required – otherwise a stand mixer on a slow speed, fitted with a dough hook, will do the job.

Add the butter of step 3, and continue to knead until fully incorporated – perhaps 5–10 minutes more, as cold butter works in slowly. Let the dough rise in the fridge for at least 6 hours, but no more than 15 (it will be ready after 6, but you can leave it longer if it suits your schedule). Do not be tempted to let it rise in a warm place – the butter-fat must remain solid, or the dough will be hard to work, and it may split as it bakes.

When you are ready to form your cake, make the butter spread by working the butter and sugar to a soft paste. Roll the brioche out on a lightly floured surface to a rectangle 3/16in thick, perhaps 16 x 20in, and spread evenly with the sweetened butter. Roll it up, butter on the inside, to make a 20in-long roulade. Put it in the fridge for half an hour or so to make it firmer and easier to handle. While it chills, line the base and sides of a 9 or 10in cake pan with parchment paper. Cut the chilled roll of dough across into 1½–2in-thick pinwheel slices (you'll get 10–12 of them) and stand these up in it on their cut sides, leaving a little gap between them to allow for expansion. Cover lightly with a fine cloth, until risen to fill the cake pan and a bit (3/4in) over the rim – anywhere up to 4 hours.

Bake at 350°F for 45 minutes to an hour, until deep gold and firm. Let cool before serving (it is best still slightly warm). As good at the start of the day as at the end of a meal, and just as sinful.

SCIASCIA / GIANNI'S HAZELNUT AND PISTACHIO COOKIES EMILIA-ROMAGNA

This recipe was given to me by Gianni Figliomeni – the very same who shared his formula for persimmon sorbet (page 415), which I hope you'll try. He is a calm, generous soul, with a temperament designed for making *gelati,* but also ideal for baking. He spends hours almost every day, tirelessly refining recipes that, to the outsider, seem perfect already. It is a very different approach from my brash, impatient cooking. But then Gianni is one who savours, I am one who consumes.

At any rate, here is his recipe which, I think, takes the biscuit. It's named after Leonardo Sciascia, the Sicilian author.

Makes about 24 large cookies

6 large egg whites, at room temperature
1 3/4 cups superfine sugar
1/2 cup plus 2 tablespoons shelled raw pistachios

1/2 cup plus 2 tablespoons shelled raw hazelnuts
Finely grated zest of 2 lemons
Scant 1 cup all-purpose flour

Beat the egg whites with about 1/3 cup of the sugar at high speed, until they turn white, then very gradually add another scant 1/4 cup sugar as the eggs beat, until they form very stiff but still glossy peaks – 10–15 minutes.

Meanwhile, grind the pistachios and hazelnuts together in a food processor until they look granular – 1/16in chunks. Put the nuts in a bowl with the lemon zest and the remaining sugar. Stir together, then add the flour and stir again. Slowly fold this aromatic nut mixture into the egg whites.

Have ready a few baking sheets, lined with parchment paper. Spoon the nut mixture carefully into little mounds, about 3 x 2in, each around 1/2in high, and leave gaps between them. Bake in an oven preheated to 400°F for 13 minutes.

Let cool before serving. As you might imagine, these are as delicious served with *gelato* as with a coffee.

CENCI / CRISPY RAGS OF DOUGH

These strips of fried dough, thin and blistered, are not very sweet, but dusted with confectioners' sugar they are without doubt the best accompaniment to a coffee at the end of a meal. *Cenci* (rags) are proof that texture is as important as taste, so roll them thinly and fry them crisp. The sight of a heap, white with sugar, is as celebratory as fireworks, and perhaps one of the reasons they are ubiquitous at *carnevale*. I've always known them as *cenci,* but elsewhere they are known as *frappe,* or *lattughe* (lettuce leaves), or *bugie* (lies), or *chiacchiere* (gossips).

It is imperative the oil be fresh as a daisy, as the taste is so subtle that any hint of the fast food restaurant would ruin the experience. This is why *cenci* are perhaps the only thing I would choose to deep-fry in olive oil.

Makes about 30 *cenci*, enough for 6–12

Scant 2½ cups all-purpose flour
1 large egg
Scant ½ cup white wine
2 tablespoons superfine sugar
1 teaspoon baking powder
Finely grated zest of ½ lemon

Vegetable oil, for frying (I use a
   light olive oil, or half extra virgin
   olive oil, half sunflower or corn)

To serve
Confectioners' sugar
A little Sambuca (optional)

First make the dough by combining the flour, egg, wine, sugar, baking powder and lemon zest and kneading to make a smooth dough. Let rest, covered, for at least half an hour in the refrigerator.

Roll the dough very thinly, 1/32in – this can be achieved with a rolling pin, or more easily a pasta machine. Cut it into irregular strips (3/4–2in wide, 4–6in long) and fry them in oil heated to 300°F until golden and crisp all the way through. Drain well and serve dusted very liberally with confectioners' sugar. Some families sprinkle the *cenci* with a little Sambuca when they serve them, but not so much as to make them soggy – this tastes as good as it sounds.

CROSTATA DI MARMELLATA / JAM TART
EMILIA-ROMAGNA

Every bakery, and every home, makes *crostata*, a simple jam tart, one which says a lot about its maker. The *crostata*, so ubiquitous, is a sign of the values the cook holds dear. Some are gnarled yet delicious; some wholemeal; some soft, spongy and supple; and others crisp and fine. Poor examples may be too sweet, or too hard, or too doughy. Perfection is not refinement, but the perfect expression of the cook's heart. Mine has a slightly spongy, soft dough, yellow with Italian eggs, and the jam is cooked only briefly, so the taste of the fruit is as fresh as it was on the tree. Make of that what you will.

Serves 8

Sweet pastry
Scant 4 cups all-purpose flour
1²/₃ cups confectioners' sugar
A pinch of salt
1 tablespoon baking powder
3/4 cup unsalted butter, cold, diced
2 large eggs

1 large egg yolk
1 tablespoon vanilla extract
Finely grated zest of 1 small lemon

Filling
1½ cups jam (see overleaf)
1 large egg yolk, to glaze

For the pastry, sift together the flour, sugar, salt and baking powder. Add the butter, and quickly work it in with your fingers, trying not to warm it up too much. Add the whole eggs, the yolk, the vanilla and the lemon zest. Bring the dough together, but do not overwork as it would become tough if really kneaded, then wrap it in plastic wrap in a flattened patty and rest in the refrigerator until firm – half an hour or more.

Roll the dough about 5/16in thick – it is very soft, and best worked on a floured sheet of parchment paper. Pick it up by wrapping round the rolling pin, and line an 11in fluted metal tart pan with it, right to the rim. Trim any excess, gather into a ball, roll out to a thickness of 3/32in and cut into ½–3/4in-wide strips. Spread the tart with the jam, which won't quite reach the top. Make a lattice of pastry strips over the top, and brush this with the other yolk.

Bake the tart for about 50 minutes in a 350°F oven. If your oven allows you to, it is a good idea to direct the heat from the bottom for the last 20 minutes, to help the base to crisp. It is done when the dough is cooked through, the lattice on top golden and crisp at least half the way through. Let cool to room temperature before serving. The tart can be kept for a few days, but never refrigerated – it would go soggy – and life is simply better if the tart is kept at room temperature, ready to grab a sneaky slice from.

JAM

Jam-making is an art we are, I fear, losing all too quickly. It need not intimidate you: the days of standing over a great cauldron for hours, splattered by boiling, sticky juices, are long gone. Two modern(ish) advances have made life easy. First, pectin: this can be added to a jam, so it is ready to set as soon as it boils. Secondly, the fridge: we no longer need to preserve fruit for the whole year, and can keep a fresh jam chilled for weeks, so small batches can be made, and there is none of the hassle of sterilising jars.

Play around with the fruit: pulped coconut is great, as are weird things like grated watermelon rind, or citrus in winter. Listed here are summer affairs, but almost any fruit makes good jam. If the fruit isn't naturally acidic, add a bit more lemon juice into the mix.

The pectin, which sets the jam so quickly, means you can keep the fruit taste as fresh as can be. If you can't find pectin, use 'jam-making sugar' instead of normal – it already has pectin added, although you can't control how much...

Makes about 3lbs

2lbs prepared fruit flesh (see below – start with about 3lbs peaches, or apricots, or sweet or Morello cherries)
1/3 cup lemon juice
2 1/2 cups superfine or granulated sugar

2 tablespoons plus 1 1/2 teaspoons powdered apple pectin (2 tablespoons for slightly softer jam, plus 1 1/2 teaspoons for a very firm one)

First prepare the fruit. Peel peaches, and cut the flesh from the stone in wedges. Quarter apricots, discarding the stone. Pit cherries. Toss the fruit in the lemon juice as you go, to keep it from oxidising.

Mix together the sugar and pectin (this is important, or the pectin will form lumps). Put the fruit in the saucepan you'll cook the jam in, and stir in the sugar mixture. Leave it to sit for between a quarter and half an hour, to draw some liquid from the fruit, then set over a high heat and bring it to a boil.

Test the jam by dribbling a little of the liquor on to a cool plate: if it sets almost to a gel quickly, and almost forms strands as the last drops fall from the spoon, the jam will set well. With this quantity of pectin, setting stage should be reached within minutes of the pot coming to a boil. Transfer the jam to a container – sterilised jars if you wish to keep it – but I prefer to make small batches of jam, and often, with whatever is in season.

CHERRIES ON ICE
EMILIA-ROMAGNA

Cherries from Vignola make an impression on all the senses. Whilst many fruits lose flavour when they grow outsize, these massive, black-red cherries are meaty and packed with flavour. In demand within and without Italy, they command a high price – and although they are worth it, they can be hard to find.

Fortunately, in late June and July, excellent cherries can be bought almost anywhere: if strawberries are the first sign of summer, cherries tell us it has well and truly arrived. While most fruits are best eaten at room temperature, cherries at their peak are so sweet they should be served chilled, like grapes. Crush some ice and pile the cherries in a bed of it in a wide, chilled bowl – you cannot serve too many. Eat them outside in the setting sun, until it dips below the horizon.

STRAWBERRIES WITH MASCARPONE CREAM AND BALSAMIC VINEGAR EMILIA-ROMAGNA

Balsamic vinegar – a good, sweet, thick one – is delicious with strawberries. An ingredient that is used perhaps too indiscriminately, it does have its place occasionally at the table, and never more so than at the end of a meal. It is great with an aged Parmesan and ripe pears in the autumn, after a robust dinner that calls for a simple dessert, or in the summer with strawberries red through to their middles, as a refreshing ending to a light repast.

Serves 4

2 cups strawberries, hulled and halved
¼ cup superfine sugar
⅔ cup heavy cream

5oz mascarpone
A little well-aged balsamic vinegar
 (1–2 tablespoons)

Toss the strawberries in 1½ tablespoons of the sugar and let them steep for a minute or two. Whip the cream with the rest of the sugar until it forms soft peaks, then fold in the mascarpone. Serve this in mounds on small plates, with a haphazard cascade of strawberries. Drizzle the lot with balsamic vinegar.

STRAWBERRIES WITH LEMON AND SUGAR LAZIO

The best strawberries are grown on the walls of the crater surrounding Lake Nemi, in one of the extinct volcanoes adjacent to Rome – it is next to Lake Albano, over which Castel Gandolfo presides. The lakes were once scene to Roman boat games, but are today more sedate, home to sleepy towns and strawberry growers.

The Italians have a knack for serving strawberries – *fragoline* (wild strawberries, *fraises des bois*) and *fragole* (cultivated ones). They dress them with just a touch of lemon juice, and then just enough superfine sugar to redress the added acidity, and render the strawberries only marginally sweeter than they were naturally. Left to macerate for a few minutes, this delicate marinade brings out the perfume of the fruit – the strawberries taste more strawberry than they did before. Use about a tablespoon of lemon juice, and a rounded one of sugar, per ¼lb of fruit, which should just about be enough for one. Serve with absolutely nothing else, as you have a little bit of perfection in your bowl.

SCHIACCIATA CON L'UVA / WINE GRAPE PIE
TUSCANY

Wine grapes, with the exception of Muscat, are not very nice – at least, not nice until they become wine. Their skins are thick, bitter and tannic, they are often as sour as they are sweet, their seeds large and abundant and their flesh small in proportion. Nobody does much with them except make wine and grappa.

The Tuscans are a stubborn lot, set in their ways. I have moaned elsewhere about their saltless and soulless bread. They are also the only people who seem to do anything with wine grapes, and they happen to do something quite lovely.

Around grape harvest-time, almost every bakery will have a rectangular tray of a low, slightly sinister but delicious-looking cake, studded with purple-black grapes. It is one of those things you see and immediately decide to eat a slice of, even if you have just had breakfast, or are groaning after an epic lunch. *Schiacciata* ('crushed') is only slightly sweet, as it is made from a plain (and characteristically saltless) bread dough, the grapes providing the same balance as they might in a fine bottle of Chianti – round, ripe, tannic, earthy, fruity. Their prolific seeds give a tremendous crunch – one that will even please some of those who normally spit grape seeds out.

Serves 10

1 tablespoon dried yeast, or 2 tablespoons fresh
About 1¼ cups lukewarm water
Scant 4 cups bread flour
About 2lbs red wine grapes (Sangiovese/ Merlot/Cabernet, etc), or *concord* grapes, picked from their stems, washed and dried

½ cup superfine sugar
½ cup extra virgin olive oil, plus a little extra to grease the pan
1 teaspoon aniseeds or fennel seeds (optional)

Disperse the yeast in the water, then add the flour to make a dough, kneading it very well until it becomes smooth and highly elastic – a good 10–15 minutes. Let rise, covered, until doubled in bulk – 2 hours or so in the airing cupboard or any gentle warmth.

Divide the dough into two equal parts. Find a baking sheet, about 8 x 12in. Roll one lump of dough out until quite thin, and 4in wider and longer than the baking sheet (12 x 16in). Lay it on the tray, so the excess comes up the side. Fill the base of this lined tray with two-thirds of the grapes, and sprinkle over them one-third of each of the sugar, oil, and aniseeds (if using).

Roll the second part of the dough out, the same size as the baking sheet (8 x 12in), and lay it over the top, completely enclosing the grapes beneath. Press down slightly, so it snuggles on to the grapes, and fold the loose edges of the lower tray of dough inwards, towards the centre of the pie, to seal it. Dot the remaining grapes over the top, quite evenly. Sprinkle the top of the *schiacciata* with the remaining sugar, oil and aniseed.

Let rise for about an hour until it looks a little puffy (with the weight of the grapes, it won't rise a great deal), then bake at 400°F for 1 hour, until the crust on top is an even and deep gold. Let it cool for at least 2 hours before serving. The leftovers make for a particularly fine breakfast.

RICCIARELLI / SOFT ALMOND COOKIES
TUSCANY

Ricciarelli are voluptuous almond cookies originating in Siena, famous and much loved in Tuscany and beyond – especially around Christmas, when they are eaten with coffee or Vin Santo. They were reputedly brought to Volterra in the fourteenth century, when Ricciardetto della Gherardesca returned from the Crusades. Despite the relative economy of their ingredients, they command a high price – better to make them at home.

Makes about 25 cookies

3 large egg whites
½ cup confectioners' sugar, plus extra for dusting
2 tablespoons bitter almonds or 1 tablespoon almond extract

1¼ cups superfine sugar
1½ cups ground almonds
Grated zest of 1 orange

Beat the egg whites with the confectioners' sugar to stiff peaks. Grind the bitter almonds finely with a little of the superfine sugar to help them along – use a mortar and pestle, or small food processor. Fold all the ingredients together to make a thick paste.

Now shape the *ricciarelli*. Put some extra confectioners' sugar out on a plate, and drop heaping tablespoons of the almond mixture on to this. With sugared hands, form each dollop into a lozenge shape and press down slightly in the middle. Arrange these on a baking sheet, leaving a little space between them, and sift over a generous layer of confectioners' sugar – thick enough that they look completely white.

Bake at 325°F for 15–20 minutes, until the surface cracks.

BRUTTI MA BUONI (UGLY BUT GOOD)
TUSCANY

Everyone knows a good name when they hear one, and 'ugly but good' tops the list. All over Italy they sell these, adapting the name to the local dialect – *brut ma bun* in Tuscany, *brut e bun* (ugly and good) in Lombardy, *brutti ma buoni* and *brutti e buoni* elsewhere. Confusingly, in Tuscany they are also known as *ossi di morti* – 'bones of the dead' – which is the equally brilliant name of a very different cookie in Basilicata, shaped actually like bones.

Essentially a nut meringue, those in the know say *brutti ma buoni* originated in Prato, in Tuscany, as a way of using up egg whites left over when they made rich egg yolk and nut *mantovana* (Mantuan cake, another result of the Gonzaga–Este union, page 351). *Mantovana* is fickle to make. But here's the famously ugly by-product, which is equally good.

Makes about 30 cookies

6 large egg whites
1½ cups superfine sugar
3 cups confectioners' sugar
2⅔ cups skin-off hazelnuts (or almonds, or both), chopped

1 tablespoon coriander seeds, crushed but not quite to a powder (optional)
A little unsweetened cocoa powder, to serve

Whip the egg whites to soft peaks, then gradually add the sugars to obtain a luscious and dense meringue. Set a shallow pan of water over a flame and, as it boils, put the mixing bowl over this, without it touching the water, to slightly warm the meringue, turning with a metal spoon until it is a little less dense, and becomes glossy. Fold in the chopped nuts and coriander seeds.

Prepare a baking sheet, either with butter and flour, or a lining of parchment paper. Use a tablespoon to dollop spoonfuls of the mixture on to the sheet, leaving about 3/4in gaps between them. Don't worry if they are somewhat irregular – that's the point. Bake at 300°F for an hour, until amber and crunchy, dust them with cocoa powder while still hot, and let cool before serving. They are also quite delicious coated in bittersweet chocolate.

BACI DI CAFFÈ
LAZIO

There is a café, Sant'Eustachio, near the Pantheon in Rome. Or perhaps I should say *the* café, because it serves the best coffee in the world. The *baristas* have a green hue to their skin from all that caffeine, and the *crema* (brown froth) on the espresso they make is thick enough to stand a spoon up in. They sell little cookies, *baci di caffè*, with a rich and layered taste of coffee, chocolate and hazelnuts. Like French *macarons*, they are crunchy on the outside and have gooey middles, only less so and more so respectively. I don't know how they make them (any more than I know the secret to their coffee), but here's a guess.

Makes about 30 tiny cookies

3 large egg whites
Generous 1 cup superfine sugar
½ cup plus 2 tablespoons blanched (skin-off) shelled hazelnuts
Scant 3 tablespoons finely ground coffee
Scant ½ cup good unsweetened cocoa powder

Whisk the egg whites to stiff peaks with a tablespoon of the sugar. Put all the remaining ingredients in a food processor and grind finely, to a powder. Fold this ground nut mixture into the meringue you just made.

Transfer the mixture to a piping bag with a wide tip. The *baci* can be piped either on to a baking sheet lined with parchment paper, into little (1in) hemispheres, or into flexible silicone petits-fours moulds, should you have any.

Bake at 350°F for just 8 minutes, or until a thin and unconvincing crust has formed on the outside. Let cool before removing from the baking sheet, and serve lightly dusted with confectioners' sugar and little cups of strong coffee.

BURNED RICOTTA PIE
LAZIO

There is a tiny Jewish bakery in the Ghetto in Rome, on the corner of Via del Portico and Via della Reginella. It is called Antico Forno del Ghetto, but that's no help as there's no name outside. They burn everything – croissants come out completely black, as do the ricotta cakes (either chocolate or cherry flavoured) for which they are famous. This signature char is delicious – only skin-deep, but it adds that slight bitter edge that makes Roman pizza so exquisite, and grounds this rich but refreshing ricotta cake in the earth.

Serves 8–12

1 quantity sweet pastry (page 355)
Generous 2lbs fresh ricotta, sheep's milk if possible
1 small egg, or ½ large one
⅓ cup superfine sugar

⅔ cup sour cherry jam, or 3½oz bittersweet chocolate, finely chopped (not both)
1 large egg yolk
Generous ¼ cup confectioners' sugar

Divide the pastry into two unequal balls, one of them one-and-a-half times the weight of the other. Roll the smaller into a 7in disc, and the larger one 9¾in. The dough is fragile, and it is easiest to roll it between two sheets of parchment paper, flouring the sheet below and the top of the dough to prevent sticking. Peel off the top sheet of paper, and leave the rolled pastry on the lower one. Put the smaller disc of pastry, still on its sheet of parchment paper, on to a baking sheet. If using jam, spread it on this disc, leaving about a ¾in border.

Mix together the ricotta, egg and superfine sugar with a wooden spoon, as well as the chocolate, if using. Pile this filling in a tall, domed heap in the centre of the smaller round of pastry, leaving about a ¾in border. Carefully pick up the larger circle of pastry (to prevent it breaking, it is best to wrap it, with its under-paper, around a rolling pin) and lay it over the filling. Peel off the top sheet of paper, and crimp the edges all the way around.

Mix together the egg yolk and confectioners' sugar, add a drop of water if needed to make a thick glaze, and paint it over the top of the pie to help it burn. Bake the pie in an oven preheated to its very maximum – best with the fan off for that perfect *brûlée*. The pie will spread a little, crack in a couple of places, and ebonise. As soon as the whole surface of the pie is blackened, or very dark chocolate brown, turn the oven down to 300°F and continue to bake, until the cake has cooked for a total of 45 minutes. Turn off the oven, and leave the cake inside for 20 minutes to rest. Take it out, let cool and serve at room temperature. As with many Italian desserts, it is just as good for breakfast as for dessert.

BOMBE CALDE / FILLED DOUGHNUTS
LAZIO

Particularly in the summer months, when the evening *passeggiata* becomes more extended and alcoholic, bars and *gelaterie* hang out signs proclaiming '*bombe calde*' – 'we have fresh, still-warm filled doughnuts!'

With either chocolate or pastry cream within, *bombe calde* are large, plump and giving, well-equipped to absorb that last cocktail or grappa – this nocturnal feast goes on until the early hours when the crowds retire. Although these beauties are always delicious, mine are, I like to think, even better: I use my grandmother Agnes' recipe for doughnuts, which is by far the best I have ever encountered. And then I fill them with far more of a far more chocolatey cream than is sensible.

Makes 12–14 large doughnuts

Dough
1 tablespoon dried yeast, or
 2 tablespoons fresh
Scant 1¼ cups lukewarm whole milk
Scant 5½ cups all-purpose flour
¼ cup superfine sugar
A tiny pinch of salt
8 large egg yolks
3 tablespoons dark rum
Finely grated zest of 1 lemon
7 tablespoons unsalted butter, melted

Filling
¾ cup heavy cream
4 large egg yolks
½ cup unsweetened cocoa powder
Generous ¾ cup superfine sugar
Generous 2 tablespoons cornstarch
2¼ cups whole milk
¾in piece cinnamon stick
4oz bittersweet chocolate, broken
 into pieces

To cook and serve
Vegetable oil
Confectioners' sugar

Start to make the dough, allowing 3 hours before you wish to fry and serve. First make a yeast sponge, mixing the yeast, half the milk and a tablespoon each of the flour and sugar. Let rise until frothy.

Mix the remaining flour and sugar with the salt in a large bowl, make a well in the middle and in it put the yeast sponge and all the other ingredients except the butter. Work the flour in gradually from the sides to make a sticky dough, which should be very well kneaded. When glossy and elastic, add the butter, gradually, and work until fully incorporated. Let the dough rise, covered, until doubled in bulk, a bit over an hour.

Roll the dough out about 5/8in thick on a floured surface, and cut about 4in rounds with a pastry cutter. Dust these very lightly with flour, cover with a light cloth, and let rise until doubled in bulk – again, about an hour.

While the doughnuts are rising, make the filling. Whisk together the cream, egg yolks, cocoa, sugar and cornstarch to make a thick paste. Bring the milk to the boil with the cinnamon stick for flavour, and whisk it gradually into the cocoa paste. Return the lot to the pan and, over the lowest flame, bring it to a gentle boil, stirring constantly with a wooden spoon or whisk. The mixture will thicken suddenly. As soon as it has boiled, take it off the heat, remove the cinnamon stick and stir in the chocolate until it has melted. Transfer it to a squeeze bottle with a pointed tip and keep warm until ready to serve – I stand the bottle in a pan of hot water over the lowest heat.

To cook the doughnuts, fry them in at least 1½in of clean oil at 300–320°F, turning them once when the first side is golden. They will take about 4 minutes on each side at this temperature, necessary to give them time to cook through. Drain them on paper towels and fill with a generous slug of chocolate filling from the squeeze bottle. Dust the *bombe* with confectioners' sugar and serve them warm – there is no point to a cold doughnut.

Variation: Dipping Doughnuts Make exactly the same dough, but cut it into scant 2½in rounds. Let them rise, then fry as above. Instead of filling them, serve with a dip of jam (store-bought, or home-made, page 357), warmed and thinned with a good hit of rum.

BABÀ
CAMPANIA

The French have left Naples a splendid culinary legacy, of which the best bit to my mind is the *babà*. The Neapolitans make it a great deal better than the French ever did. It is a lighter, springier affair, like a natural bath sponge made of the finest yeast dough.

My recipe took a great deal of time to perfect, and I should warn you that it is more exacting than any other in this book. The tall buns, which are initially difficult to make, become easier with practice. The ingredients for the dough are cheap, so if they don't turn out right the first time, pretend it never happened, throw them out and start again before wasting all that rum. When you've got it right once, I can almost guarantee you'll never fail again.

The flavour of the rum is, of course, an important component of this dish. Don't waste the very finest, but use the best everyday rum you can find. I don't like to promote particular brands, but my favourite is rather gay...

The recipe just makes 16 individual *babà*, for which you will need sixteen 2¾ x 2¾in *babà* moulds (tall, straight-sided aluminium or non-stick ramekins). Or it makes two large ones, for which you will need two ornate *bundt* (*kugelhopf*) pans, the more ornate, the better.

Serves 16

Dough, step 1
Scant 2 cups bread flour
6 large egg whites

Dough, step 2
1½ tablespoons dried yeast,
  or 2½ tablespoons fresh
About 3 tablespoons bread flour
2 tablespoons water

Dough, step 3
6 large egg yolks
Generous 1 cup bread flour
¼ cup superfine sugar
Generous 1 teaspoon salt

Dough, step 4
5 tablespoons unsalted butter, cubed,
  at room temperature (softish)

To coat the pans
Unsalted butter
All-purpose flour

Syrup
1 quart water
Generous 2 cups superfine sugar
Strips of zest from 1 lemon, made with
  a potato peeler, and the juice
1½ cups rum

To serve
1 quart heavy cream, whipped with
  1 cup confectioners' sugar
1 large or 2 small pineapples,
  peeled, cored and cut up, or 2½lbs
  strawberries, hulled and halved,
  or 1¾lbs wild strawberries

To make the dough well, be precise with your measurements. It is best to measure out scant 3¼ cups bread flour precisely first, and then divide it between steps 1, 2 and 3, as your result will be more accurate.

Before you start, it is vital that you understand the reasoning behind a seemingly convoluted process. The gluten in the flour needs to be worked to the utmost to make the dough light, spongy and elastic even when soaked in the syrup. Fat (from egg yolks or butter) interferes with this, so we work the maximum amount of flour with just egg white that we can, whilst being sure that it is fully hydrated (like a batter – too much flour and we'd make a hard lump). We then let it rest for half an hour, to ensure full hydration of the starch, then gradually work in the yeast and the fatty ingredients. The syrup is diluted with water to keep the taste and texture light – this is also made with care to keep the fresh taste of the lemon, and not to lose the alcohol from the rum.

This recipe is best made in a stand mixer, using both a dough hook and paddle. A paddle kneads the dough better, but at points where it stiffens, the dough may 'ball up', and cease to be worked well. If this happens, switch to the dough hook until, with addition of liquid or fat, the dough softens enough to use the paddle again. Work always on the lowest speed.

Time to bite the bullet and begin. Combine the flour and egg whites from step 1, and mix well for 15 minutes (literally). Let rest for 30 minutes, still in the mixer bowl.

Meanwhile, make the sponge. Combine the yeast, flour and water of step 2 to make a thick paste, and leave to rise in a warm place for 30 minutes, until it at least doubles in bulk.

Turn the mixer on again. Start to add the egg yolks from step 3, one by one, mixing with the paddle for a full minute before adding the next egg yolk. With each yolk add a bit of the remaining flour (about 2 tablespoons each time). With the first yolk, add the yeast sponge made in step 2. With the second, add the sugar, and with the third the salt. When all the egg yolks are in, allow the mixer to work the dough for another 15 minutes. Only now do you add the butter of step 4, and work for a final 2–3 minutes until incorporated and shiny. The resulting dough should be incredibly wet, gorgeous and glossy. The strings it forms when you lift the paddle will be almost mucus-like – all the gluten has been worked into a proteinous mass.

Allow the dough to rise, covered with plastic wrap well above the surface, at room temperature until doubled in bulk. Do not allow it to over-proof or the texture will be ruined. As it rises, prepare the moulds.

Butter the moulds and dust them with flour. It is vital that every nook and cranny be coated, especially with the butter, and that all excess flour is tapped out. Divide the dough between the moulds. If using two large ones, just divide the dough in two and manoeuvre it into evenish rings – this is a bit like handling a live, slippery snake. If using small ones, weigh out (fairly precisely) generous 1½oz portions of dough. A teaspoon under and they won't rise high enough; a teaspoon over and they will spill over the edge in the oven like lava, rather than ballooning up. Form the dough into a smooth ball, for the perfect texture and pattern of bubbles in the sponge it will become. As it is too sloppy to put down, hold it suspended between thumb and two fingers of one hand. Use one finger of your other hand in a stroking motion, upwards from the base, working around the ball until it is nicely rounded, and falls from your fingers into the buttered and floured mould below. Easier done than said – look at the pictures if my words sound Greek.

Let rise until risen a good 3/4in above the top of the moulds. This will take about an hour (to almost quadruple in bulk).

During this time, make the syrup. Put the water and sugar in a saucepan over a high heat. The moment it boils, take it off the heat and add the lemon zest. Let cool to around 160°F (no longer steaming much) and add the rum and lemon juice. Immediately cover tightly with plastic wrap – the alcohol will evaporate from the heat, and you want to catch the vapours so they condense back into the syrup. Let cool, but not completely – it should still be warm when you come to soak the *babà*.

Bake the *babà* at 350°F for 20 minutes, until browned on top and against the sides of the mould if you peek in (with the help of the tip of a knife). They should balloon up in a manner at once immensely satisfying and slightly ridiculous. Let cool in their moulds until you can hold the metal without it hurting – try to unmould them straight from the oven and they will likely break. Still warm, submerge one *babà* at a time in the syrup. Press down gently but firmly with the flat of your hand to expel all the air, then let it expand again and soak up the syrup. Repeat once more to be sure it's fully drenched, as any dry pockets of dough will be unpalatable. Remove the *babà*, stand it on its head in a tray to drain, and start on the next. If you run out of syrup, just add that which has run from the preceding *babà*.

Serve cool, or chilled (they will keep for up to a week in the fridge, but are best fresh). Small *babà* should be split in half down the middle like a hot dog roll, filled with whipped cream and topped with fruit. Large *babà*, in a decorative ring shape, are best served plain, to be cut at the table on which are ready bowls of cream and fruit.

They are well worth the effort.

PASTIERA NAPOLETANA / NEAPOLITAN EASTER CAKE CAMPANIA

An unusual recipe, this, a cake of ricotta and grain, aromatic with candied oranges, and the essence of their flowers. Heavenly, and making it is the surest way I know to befriend a Neapolitan. *Pastiera* can be made like a deep cake, or shallow tart. Neapolitans tell me my rich filling is too much for a deep cake, though even they admit it does make a good tart.

Serves 14–16

Pastry
Scant 5 cups all-purpose flour
2 cups confectioners' sugar
2³⁄4 sticks unsalted butter
Finely grated zest of 1 lemon
6 large egg yolks
1 teaspoon vanilla extract

Filling
9oz *grano cotto* (cooked wheat sold in jars – otherwise 4oz wheat berries, *farro*, or small barley, boiled until tender, will do)
3/4 cup whole milk

2 tablespoons unsalted butter
3/4lb fresh ricotta cheese
Finely grated zest of 1 lemon
1 teaspoon orange-blossom water (optional)
2 large egg yolks
1 teaspoon vanilla extract
13/4 cups superfine sugar
1 teaspoon ground cinnamon
1oz candied orange peel, finely diced to the same size as the wheat
3/4oz candied lemon peel, diced the same way (or 3/4oz more orange peel)
1 large egg white, whisked to moist peaks

To make the pastry, combine the flour and sugar, then work in the butter until almost evenly incorporated – a few golden flecks won't hurt a bit. Add the lemon zest, egg yolks and vanilla and bring the pastry together; wrap in plastic wrap and let it rest in the fridge until firm – a flattened patty will chill fastest.

Meanwhile, make the filling. Combine the cooked grain, milk and butter, and simmer over a medium heat until creamy and viscous, stirring as though for a risotto. Let it cool to room temperature, then add all the other ingredients (apart from the egg white) and stir vigorously with a wooden spoon until well mixed and sloppy. Fold in the beaten egg white, and the filling is ready.

If you haven't already decided whether to make a cake or two tarts, do so now. To make a homely cake, line the bottom and sides of a 9 or 10in springform cake pan with parchment paper. Roll the pastry about ¼in thick, line the pan well, and trim the pastry level with the top – keep the trimmings for later. To make fancier tarts – and this quantity will suffice for two of them – roll the pastry out thinner, $1/8$in. Line a pair of 11in fluted tart pans, trimming the pastry nice and level to the rim. Prick the bases all over with a fork.

In either case, pour the filling into the lined pan(s), and roll the leftover dough out thinly, about $3/32$in. Cut it into about $1/2$in-wide strips, and use these to decorate the top of the *pastiera* with a lattice. Bake for about an hour (just more for a cake, just less for tarts) at 350°F, until the top is browned, and doesn't wobble when shaken gently. Let cool completely before cutting – *pastiera* is best in the evening if made that morning, but will keep a few days if you can resist finishing it.

TORTA CAPRESE 'BILIVELLO' / MY LEMON AND CHOCOLATE NUT TORTE CAMPANIA

Order a *Caprese* in an Italian restaurant and you will get one of two things – a tomato and mozzarella salad, or a nut torte. On Capri, they make two versions of this delightful cake. One is golden yellow, flavoured with lemon, the other black with chocolate. Important decisions I can make easily (open a restaurant? buy a house? fall in love?), but the most trivial I find perplexing. Faced with a choice between lemon and chocolate, I crumble.

One day, trying to have the best of both worlds, I made a *torta Caprese* in two layers, dark and light. The lemon and chocolate cakes, united by the almond they have in common, eat beautifully together. Making two in one is double the effort, and you may be as happy if you double the quantities of one mix below, and omit the other.

Serves 10

Lemon mix
3/4 cup blanched almonds
2 tablespoons cornstarch
Generous 1/2 cup superfine sugar
2 large eggs
1 large egg yolk
7 tablespoons unsalted butter, softened
Finely grated zest and juice of 1 lemon
1/4 cup limoncello (lemon liqueur)
1 teaspoon baking powder

Chocolate mix
3/4 cup blanched almonds
1/4 lb bittersweet chocolate, chilled
1/4 cup unsweetened cocoa powder
2 large eggs
Generous 1/3 cup superfine sugar
1/2 teaspoon vanilla extract
Finely grated zest of 1 small lemon
7 tablespoons unsalted butter, melted

To serve
Confectioners' sugar

Have ready a 9in round cake pan, bottom lined with greased parchment paper. A low one with sloping sides (in other words a *tarte tatin* pan) is ideal, giving the classic shape, but taste and texture make the cake, not its form.

Make the lemon mixture first. Grind the almonds finely with the cornstarch and scant 2 tablespoons of the sugar in a food processor, leaving just a little texture – they should almost be as fine as store-bought ground almonds. Whisk the whole eggs and egg yolk with the remaining sugar until pale, thick and fluffy, then combine with the ground almond mixture and all the other ingredients. Fold together until just incorporated, then pour into the baking pan. Level it approximately with the back of a spoon, and par-bake at 350°F for barely 15 minutes until half set.

Meanwhile, and quickly, make the chocolate mixture: it needs to be ready before the almond cake comes out of the oven. Combine the almonds, chocolate (broken into pieces) and cocoa powder in a food processor and grind as finely as you can without the chocolate heating up and clumping the lot together. Separate the eggs, and whisk the yolks with the sugar, vanilla and lemon zest until very thick and pale. Add the chocolate and almond mixture. Start to stir – the mixture will be so thick it won't come together, so add the melted butter to help it along. Whisk the egg whites to soft peaks and fold them in gently, transforming the mess into a cake batter.

Draw the half-cooked lemon cake from the oven: it should be just set enough that the chocolate can now go on top without disturbing it. Spoon the chocolate mixture over the top, and smooth it gently as best you can. Return the pan to the oven for another 30 minutes, until only just set. Remove it from the oven and let cool partially, about 15 minutes, before unmoulding on to a plate. Let cool to room temperature before dusting with confectioners' sugar and serving. The slightly impatient will be rewarded with an only slightly warm and particularly moist cake; the overly impatient will have a hot mess.

SANGUINACCIO
CALABRIA

At slaughter, nothing is wasted from a pig. Meat is salted and cured, just a little eaten fresh. Intestines and bladders are used for *salumi*, the offal quickly cooked. The precious blood, rich in iron and vitamins, is used too: it is wet, so hard to preserve, and almost every region will have its recipe for *sanguinaccio*, blood pudding. In some, combined with grain, meat, fat and onions, this blood pudding is close to the version we all know – a savoury sausage. In this one, the word 'pudding' is more literal.

This recipe is for a rich, intense chocolatey *sanguinaccio*. The Marsala adds to the depth of flavour, while the blood is almost imperceptible at first. As the moments progress, a distinctly ferrous and piggy taste pervades the mouth. If the idea of blood and chocolate sounds weird and wonderful, you are likely to find this pudding exactly as you expect it. That it tends to meet expectations is true also for those who find the idea weird and repugnant. If you are of the latter persuasion, do not be tempted to try it.

Serves 10

1 cup superfine sugar
½ cup unsweetened cocoa powder
2½ tablespoons cornstarch
1 cup sweet Marsala
½ cup milk
½ cup heavy cream
2 cups pig's blood, strained (ask your butcher nicely, or try a Chinese supermarket)

½ lb bittersweet chocolate, chopped
1 teaspoon vanilla extract
1in piece cinnamon stick

To serve
3oz finely diced candied orange peel
½ cup raw pine nuts (preferably long ones)
Sourdough bread or *savoiardi* cookies

Combine the sugar, cocoa powder, and cornstarch in a large metal bowl. Add half the Marsala, beat to get rid of any lumps, then add the rest of the ingredients. Place over a pan of simmering water (which should never come to a full boil) and cook over a very low heat for about 2 hours. It is vital to stir almost continually with a whisk (every 5 minutes or so), or the blood will clot. If it does, despite your best efforts, strain the whole mixture to remove the lumps, return the cinnamon and then return to the bowl and the heat. It is ready when thickened and steaming hot – very gloopy, but not grainy in the least.

Remove the cinnamon, ladle into 10 serving glasses and chill until set. Sprinkle with the peel and pine nuts, and serve with the bread or cookies.

CARTELLATE / FRIED COOKIES SOAKED IN GRAPE SYRUP PUGLIA

My team of Italians all miss their mammas so much, that when they tell me of their mother's recipe for this, or how she makes that, their eyes glaze over with nostalgia. Giovanni Locapo, who works behind the bar, pulled just such an act when he told me about the *cartellate* he used to eat at home. They are fried pinwheels of pastry, like Indian *jalebi*, doused in honey or *vincotto* (dark grape must syrup) – sticky and sweet, a relic of the Moors. They are particularly associated with Christmas, an edible reminder of the eastern origins of our own traditions. Anyway, Giovanni used to be a baker, so I trusted his opinion and asked him if his mother, Paola Riso, might send her recipe over. She did, and here it is.

Makes about 30 *cartellate*

Scant 5 cups flour (all-purpose, or Italian 00)
1 small egg, or ½ a big one
Generous ¼ cup superfine sugar
Generous ½ cup white wine or mandarin juice (mandarin juice used to be a sign of wealth)
¼ cup extra virgin olive oil (but unsalted butter will do)

A pinch of ground cinnamon (optional, as used by Giovanni's grandmother Grazia)
Vegetable oil, for deep-frying
1¼ cups *vincotto* (probably grape *vincotto*, possibly fig, or ½ cup honey plus ½ cup sugar and ½ cup water)
1 tablespoon granulated sugar mixed with 1 teaspoon ground cinnamon (optional)

Knead together 'energetically' the flour, egg, sugar, wine or mandarin juice, olive oil and cinnamon, along with a little pinch of salt, until you have a soft but dryish dough – add a little more flour or liquid as needed. Let rest for 30 minutes or more in the fridge, then roll out to make a thin sheet (1⁄16in thick). Paola uses a rolling pin dusted with flour, but I find a pasta machine easier. You now have two options.

Either you can cheat slightly: Cut the dough into long rectangular strips, 1in wide by 4–6in long, using a crinkly pastry cutter. Cut a 2in slit down the middle of each strip, and pass one of the ends through this hole, to make a complex, twisted and vaguely rhomboid shape.

Or you can try it the hard way: Use a crinkly pastry cutter to make long strips, 1in wide by 12–16in long. Fold loosely in half, lengthways, and pinch together at 1½in intervals, to make a chain of connected, open pockets. Coil this around and around, very loosely, such that the pockets' openings all face upwards, the folded side down on the table. Pinch together where they touch each other, to stick them together in a pinwheel, or rose-like shape. In either case, leave the shaped dough out to dry while you make the rest (they are best fried after 45 minutes, when they have gone a little leathery). With the oil moderately hot (320–350°F), deep-fry the *cartellate* until the palest gold. Drain on paper towels. Heat the *vincotto* (or honey/sugar/water mixture) until it boils and then drop in the *cartellate* a few at a time, lifting them quickly out with a slotted spoon, and leaving them to drain, but with the cups and crevices upwards, to trap the *vincotto*.

Let them air for another 20 minutes, so the syrup can soak in. Dust the *cartellate* with the cinnamon sugar, if you like, before serving piled on a plate.

CALZONCELLI / CHESTNUT AND ANISE FRITTERS
BASILICATA

These little fried parcels of dough, like crescent-shaped *ravioli,* are filled with a heady mixture of chestnut, chocolate, cinnamon and aniseed liqueur. The richness of a fried dough and density of the filling is offset only by their small size – a few go a long way. As they can be made ahead and fried en masse, they are perfect to serve to a large party, or after dessert at a long dinner and full table, when the spirits come out.

Makes about 40 – allow 2–3 per person

1 quantity *cenci* dough (page 354)
1 large egg, beaten
Lard or vegetable oil, for frying
Confectioners' sugar, for dusting

Filling
7oz cooked peeled chestnuts
  (vac-packed ones are easiest)
½ cup unsweetened cocoa powder
⅓ cup superfine sugar
1 teaspoon ground cinnamon
About ½ cup Anisetta or other anise
  liqueur (Sambuca, for example)

While the dough rests, make the filling. Combine all the ingredients in a food processor and work to a stiff paste.

Roll the dough out quite thinly, about ¹⁄₃₂in, and use a pastry cutter to make 2¾in discs (if you have a fluted one, the frilly edges will be nice). Put a tablespoon of filling in the centre of each, brush with a little beaten egg and press to seal closed in a half-moon. These can be made in advance and refrigerated or frozen; at any rate, it is best to let them rest, covered with a cloth, for at least half an hour before cooking.

Deep-fry at 320°F in lard or oil (lard is better if you are that way inclined) for 4 minutes, turning once or twice. Drain on paper towels, and serve dusted with confectioners' sugar.

GELO DI MELONE / WATERMELON AND JASMINE PUDDING SICILY

Another weird and wonderful dessert. I wonder if *gelo di melone* isn't a play on words: *'gel'* being indicative of something set, but also referring to *'gelsomino'*, the jasmine which perfumes the pudding. This exotic aroma reveals Sicily's Arab heritage – without any doubt, this is her answer to Turkish delight.

It should be noted that if you haven't an abundant supply of jasmine flowers, or can't face the thought of eating jasmine essence, you can make this pudding without. A plain watermelon flavour is just as delicious, and less challenging to fussy palates.

Serves 4–5

6½lbs ripe, ripe watermelon
   (choose one that feels heavy)
½ cup superfine sugar
100 jasmine flowers from the garden,
   2 teaspoons jasmine water, or 8 drops
   essential oil of jasmine (optional)

Generous ⅔ cup cornstarch
½ oz bittersweet chocolate, chopped
¼ cup raw shelled pistachios, peeled if
   possible, chopped

Cut the flesh from the watermelon, and discard the peel. Purée the fruit in a food processor, and pass through a coarse sieve, pressing well to extract all the juice. Measure out 1 quart, and drink the rest (this is the best part). Mix the sugar into 3½ cups of the juice in a large saucepan and set it over a medium flame.

If using fresh flowers, add them to the pan from cold, bring it to a steaming heat, and infuse at this temperature for 5 minutes before straining the flowers out and returning the juice to the pan. If not, proceed without. In either case, now bring the juice to a boil, meanwhile mixing the cornstarch with the remaining, cold ½ cup of watermelon elixir. As soon as the pan boils, whisk in the cornflour mixture. When it boils again, take it from the heat and mix in, if using, the jasmine water or oil of jasmine.

Ladle the concoction into glasses or a jelly mould and refrigerate until set. Serve sprinkled with the chocolate and pistachios.

PISTACHIO 'GNOCCHI'
SICILY

These little cookies, in the shape of dumplings, are Sicily's answer to *ricciarelli* (page 362), more decadent with expensive pistachios, and a glorious green. It is best to use peeled pistachios, for the most verdant colour and smoothest texture, but these are hard to find. (Iranian food shops often have them – Iranians are as proud of their pistachios as the Sicilians are of theirs.)

Makes about 70 little cookies

2²/₃ cups peeled pistachio kernels
1¹/₂ cups blanched almonds
2¹/₂ cups superfine sugar
2 large egg whites

2 tablespoons runny honey
Zest and juice of ¹/₂ lemon
Confectioners' sugar, as required

Put the pistachios, almonds and around three-quarters of the superfine sugar into a food processor and grind very finely indeed. Whisk the egg whites with the remaining sugar until firm peaks are formed, then add the honey, lemon zest and juice. Fold in the nuts and work by hand to make a firmish dough.

Dust a work surface with the confectioners' sugar, turn out the dough and, with plenty of the sugar on your hands as well, roll it into a long sausage ³/₄in wide. Cut it into little dumplings, about ³/₄in long, and pinch each of these across to make a couple of deep dimples. Put the cookies on a baking sheet, either greased with butter or lined with parchment paper, making sure they don't touch each other, and bake for 8–10 minutes at 350°F, until a crust has formed on the outside, which may take on a little colour. Cool before serving.

CHOCOLATE AND MARZIPAN BALLS
SICILY

I first had these brilliant balls at Maria Grammatico in Erice, where they are lovingly made by ladies not short on experience. Occasionally, when my mum wants to do something particularly nice for me, she phones this venerable *pasticceria* to plead for a box of these delights to be sent to her starving son.

Spheres of aromatic marzipan are filled with boozy raisins in a sugary, alcoholic syrup that is crunchy with sugar grains, and the lot covered in chocolate. I don't have their recipe, but have elaborated my own, which is almost as good...

Makes about 16 balls

Marzipan
2lbs good store-bought marzipan
or
2½ cups blanched almonds
⅓oz bitter almonds, or 1½ teaspoons
  of their extract
1½ cups superfine sugar
2 tablespoons light corn syrup or runny
  honey

Balls
1 cup raisins, soaked overnight in
  scant ½ cup rum
½ cup granulated sugar
7oz bittersweet chocolate, broken
  into pieces

First make the marzipan (unless you've bought it). This is an uncooked one, with less sugar and more taste than a commercial product. Put the almonds, bitter almonds (if using) and superfine sugar in a food processor and grind for ages, until the almonds are fine as sand, the mixture starting to stick together, and the motor getting rather warm. Add the corn syrup along with ⅓ cup water (and the almond extract, if it's what you're using), and continue to work to a smooth, hot paste – stop only when you fear the motor will burst into flames. Turn out into a container, cover tightly, and let cool.

The raisins should have soaked up most of the rum, and be sitting in just a couple of tablespoons of thick, sweet liquor. If it looks like there's much more left than this, pour the excess into a glass, and drink it when no-one's looking. Mix the sugar into the rum and raisins, to bind them into a sloppy filling.

Divide the marzipan into 16 portions, and roll them into balls. Use your thumb to make an indentation, and form the marzipan into a cup, like making clay pinch-pots in those early school years. Fill the hole with a little of the raisin mixture, and carefully close the marzipan around it, pinching to seal. It is absolutely vital the filling is completely enclosed, as it will become more liquid in time as the sugar starts to dissolve, and tends to seep out of any holes, exposing sloppy workmanship. Gently roll between your palms to make the sphere again spherical, and leave in the fridge while you make the rest.

Melt the chocolate (microwave or double boiler): if you know how to temper it, do so, otherwise don't bother. If the balls are well chilled when you dip them, untempered (normal, melted) chocolate will be fine. Dip the balls in the chocolate one by one, rolling them around until covered, then swiftly lifting out with a fork. Wave the fork up and down a couple of times to help the chocolate drain off, as you want the thinnest coating possible (do this over the bowl of chocolate to catch drips, and the ball, should it fall). Put the ball on a tray lined with parchment paper to set. They can be eaten as soon as the chocolate is hard, or kept in the fridge for a couple of weeks.

CANNOLI
SICILY

Canna, cane, grows in the marshes throughout Italy, and gives words for *cannella* (cinnamon, 'little canes'), *cannellini* (white beans, 'tiny little canes'), *cannelloni* (stuffed rolled pasta, 'big little canes'), and *cannoli* (fried cookie tubes filled with ricotta, 'big canes'), this last the most famous dessert from Sicily, itself *the* place for desserts. With its close links to North Africa, and the pride and enthusiasm with which its people approach sweets, there can be a tendency to use a lot of sugar, often too much for me. For my palate judicious use is key – enough to not be savoury, not so much as to mask the other flavours.

I make my *cannoli* small (one might call them *cannolini,* but no-one does), and serve them empty, dusted with a little confectioners' sugar for sweetness, with a big bowl of the classic sweetened ricotta filling and as many teaspoons as there are of us, for each to fill our own as we eat. *Cannoli* filled just before they are eaten are necessarily fresher, crisper, better. It is a trick I picked up at Al Merluzzo Felice in Milan, where I seem to learn something worthwhile and new with each visit.

For the filling I use a mixture of cow's and sheep's milk ricotta. This is largely because I like much less sugar than Sicilians do – their heavy hand with it helps to mask the farmyard taste of pure sheep's ricotta. This is, however, a matter of personal taste so let your instinct, and your local deli's stock, dictate your exact recipe.

This recipe makes up to 40 small *cannoli,* enough for ten. Allowing for accidents and other wastage, it is a good idea to make more dough than you need, so the accompanying quantity of filling here is for 6–8 people. Make more if you want to.

Serves 6–8

Cannoli
Scant 2 cups all-purpose flour
3 tablespoons unsalted butter, softened
2 tablespoons superfine sugar
Scant ⅓ cup sweet Marsala (or sweet sherry, if you don't tell anyone – but if you use Marsala, serve the rest of the bottle with dessert)
Vegetable oil, for frying
1 egg, beaten, to glue the *cannoli* tubes

Filling
18oz fresh cow's milk ricotta (or sheep's or mixed milk, if you prefer)
5oz sheep's milk ricotta (or fresh cow's or mixed milk, if you prefer)
¾ cup superfine sugar
2oz bittersweet chocolate, very finely chopped

To serve
1¾oz candied orange peel, finely diced
¼ cup peeled pistachios, chopped
Confectioners' sugar

To make the *cannoli*, be sure you have a mould to fry them around. Without investing in *cannoli* moulds, which in any event are for tubes wider than I like to make them, the best thing is to go to a plumbing shop and have some scant 7/8in copper pipe cut into sections that will fit the width of your pan. *Cannoli* can also be made successfully by wrapping the dough around dried, uncooked *cannelloni* pasta bought from a shop.

First make the dough, by combining the flour, butter, sugar and Marsala, and kneading to make a smooth dough. Let rest for 30 minutes.

While the dough rests, make the filling. Purée all the ricotta with the sugar until very smooth in a food processor. Stir in the chocolate, and refrigerate until ready to serve (at least half an hour is best).

Roll the dough out 1/32in thick. Many Italians, and enlightened foreigners, use a pasta-rolling machine for this. Cut this rolled sheet into about 3in discs (the trimmings can be re-rolled and re-used). Let these discs rest for at least half an hour, covered, if you want the lightest possible *cannoli* – but they can be fried straightaway if you're in a hurry.

Heat to 300°F just enough of a depth of oil to deep-fry them in (1½in or more). Oil your *cannoli* moulds well on the outside before you start and between frying one batch of cannoli and the next. Wrap a disc of dough around the mould, using a little beaten egg to join the ends and make a tube, then fry it until golden brown, blistered and crispy all the way through. Lift the mould from the oil and, using a cloth to protect your hands, slip the *cannolo* off before forming and frying the next. Drain on paper towels, and let cool before serving. Although best on the day they were fried, they can be kept longer in a well-sealed container.

Serve the filling piled in a nice bowl, scattered with the candied orange, and pistachios. On a separate dish, pile up the *cannoli*, dusting each layer with quite abundant confectioners' sugar. One teaspoon per guest is all you need to serve; plates might be helpful too.

Variation: Frozen Cannoli These are delicious, fancy treats. The dough, being fried, stays crisp for a few days in the freezer even if you fill them in advance. Use a piping bag to fill *cannoli* with *gelato* – particularly ricotta *stracciatella* (page 423), chocolate sorbet (page 416) or pistachio *gelato* (page 418).

CASSATA / LAYERED RICOTTA CAKE
SICILY

If *cannoli* are the most famous Sicilian dessert, and I am sure they are, *cassata* is the crowning glory of the island. It is an elaborate cake, low, with tapered sides (the shape of a *tarte tatin* pan). From outside in, there is first white frosting, semi-transparent, then marzipan, then *pan di spagna* (which the French would call '*genoise*', and the English 'sponge') moistened with Marsala, then a sweetened ricotta filling studded with chocolate. The cake is topped with candied fruits, often in a tall pile reminiscent of a rococo fruit display.

There is a lot of scope for sweetness here – candied fruits are by definition sweet, as is frosting, as is marzipan. Sicilians make the filling quite sweet too, and the lot is enough to make an adult nervous, a child ecstatic, and a dentist rub his hands in anticipation. The best I had in Sicily was at La Casa del Brodo in Palermo, where it wasn't so sweet at all.

I make mine with a thin, lemony frosting, a judicious decoration of candied fruits, and a filling that is too savoury on its own, but perfect with the marzipan. I also, unusually, stain the decorative parts of the marzipan with pistachio paste, as I feel convinced this is where the tradition started – but you can do as modern Sicilians do, and use food colouring if it's easier.

Serves 12–16

Pan di spagna
8 large eggs
1¼ cups superfine sugar
Scant 2½ cups all-purpose flour
1 heaped teaspoon baking powder

Filling
1lb 5oz fresh cow's milk ricotta (or sheep's milk, for an earthier taste)
¾ cup superfine sugar
18oz sheep's milk ricotta (or buffalo's or cow's, if easier to find)
2oz bittersweet chocolate, very finely chopped

Cassata
1½lbs best-quality marzipan (high nut content, or make your own, page 393)
2 teaspoons pistachio paste, or a few drops green food colouring
Sweet Marsala – a little, around ¼ cup
Scant 4 cups confectioners' sugar
½ cup water
Juice of 1 lemon
2 quarters of candied orange peel
1 good wedge of candied citron (*cedro*) or candied lemon

For the *pan di spagna,* whisk the eggs with the sugar to make a very thick, luscious, pale cream that forms ribbons when poured or dribbled from the whisk. Sift the flour and baking powder together, directly on to the eggs a bit at a time, folding them in with a light

touch. Line a wide baking sheet (12 x 16in) with parchment paper, pour the cake batter in, and level it as best you can without playing with it too much. Bake at 350°F until golden and set, around 15 minutes for such a thin cake. Let cool before using. This makes a little more than you need, but leftovers can be frozen and later used for *gelato* cakes (pages 437 and 438), or trifles and the like.

To make the filling, purée the 1lb 5oz cow's milk ricotta and sugar in a food processor to a smooth paste. Turn it into a bowl and add the 18oz sheep's milk ricotta and chocolate, and beat with a sturdy balloon whisk until well incorporated and smooth. A wooden spoon will work too, but takes longer.

To start making the *cassata*, line a pan with plastic wrap. For the classic shape, use a *tatin* pan – about 9½in wide, 1½in high, with gently tapering sides.

Take scant 3oz of the marzipan and work together with the pistachio paste to make a nice green colour. Roll into a thin sausage, roll this flat to make a ribbon, and cut lengths of this to press against the sides of the pan, to make vertical stripes. Roll the remaining marzipan 3/32in thick (easiest on a sheet of parchment paper, with a rolling pin dusted with confectioners' sugar), and line the whole pan, covering the green bands. Press into the corners and against the sides, so the green sticks to it.

Cut the *pan di spagna* horizontally, to make two sheets a scant ½in thick. Cut a disc to line the bottom and strips to line the sides of the pan, a layer within the one you've already made of marzipan. Sprinkle with a little Marsala to barely moisten, and fill the cake up to the top with the ricotta filling. Cover the top with another disc of sponge, and again moisten with Marsala. You need to press the *cassata* – to help, find a plate just a little smaller than the pan (which will help later when you ice it). Upturn the plate on top of the cake, and refrigerate under a heavy weight to set – at least a couple of hours, up to a couple of days.

Turn the *cassata* out on to the plate used to press it and remove the plastic wrap. Mix together the confectioners' sugar, water and lemon juice and ice the cake thinly and evenly. Any excess frosting will drip off, so stand the cake over something you don't mind dirtying. Cut the candied peel into fine strips and decorate the cake – an artful hand will make a thing of beauty, a clumsy one will give a charming result. Refrigerate until ready to serve.

This cake will feed more than fit around the average table, but is equally good at breakfast, lunch and dinner. I have a great appetite for it, and so have never had the opportunity to find out exactly how long it keeps in the fridge. Suffice it to say, *long enough.*

FROZEN DESSERTS

I hate growing up. I always think myself to be a few years younger, so when asked my age I'll falter for a moment. I loathe gravitas (which is a shame as I can be quite serious), and anything that reawakens my inner child is more precious to me than gold.

Nothing works better than *gelato*. I challenge anyone to frown while they eat a fine ice, or not to recall what it was like to be a child. The years melt away, and the world becomes sweeter, as if observed through sugar-glass. There – did you notice? I was thinking like a grown-up again. Time for another scoopful of the elixir of youth…

Take care when ordering in a *gelateria*, and watch the face of the person serving you. A scowl may hint that you have ordered badly. Each *gelato* may be good on its own, but it is the combination that dictates the greatness of your cup. Nuts always go well together, or with chocolate. Dark chocolate and coffee are eye-openers with nuts or red fruits, and red fruits great with white-coloured *gelati* (rice, yogurt, coconut) and exceptional with liquorice. Citrus sorbets are delicious with each other, but disastrous with coffee. The same rules apply when making a *gelato* cake, which is essentially a big, baroque cup – it will only be as good as the *gelati* together. The ideal cup or cake, for me, has three flavours, every possible combination of which must be perfection.

But first you have to get the good stuff. This is no mean feat – even in Italy the best *gelaterie* are few and far between. The measure of a great *gelato*, which may be only ten percent pistachios, or half strawberries, is that the ice itself should always taste more strongly and credibly of pistachios or strawberries than the nuts or fruit do themselves. My very favourite three *gelaterie* of them all are for some reason in Bologna, where they use a little less fat for a purer taste, and a little less sugar in their creations. The best of the lot is Gelatauro, where flavours are so clean that after eating a peach sorbet, a real peach tastes somehow hollow and artificial. A flawless representation, like that of Dorian Gray, the picture is so perfect it steals its subject's soul.

WATERMELON GRANITA
SICILY

Granite are ice slushes, crystals of frozen water in a flavoured syrup. They are the easiest frozen dessert to make – mix juice and sugar, freeze, and stir occasionally. Coffee, almond, lemon and mulberry are the true classics, but many watery fruits lend themselves to the task – blood oranges, cherries and, of course, watermelons.

Watermelons are the ultimate summer fruit – so refreshing, and satisfyingly massive. The heavier they feel, the better, and the more juice they will yield for this *granita* – possibly the one thing in the world more refreshing than a big slice of watermelon. Every 2lbs of watermelon will yield about 2 cups juice, enough for two to three people.

Watermelon
Superfine sugar

Blend. Strain. Sweeten. Freeze. Eat.

For those who like everything spelled out, cut the green and white peel from the watermelon (easiest to slice it first – be sure to get rid of all the white pith or the *granita* will taste of compost). Purée the fruit with a stick blender or food processor (not in a blender, which would crush the seeds), and pass it through a coarse sieve to get rid of seeds and pulp. Press down hard on the mush to extract as much juice as you can. Measure the juice, and add a generous ½ cup sugar per quart watermelon juice (or ½ cup per quart if your watermelon is super-sweet). Stir well until the sugar is fully dissolved (this will be quicker if the watermelon was at room temperature to start with).

Pour the liquid into a deep tray that will fit in your freezer (metal is best, as it will conduct heat from the *granita* fastest – but this is only a question of time, rather than quality). Place it in your freezer, and check after half an hour. Once ice crystals start to form, stir every 15 minutes or so with a fork or sturdy balloon whisk until you have a satisfyingly thick slush. If it gets too hard, you can always thaw it a little before serving – and it can be stored this way (frozen solid) for weeks. Serve on a hot day.

Mixed 2:1 with vodka, this makes for an excellent cocktail, too.

BLOOD ORANGE GRANITA
SICILY

As watermelons are the ultimate fruit of summer, blood oranges are the highlight of winter. I can think of no food more intriguing, even slightly sexual, than an orange so red it bleeds when its skin is cut. And there is no greater relief from winter than its flesh, a sweet reminder that once there was sunshine, and there will be again.

Every generous 3lbs of blood oranges will yield about 2 cups juice, enough for two to three people, but make more, and keep it in the freezer for breakfast.

Blood oranges
Superfine sugar

Juice the blood oranges, removing any seeds but straining only through a colander or coarse sieve to do so, so some pulp remains. Add generous ½ cup superfine sugar per quart of juice, and proceed exactly as for watermelon *granita* (see opposite).

And just like watermelon *granita,* it makes an excellent cocktail with vodka added, or perhaps Campari.

PEACH, WINE AND VANILLA GRANITA

This *granita* is dramatic, delicate and complex to taste, but so easy to make. It is a great thing to do with less-than-perfect peaches, especially if they have dark red skins – but is one of the only dishes I can think of which is excusable to make with good peaches too (such peaches are so hard to find it is normally a travesty to do anything other than eat them as they are). The recipe, or the principle behind it, came from my dear friend Zaki, who made it for me after eating something similar at The Eagle in Farringdon. He decorated his with frozen grapes, which I absolutely loved – only recently have I become so austere in my outlook as to omit them. With or without, it is summertime perfection.

If you have a choice, choose peaches that have very dark skins and a good aroma, and are pretty much ripe but ever so slightly firm – the ones that would be perfect to eat tomorrow. These will be the best to cook today.

Serves 4–6

6 large or 12 tiny white or yellow peaches, with dark red skins
2 strips lemon zest, made with a potato peeler
½ vanilla pod, split lengthways
1in piece cinnamon stick
2 cups white wine
¾ cup superfine sugar

Put everything into a pot, and add water to just cover the peaches – 2 cups or so. Bring it to a simmer, and cook until the peaches are tender, the skins ready to slip off. This may be as little as 3 or 4 minutes if they are ripe, or 15–20 if they are firm.

Use a slotted spoon to lift them from the syrup, and let cool until you can just handle them (if you wear rubber gloves, you needn't have as much patience). Remove all the skin with your fingers and return it to the liquor; put the peeled peaches, covered, in the fridge. Allow the syrup to simmer with the skins in it for at least 20 minutes longer (to extract all the colour and flavour), and taste for sweetness. If too watery, you can either boil it down a little, or add more sugar to taste. Strain the rosy pink liquid, let it cool and freeze as for any *granita* (page 402).

Serve the ice (whose colour is about as beautiful as can be, especially on a sunny day) with the whole peaches on top.

SOUR CHERRY GRANITA

My grandmother used to make me yogurt soup as a child, by opening a jar of Morello cherries and spooning yogurt into it. I loved it, and still do – sour cherries have a special place in my heart. In Sicily they make a mulberry *granita* that is exceptional, but it is hard to find black mulberries these days if you don't have a tree. Morello cherries are my replacement – tarter, but just as full of fruity goodness, and full of happy memories.

Serves 4

1lb Morello or other sour cherries, stemmed
2½ cups water
¾ cup superfine sugar

Put everything into a pot, bring it almost to a simmer, turn it off immediately and let cool. Put the lot in a food processor (*not* a blender, which would crush the cherry stones) and purée until the flesh has come from the pits, and broken down to a red liquid. Pass through a sieve, pressing down to extract the juice, and discard the stony residue. Freeze this liquor as for any other *granita* (page 402).

If you can't get fresh Morello cherries, or they are out of season, you can use cooked ones from jars, which can be blended and strained. Alternatively, use fresh, eating cherries and the method above. In either case, add sugar to taste if necessary, remembering the *granita* will taste slightly less sweet when frozen.

ALMOND GRANITA, BLONDE OR BURNT
SICILY

I first had almond *granita*, a Sicilian classic, at Mastrociliegia, where unusually they toasted the almonds for it. I make two versions: 'blonde', with untoasted almonds and an ambrosial flavour (basically frozen almond milk, page 453), and 'burnt', with dark-toasted almonds providing depth and almost a hint of bitterness. Each is delicious on its own, and they taste great together. The blonde version is great with fruits – fresh fruit, fruit *granite* (pages 402–406), or sorbets (pages 411–15), while the burnt one is better with other nut *gelati* (page 418), chocolate sorbet (page 416) or *espresso gelato* (page 426).

Serves 4

Generous ½ cup blanched almonds
1½ teaspoons bitter almonds,
 or 1 teaspoon almond extract

Generous ½ cup superfine sugar
3 cups water

For burnt almond *granita*, roast the blanched almonds in the oven until as dark as they can be without quite being burned, best to do this in a 350–400°F oven, spread out in a single layer on a baking sheet. Shake the baking sheet every 5 minutes until as dark as you dare – the colour of milky coffee – likely to take 20 minutes but trust your eyes and nose, not the clock. For a blonde *granita,* use the almonds untoasted, as they are.

Combine the almonds, bitter almonds and sugar in a food processor and work for a long time until as fine as they will get – 5 minutes at least. Add ¼ cup of the water, just enough to make a thick paste, and work until the bowl of the processor is hot, and you fear the motor may overheat – at least 5 minutes more. Gradually add the remaining water. Transfer the mixture to a wide dish and put in the freezer, stirring with a fork until the mixture is almost completely frozen and icy. It is ready to serve in this slightly wet, slushy state. To keep it a while, let it freeze solid, and take it out to thaw for 20 minutes or so before serving.

ESPRESSO GRANITA

Granita di caffè is made in almost every good *caffetteria* in Italy, and is as good as the coffee that makes it, and therefore as the café. This poses a challenge to the home cook, unless you have a proper espresso machine. The best alternatives are to use a stovetop *'moka'* machine, or to get friendly with a local coffee-shop owner. Once you have made a good coffee (page 444), the rest is impossible to get wrong.

Serves 6–10, depending how much coffee they like

2¹⁄₂ cups espresso
³⁄₄ cup water

1 cup superfine sugar, plus extra
  for the cream
Whipped cream, to serve

The espresso should be mixed with the water and sugar, and stirred until the sugar has dissolved. The mixture can then be frozen – see watermelon *granita* (page 402) if you need any assistance here.

Serve with plenty of cream, slightly sweetened and whipped to soft peaks. I use 2 tablespoons superfine sugar per cup of whipping cream. Italian cafés often layer the *granita* and cream, but the cream in the middle may freeze, which I find unpleasant. Better just to fill glasses two-thirds full with the *granita*, and mound the cream up above the rim.

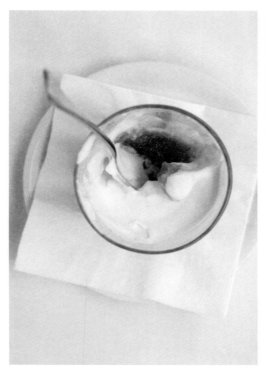

SIX FRUIT SORBETS

A fruit sorbet need be no more complicated than fruit and sugar, although a blend of sugars, and a little stabiliser as I recommend here, will have a smoother result. Since such a mixture requires heating, and I like to keep the fruit raw and fresh, I make a sorbet syrup and leave it to cool before blending with the fruit. This also makes it easy to make a variety – a big batch of syrup can be used to make a myriad of ices, six of which are on the following pages.

Serves 4

Sorbet syrup
1 cup water
3/4 cup superfine sugar
1/4 cup light corn syrup or very light runny honey

1 teaspoon unflavoured gelatin, or 4 teaspoons agar-agar

Bring the water, sugar and corn syrup to a boil, then turn off the heat immediately. Bloom the gelatin (soak it in cold water, then drain) and stir it in, or if using agar-agar, sprinkle the flakes on the surface of the liquid and leave them to hydrate for 5 minutes before stirring to dissolve. Let the syrup cool before using – it will keep for up to a week in the fridge.

MELON SORBET

Generous 2lbs whole melon
1 quantity sorbet syrup (see above)
Juice of about 1 lemon, to taste

Take a ripe orange-fleshed melon. You can tell it's good if it smells deliciously of melon from the base end (opposite the stem). If it doesn't smell, it's either not ripe or not tasty. If it is soft and smells like an off melon, you've guessed it – the melon is off. Scoop out and discard the seeds, and scoop the flesh from the skin. Purée the fruit finely and pass through a sieve. Measure out 2 3/4 cups, and mix with the syrup and lemon juice.

Freeze in an ice-cream machine until quite solid and dry-looking, forming deep lines as the paddle turns, then leave to firm up for at least half an hour in the freezer before serving.

BERRY SORBET

1¼lbs strawberries, weighed after hulling, or raspberries, blackberries or mulberries
1 quantity sorbet syrup (previous page)
Juice of about 1 lemon, to taste

Blend the berries with the syrup and about 1 tablespoon lemon juice to start with. Taste the mixture – add a little more lemon if needed. Don't strain the mixture (the seeds offer a lovely texture, and proof of natural origins) but freeze it in an ice-cream machine as usual.

PEACH SORBET

About 2lbs ripe peaches (white or yellow), with red-blushed skins
Juice of about 1 lemon, to taste
1 quantity sorbet syrup (previous page)

Cut the flesh from the peach stones, but leave the skins on. Add just a squeeze of lemon juice to start, to keep them from browning, and purée finely. Pass the puréed peaches through a coarse sieve to remove the skins, which will by now have released some of their colour and flavour to the mix. Press firmly to help get all the goodness. 2¾ cups of this purée, mixed with the syrup, and tasted for acidity (add lemon as needed), can be stirred and frozen in an ice-cream maker as usual.

PINEAPPLE SORBET

About 2lbs pineapple flesh, skin removed
1 quantity sorbet syrup (page 411)
Juice of about 1½ lemons

Purée the pineapple finely, then pass it through a coarse sieve, pressing down with force to improve economy. Measure out 3 cups of this purée, and stir in the syrup and lemon juice to taste (a little more fruit is used here, and a little more lemon, as the sugary pineapple needs a different balance with the sugary syrup). Freeze in an ice-cream machine, as usual.

COCONUT SORBET

1¼lbs puréed coconut, fresh or frozen
1 quantity sorbet syrup (page 411)
¼ cup superfine sugar

3 tablespoons light corn syrup, or very light runny honey

Coconut makes a most exquisite sorbet, one that is easily mistaken for an ice-cream, as the fat from the coconut gives a texture not dissimilar to milk-fat. I use the blended flesh and juice from whole, ripe coconuts, for the freshest taste. You too could break open a brown-hulled coconut, remove the inner brown membranous skin with a peeler, and pulp the white flesh with the milk – or you could use a frozen purée.

Blend together all the ingredients, and freeze in an ice-cream maker as usual.

AVOCADO SORBET

1 large or 2 small ripe Hass avocados
Generous 2 tablespoons runny honey

Juice of 1 lemon
1 quantity sorbet syrup (page 411)

This is an unusual sorbet, inspired by my grandfather John's failed attempt to farm avocados in Italy in the 1960s. The thought of sweet avocado should not put you off – Brazilians make exquisite avocado milkshakes, and Indonesians mash avocado, coffee and sugar together as a sweet treat. The end result tastes surprisingly like green apples, only nicer and more interesting.

Blend all the ingredients together with 1⅓ cups water, strain through a sieve, and freeze in an ice-cream maker.

PERSIMMON SORBET
EMILIA-ROMAGNA

Gianni Figliomeni taught me everything I know about *gelato*. At Gelatauro in Bologna he serves the best in the world – he's far too modest to admit it, but all who have been to his shop agree. If I want a good *gelato* I go to my little Gelupo, but for a great one I see Gianni.

He absolutely loves fruit, and is quite obsessive about sourcing the very best for his sorbets. When *cachi* – persimmons – are in season, he waits for their evening-sunshine globes to turn jelly-like and wobbly, and then pulps them to make *gelato*. His recipe is deceptively simple – it is as finely tuned as a Maserati, and has a more persimmony taste, and more persimmony texture, than persimmons do. Here it is.

Serves 6

Light syrup
Scant ½ cup dextrose (glucose powder)
¾ teaspoon carob or guar bean powder
  (or unflavoured gelatin)
1½ cups boiling water

Sorbet
1½lbs persimmon flesh (start with
  a generous 2lbs persimmons, skin
  and core them)
1¼ cups cold water
Generous 1½ cups superfine sugar

To make the syrup, stir together the dextrose and carob/guar/gelatin powder, then stir into the boiling water until dissolved.

To make the sorbet, combine the cooled syrup with the persimmon flesh, cold water and sugar in a blender and purée – you may need to do this in batches. Freeze in an ice-cream machine until firm and smooth.

CHOCOLATE SORBET

Asked why I serve a chocolate sorbet as opposed to a milky *gelato*, there are three answers I can give. The first is that it is simply better – cleaner tasting and more intense. The second, that I like bitter, dark chocolate – milk kills the flavour like nothing else can. The third, that I use so much chocolate in it, there simply isn't room for milk...

Serves 4

½ cup unsweetened cocoa powder
1 cup superfine sugar
¼ cup light corn syrup or pale,
   mild runny honey

9oz bittersweet chocolate (70–74% cocoa
   solids), broken into pieces

Mix together the cocoa powder and sugar. Stir in generous 2 cups water, slowly, to try to avoid lumps (don't worry if you get a few – they will cook out), then add the corn syrup. Bring to the boil, take off the heat as soon as it bubbles, add the chocolate and stir until evenly mixed. Cool to room temperature and then blend (a stick blender is fine) if you want it extra smooth. Freeze as usual in an ice-cream machine.

YOGURT GELATO

Yogurt makes a refreshing *gelato*, the natural acidity creating a lightness of taste that cleans the palate. It is delicious served with fruit (or sorbet, pages 411–15), or as a bridging flavour between fruit and nut (pages 418 and 421).

Serves 4

²/₃ cup egg whites (from 3 or 4 large eggs)   1 teaspoon unflavoured gelatin or
3 tablespoons light corn syrup   4 teaspoons agar-agar
Scant ³/₄ cup superfine sugar   18oz strained ('Greek') yogurt

Put the egg white, corn syrup and sugar in a metal bowl and stir with a whisk until incorporated (but not beaten). Put this over a pan of boiling water and cook, still stirring constantly, until it steams and starts to thicken (at about 165°F). Take it off the heat and add the gelatin, already bloomed in cold water, or sprinkle the agar-agar flakes on top and wait 5 minutes for them to hydrate. In either case, stir in until dissolved. Allow the mixture to cool to room temperature, then mix the yogurt in until well incorporated. Freeze as usual in an ice-cream maker.

PISTACHIO OR HAZELNUT (OR PEANUT OR SESAME) GELATO

I apologise for asking the impossible – you do need pistachio or hazelnut paste to make these ices, and these are hard to find.

The best hazelnuts come from Langhe in Piedmont, and the best pastes are made from these very nuts, dark-roasted and ground to a fine purée, as sesame seeds are for tahini. Similarly, the best pistachios come from Bronte in Sicily. These are also roasted (darker by some makers, lighter by others) and ground. These pistachios are so ridiculously expensive that, despite their indisputable superiority, many *gelaterie* use Syrian or Iranian pistachios (still good, if not quite the real deal) or, even worse and even commoner, a paste of almonds, with a small amount of pistachio for taste and green food colouring to compensate. If ever you have a pistachio *gelato* that tastes of almonds, try another *gelateria*. Only almond *gelato* (page 421) should taste of almonds.

Serves 4

Base bianca (white base)
2 cups whole milk
3/4 cup heavy cream (preferably 38% fat)
3 tablespoons light corn syrup or light runny honey
1/2 cup superfine sugar
1/2 cup skim milk powder
1 teaspoon unflavoured gelatin, or 4 teaspoons agar-agar

Gelato
Scant 3oz pistachio paste, or 3 1/2 oz hazelnut paste (or scant 3oz smooth peanut butter, or 3 1/2 oz tahini)
1/2 cup confectioners' sugar (or dextrose powder, if you can get it)

For the *base bianca*, put the milk, cream and corn syrup or honey in a pan. Heat over a low flame and, in a separate container, mix together the sugar and milk powder. When the pan is steaming, add the sugar mixture in a steady stream as you stir. When the mixture approaches a simmer, remove it from the heat and add either the gelatin (already bloomed for a few minutes in cold water, then stirred into the mix) or the agar-agar (sprinkled on the top of the hot mixture and left for 5 minutes, then stirred in). Let cool, covered, to room or fridge temperature.

Blend the nut paste and confectioners' sugar into the *base bianca* and freeze in an ice-cream machine as usual. For the creamiest texture let the *gelato* freeze as hard as it will go in the machine before taking it out.

RICE GELATO
LAZIO

Even proud Romans will concede that they don't live in the *gelato* capital of Italy – a new wave of *gelaterie* may have swept the city, but they pale in comparison to those of Bologna or Sicily. There remain a delightful handful, however, whose clean modernist lines and polished travertine date from the 1950s. These stalwarts serve, amongst a colourful riot of other flavours, bone-white rice *gelato* – a plain milk ice, studded with crunchy grains of sweetened cooked risotto rice. I like it best when it is served with fresh strawberries and comforting cinnamon.

Serves 4

¼ cup risotto rice (any kind)
¼ cup superfine sugar

¼ cup sweetened condensed milk
1 quantity *base bianca* (page 418)

Cook the rice with the sugar in about 2 cups water at the gentlest of simmers for 1 hour, until completely soft. The water will reduce as it cooks – this is okay as long as there is enough to cover the rice, but top it up if it starts to run dry. Drain the rice well in a sieve, and spread it out on a plate to cool.

Mix the condensed milk into the *base bianca* and freeze as usual in an ice-cream machine. When the *gelato* is as frozen as it will get, add the rice grains and let the paddle stir them in. If this softens the *gelato* too much, leave it in the machine until stiff again, then take it out and let it firm a little in the freezer before serving.

Variation: Rice *Gelato* with Strawberries Some 10 minutes before you serve the *gelato*, hull and halve 1lb strawberries, toss them in 3 tablespoons sugar, and leave them to macerate. Scoop the *gelato* into serving bowls after the berries have released a few ruby drops of liquid, top it with the fruit, and sprinkle with a little ground cinnamon. It is worth noting that rice *gelato* and strawberry sorbet (page 412) make an excellent combination, whether at home or in a Roman *gelateria*.

ALMOND GELATO

Instead of adding a flavour to plain *base bianca*, you can infuse it into the milk first. You just can't capture the perfect almond flavour without infusing almonds into milk. And you can do extraordinary things with fig leaves (which give the flavour of the smell of a fig tree – the very perfume that makes their fruit so delectable) or black currant leaves (which have as strong a taste of black currants as the fruit). The method below works well also for walnuts, roasted a little less dark than the almonds, or cinnamon, or citrus leaves, or cloves, or...

Serves 4

2 cups whole milk, plus a little extra

1 cup blanched almonds, roasted very dark (not burned)

2/3 cup heavy cream

3 tablespoons light corn syrup or light runny honey

½ cup superfine sugar

½ cup skim milk powder

1 teaspoon unflavoured gelatin, or 4 teaspoons agar-agar

½ teaspoon almond extract

Put the milk and almonds in a pan. Heat to 175°F, just before a simmer, and steep at this temperature for 45 minutes. Strain out the almonds, put the milk in a measuring jug and make it back up to 2 cups with a little extra milk (the almonds will have absorbed some moisture as they infused).

Return the milk to the pan, adding the cream and corn syrup or honey. Heat over a low flame and, when steaming, mix together the sugar and skimmed milk powder and add them in a steady stream. When the liquid approaches a simmer, remove it from the heat and add either the gelatin (already bloomed for a few minutes in cold water, then stirred into the mix) or the agar-agar (sprinkled on the top of the hot mixture and left for 5 minutes, then stirred in) and the almond extract. Leave to cool and freeze in an ice-cream machine.

Variation: Fig Leaf or Black Currant Leaf *Gelato* Omit the roasted almonds and almond extract, and use instead 5 medium fig leaves, or a big handful of black currant leaves. Infuse them for only 15 minutes, or until the taste is strong enough – too long and the ice-cream will become bitter. Fig is particularly challenging in this respect – too little and you can't taste it, too much and the ice-cream becomes suddenly distasteful, or the sap curdles the milk. Be cautious, and taste often. Otherwise, proceed exactly as for almond, above.

RICOTTA, COFFEE AND HONEY GELATO

This has fast become a signature *gelato* at Gelupo, and is based on the *crema pastore* that my tutor, Gianni at Gelatauro in Bologna, makes so beautifully. It is at once ethereal and earthy, the complex, autumnal flavours not even threatening to mar the lightness of a fine *gelato*. One of the best things to eat at any time of year.

Serves 4

Ricotta base
1⅓ cups whole milk
¼ cup light corn syrup or light
   runny honey
Generous ½ cup superfine sugar
2 tablespoons skim milk powder
1 teaspoon unflavoured gelatin,
   or 4 teaspoons agar-agar

¾ lb fresh ricotta cheese (sheep's milk
   if possible)

Gelato
2 tablespoons chestnut honey – or any
   dark, aromatic one
A heaping teaspoon ground coffee

To make the base, bring the milk to the boil with the corn syrup. Mix together the sugar and powdered milk and stir into the hot milk in a steady stream. Turn off the burner and add the gelatin (if using), bloomed in cold water, and stir. Add the ricotta to the hot mixture and use a stick blender until the mixture is homogeneous and smooth. Return the pan to a low heat and cook to 160–165°F to re-pasteurise the cheese. (If using agar-agar, now is the time to sprinkle it on top, leave for a few minutes, then stir it in.) Cool to room temperature.

To make the *gelato,* stir in the chestnut honey and coffee grounds, and freeze as usual in an ice-cream machine.

STRACCIATELLA / CHOC-FLECK CLASSIC, ALMOND, OR RICOTTA

Stracciatella is chocolate chip, only nicer. Rather than adding chocolate chips, liquid chocolate is stirred into the frozen *gelato,* making delicate fragments – *stracciatella* more or less means 'raggedy'. You taste the *gelato* base first, then the chocolate on the finish. A plain milk *gelato* is the perfect background to the chocolate, while almond or ricotta add a splendid depth and complexity. I especially use ricotta *stracciatella* to fill frozen *cannoli* (see the variation on page 396), and to make my *gelato* cake '*cassata*' (page 438).

Serves 4

1 quantity *gelato* – plain *base bianca*
  (page 418), almond (page 421), or
  ricotta (page 422)
2oz bittersweet chocolate, broken
  into pieces

2 teaspoons flavourless vegetable oil
  (groundnut or similar), or 1 tablespoon
  cocoa butter or coconut oil

As the *gelato* is churning in the machine, melt together the chocolate and oil/cocoa butter in a double boiler (the oil acts to thin the chocolate, so it can form fine strands as opposed to obnoxious lumps). Let cool to lukewarm. When the *gelato* is fully frozen, with the paddle still turning, add the chocolate in a steady stream. The turning paddle will break the chocolate into tiny flakes. Set in the freezer for a while before serving.

Variation: *Stracciatella alla Menta* Chocolate-flecked mint (mint-choc-chip) is as popular and pleasing in Italy as elsewhere. To make it, take a decent bunch of mint and pick the leaves from the stems. Blanch them for 10 seconds in boiling water, refresh in cold, and drain. Put this in a blender with cold *base bianca* and blend until smooth, then proceed exactly as above.

BRIOCHE WITH GELATO
CAMPANIA

Most *gelaterie* worth their sugar have brioche buns available to fill with *gelato* and whipped cream, although the tradition is strongest in Naples. In Sicily they fill a brioche with espresso *granita* (page 410) and cream for breakfast, which I cannot fault in principle, although I prefer to eat the brioche and *granita* side-by-side (and do so often). A filled brioche I prefer with a stuffing of ice-cream, a *gelato* burger. The warm, slightly sweet yeast dough, billowing cream and silken *gelato* disappear frighteningly quickly.

Serves up to 16

1 quantity brioche dough (page 351, optionally enriched using an additional 7 tablespoons unsalted butter in step 3)
1 large egg, beaten, to glaze
2 tablespoons heavy cream and 1 teaspoon superfine sugar per person

3 complementary flavours of *gelato* (I like pistachio, hazelnut and chestnut together, but it is your preference that counts)
Confectioners' sugar, to serve

Let the brioche dough rise for 6 hours in the fridge, as normal, until doubled in bulk, then divide it into even portions, around 2½oz each. For perfect brioches, you need to roll the dough into perfect balls. Working on a smooth surface, not floured, dust a portion of the fridge-cold dough with flour. Put it in the centre of the clean surface. Very loosely cup your hand over it, and roll in a circular motion – the flour will keep it from attaching to your hand, while it actually helps if the ball sticks slightly to the surface at its base.

Transfer as many as you need of these glossy and perfect balls to a baking sheet covered with parchment paper, leaving about 6in gaps between them. Freeze the rest on a tray, and when solid, transfer to a sealed container – they will keep like this for months unrisen, and you will be thankful to have them on hand. Brush the ones you are going to cook today with the egg, and let them rise at room temperature. Mist them with water from time to time as they rise. They should quadruple in bulk, until they look like little domed burger buns, about 2½in high and 4½in wide. This will take around 4 hours, depending on the climate.

Bake them for just 7–10 minutes in an oven at 350°F, until risen more and golden brown. Serve them only slightly warm. To make the dish, cut the buns open horizontally. Whip the cream to soft peaks with the sugar. Put 3 smallish scoops of *gelato* on the bottom half, top with a dollop of cream, cover with the rounded brioche top, sprinkle with confectioners' sugar and serve before the *gelato* melts.

MY AMAZING MILK-FREE ESPRESSO GELATO

I made perhaps my greatest invention by accident. My mum had, a few weeks before, made me my first *caffè allo zabaione*, an indulgent mixture of espresso and egg yolks beaten with sugar (page 450). I started having them for breakfast, then over-indulging morning, noon and night. One day, I made far too much even for me to finish – it was late in the evening, and I could face neither drinking the remnants, nor discarding them as they were so delicious. Emboldened as I was by the caffeine, I tossed the leftovers into the ice-cream machine to see what would happen. So amazing was the result that, against my better judgement, I ate it all and suffered a restless night as a result.

I have made it ever since, but learned my lesson and serve small portions.

Serves 4

³/₄ cup espresso (make it strong) plus ½ cup water, or 1¼ cups very strong coffee
½ cup superfine sugar

1 tablespoon light corn syrup or light, runny honey
6 large egg yolks

Combine the coffee, sugar and corn syrup in a small pan and bring to the boil. As soon as it has boiled, gradually whisk it into the egg yolks, which should be ready for action in a bowl. If you care that the eggs become pasteurised, make sure the mixture reaches 160°F (if not hot enough, return to the pan and carefully bring up to temperature using a low flame and a whisk, and keep a sharp eye for curdling).

Cover the coffee 'custard' and let cool to room temperature – it will thicken in a very satisfying way. Freeze in an ice-cream machine as usual, and serve small portions as dessert, or afterwards instead of coffee.

SEMIFREDDO DI ZABAIONE
PIEDMONT

This *semifreddo* is reasonably involved, and rather spectacular. Its high sugar content would seem sickly to my somewhat austere palate were it not for the booze and the toasted nuts and the bittersweet chocolate, which make it just grown-up enough. The result may seem almost plain to look at, but looks can be deceptive – this tastes absolutely brilliant.

Serves 4

4 large egg yolks
Generous ¼ cup superfine sugar
A few gratings of lemon zest
5 tablespoons sweet Marsala
1 tablespoon rum
½ teaspoon vanilla extract
1¼ cups heavy cream

2oz *torrone* (hard honey nougat), chopped
2oz bittersweet chocolate, finely chopped
Generous ¼ cup toasted hazelnuts, coarsely chopped
2oz crunchy white meringue (overleaf), chopped

First make a *zabaione*. Combine the yolks, sugar, lemon zest, Marsala, rum and vanilla and whisk in a bowl over a pot of simmering water (don't worry whether the water touches the bowl or not – it will work either way) until very thick and lustrous. Remove the bowl and float it in iced water, continuing to whisk until the mixture is completely chilled.

Whip the cream until stiff. Fold it together with the *zabaione,* then stir in the *torrone,* chocolate, hazelnuts and meringue. Transfer to a mould of sorts (I use a brick-shaped 1-quart plastic container), lined with plastic wrap. Freeze until set. Due to its high sugar content the *semifreddo* will need a good few hours before becoming hard enough to serve.

MERINGATA / MERINGUE GELATO CAKE
PIEDMONT

There are easier ways to make an ice-cream cake (page 437), but there is something special about a crisp meringue. With all the sweetness of a baked Alaska, it has the added benefit of crunch, the perfect contrast to an ultra-smooth *gelato*. It also takes quite a while to make the meringue shell, and a delicate hand to fill it. As with so many things, work beforehand makes for easy service. All you have to do is pull the snow-white confection from the freezer, and present it at the centre of a table, with a knife and chilled plates at the ready. The result oozes glamour and sophistication.

Serves 12–15

1 cup superfine sugar
2 cups confectioners' sugar
6 large egg whites
1 tablespoon lemon juice
Unsalted butter, for greasing
2oz white chocolate (only necessary if making the cake long in advance)

4 quantities *zabaione semifreddo* (page 430)
or
3 quantities *gelato* or sorbet, chosen to complement each other
or
3 quarts store-bought ice-cream

Mix together the superfine and confectioners' sugars. Whisk the egg whites with half the mixed sugars and all the lemon juice until very frothy, but still a touch sloppy, then gradually add the remaining sugar as you continue to whisk to very stiff peaks.

Line a baking sheet with parchment paper, and find an 8½in ring form (the outside of a springform cake pan will do), 2¾in high. Draw a circle the size of the pan on the paper, then turn the paper over, so the ink/graphite is against the baking sheet, not the meringue. Set the ring form on a second baking sheet, also covered with parchment, or on the same sheet if there is room next to the circle you've drawn.

Butter the inside of the metal ring, and line the sides with a 2¾in ribbon of paper (which may stick up over the top; the butter is just to stick the paper to the metal). A piping bag with a scant ½in tip is the easiest way to manipulate the meringue, but you can make do with a spoon and a spatula, and a steady hand. Form two circular discs of meringue, each a scant ½in thick, one inside the ring, and one on the circle you've drawn (work in a spiral from the perimeter to the middle, or fill it with little dabs of meringue). Carefully pipe a scant ½in-thick circular wall of meringue one-third the way up the inside of the lined ring – two circular rows will do. Keep the rest in the bag, in the fridge for later.

Bake the meringue in a very cool oven (160°F, or just the pilot light if you have a gas oven) for 2 hours until partly set. Take it from the oven, and carefully pipe another couple of rows of meringue to come two-thirds the way up the side of the pan. Put it back in the oven for another hour, then pipe a final two rows to the very top of the pan, making sure it is good and level. Use any excess meringue to decorate the top of the lid, if you like. Return it to the oven for 5 more hours, until it's crunchy all the way through. Let cool before filling.

You can assemble the cake a couple of hours before serving and omit the white chocolate. If you plan to keep it longer, melt the chocolate and brush it evenly over the inside of the meringue shell, and the underside of the meringue disc that will become the lid – the chocolate will protect the meringue from absorbing water from the filling.

Leave the ice-cream in the fridge until it is malleable, but not defrosted – mix it with a spoon and some force until it is gooey. Fill the meringue shell to the very top with layers of ice-cream, then lift the metal ring from the filled meringue cake within. If you have a touch too much ice-cream, eat the excess, whilst if instead the meringue walls are too high, trim them with a sharp serrated knife and again consume the evidence. Top with the meringue lid and press down gently to close. Freeze for at least an hour to set.

SEMIFREDDO MONTEBIANCO / CHOCOLATE AND CHESTNUT PARFAIT

Semifreddi can be complicated to make, but this one isn't. They are better suited to chillier weather than refreshing *gelati*, being richer, and served not quite so cold. Think of this as a frozen *Mont Blanc*. A chestnut *semifreddo* seems especially autumnal, and therefore somehow warming, despite its frigidity.

Serves 4–5

2 cups heavy cream
3 tablespoons unsweetened cocoa powder
⅓ cup superfine sugar
2oz bittersweet chocolate (70% cocoa solids), chopped
11oz sweetened chestnut purée*
¼ cup rum

4 *marrons glacés*, chopped (optional)
2 large egg whites plus 2 tablespoons superfine sugar (optional, for lighter texture)
½ cup heavy cream, whisked to soft peaks with a scant tablespoon of superfine/confectioners' sugar, to serve

*To make your own purée, if you prefer, take 7oz vacuum-packed cooked chestnuts, chop them, and put them in a small pan with 2 tablespoons superfine sugar, ½ teaspoon vanilla extract and 1 cup water. Simmer for 20 minutes or until very soft, then blend to a fine purée.

Stir together scant ½ cup of the cream with the cocoa powder and sugar. Heat it in a small pan until the paste is smooth and glistening, then take off the heat and stir in the chocolate until it melts. Now add the chestnut purée, rum and *marrons glacés*, if using.

Whip the remaining cream to soft peaks, and fold it into the chestnut mixture. For a lighter texture, whisk egg whites with extra sugar to stiff peaks and fold in gently, but thoroughly, after the cream.

Freeze in an appropriate mould (a brick-shaped 1-quart plastic container is ideal), lined with plastic wrap for easy extraction. It can be turned out when solid (3 hours at least – but it will keep happily in the freezer for a week or two), and should be served sliced, with a dab of whipped cream on the side.

GELATO CAKE 'OPERA'

This is my Italianate version of that French *pâtisserie* classic – a *gelato* cake in the flavour of *'opera'* – the layered delight of hazelnut, coffee and chocolate.

Serves 12

1 quantity *pan di spagna* (page 397),
  or a sponge cake
⅓ cup brandy
¼ cup sugar

1 quantity hazelnut *gelato* (page 418)
1 quantity espresso *gelato* (page 426)
1 quantity chocolate sorbet (page 416)
Unsweetened cocoa powder, to serve

Take a circular cake ring (or the outer part of a springform mould), about 9½in in diameter and 2½in high, and stand it on a serving plate or a tray lined with parchment. Cut a disc from the *pan di spagna* to fit exactly, and halve it horizontally with a bread knife, to make two thin discs, about ½in thick. Put the bottom disc, cut-side up, in the base of the ring. Mix the brandy with the sugar until it dissolves, and dribble half of this mixture on to the cake base.

Spread the *gelati* in three layers on the cake – hazelnut below, coffee in the middle, and chocolate on top. Use them straight from the machine (churn one while you layer the last in the cake), or if they are already in the freezer let them soften at room temperature, stirring forcefully until malleable. Put the cake in the freezer after forming each layer, so the last can set before you start on the next. Top with the upper layer of cake, cut-side down, and sprinkle this with the remaining sweetened brandy. Put the cake in the freezer for a couple of hours until set.

To unmould your magnum *opera*, warm the ring, either with a blowtorch, or a towel wet with hot water. A finer finish could be achieved by lining the pan with a strip of parchment (pros use acetate ribbon), but this hardly seems worth fiddling with at home. Sprinkle with cocoa powder just before you serve.

GELATO CAKE 'CASSATA'
SICILY

Cassata is not itself an ice-cream, even if sickly ices studded with candied fruits bear its name. Such a *gelato* does exist, but takes its inspiration from the queen of Italian puddings, Sicilian *cassata* cake (page 397). Here I add further to the confusion with my *gelato* cake 'cassata', but it is worth it, I promise.

Serves 12

1 quantity *pan di spagna* (page 397),
  or sponge cake
⅓ cup sweet Marsala
1 quantity ricotta *stracciatella gelato*
  (page 423)

1 quantity almond *gelato* (page 421)
1 quantity pistachio *gelato* (page 418)
2 quarters candied orange peel, cut into
  thin strips or small diamonds

Take a circular cake ring (or springform without base) that is 9½ in in diameter and 2½ in high, and stand it on the serving plate, or a paper-lined tray. You can line the sides of the pan with a strip of parchment if you like, for a neat finish, but it isn't essential. Cut a disc from the *pan di spagna* to fit exactly, and put it in the base of the ring. Drizzle the Marsala on to the cake base.

Allow the *gelati* to just soften out of the freezer for a few minutes, or use them straight from the ice-cream machine. Spread the ricotta *stracciatella* in an even layer on the bottom. Put it in the freezer for a few minutes to firm, then top with the nut *gelati* in one of two ways.

Either: Put the pistachio *gelato* in a piping bag with a wide tip, and pipe it into a ring on top of the ricotta base, such that it touches the sides of the mould but has a wide round gap in the centre. Pipe the almond *gelato* to fill the middle and smooth the top level with a palette knife, working in a circular motion to keep the line between the *gelati* distinct.

Or (pictured): Spoon smallish dollops of the pistachio and almond *gelati* over the top to create a variegated effect. Smooth the top with a couple of fast, clean sweeps of a warmed palette knife to gently marble the colours, without blending them together too much.

In either case, put the cake immediately in the freezer for a couple of hours to set, and unmould by warming the cake ring with a blowtorch or wrapping it around with a steaming hot wet towel. Decorate the top with a random scattering or considered arrangement of the pieces of candied orange peel, and serve with glasses of sweet Marsala or Muscat wine.

DRINKS / CARDS

My parents spent a year near Panzano, as a sort of honeymoon. They rented a small house from a wealthy Count, which sat on a piece of land farmed for him by some impoverished *contadini* (peasants). Here they learned what hospitality was. They went for a meal first with the *contadini*, and the family shared with my parents all they had. They ate bread and cheese, and a rabbit stew, only learning at the end of the meal that the rabbit was in fact the family pet, or had been until that morning. It was all washed down with home-made wine, from vines on what is today one of Tuscany's best estates. Two weeks later they were invited to dine with the Count. They ate a meal in four courses, seated awkwardly around a large table, largely in silence. At the very end of the meal, as they stood up to leave, the Count asked, 'I'm sorry – did you want any wine?'

Wine in Italy is like water – it is on every table at lunch and dinner. Children drink it – just a very little – and come to enjoy it for its taste, so learning over the years to drink in order to drink, rather than to get drunk. It is a good thing they do, for Italy is home to over five hundred grape varieties, and her fragmented past has led to as much diversity in wine as food. The mind boggles. I have struggled enough to convey the joy of so many of my favourite dishes, helped as I have been by an army of ingredients you know as well as I, and instructions to guide you to a conception of the finished dish as I know it. What hope would I have with wine? I have no frame of reference that I can be sure of. If you know what Arneis or Picolit or Ribolla Gialla or Pignolo or Schioppettino or Nerello taste like, you certainly don't need me to tell you. And if you don't, you can only learn by drinking some. I heartily recommend you do so.

At the end of the meal – and it has been a long one – we are sitting deep in our chairs. Any disagreements are long resolved or forgotten: the sense of bonhomie at the table is tangible. No matter how good the food was, it wasn't half as enjoyable as this moment. So, until eyelids grow heavy and conversation slows, we keep going, and stoke the fire. It is time to put the coffee pot on, and bring out the bottle of grappa that somehow survived dinner yesterday. A deck of cards is found and dealt, and those of us that do, indulge in a cigarette. The night is young.

APEROL SPRITZER VENETO

Aperol is a bitter, similar to Campari, but sweeter and perfumed with bitter orange. Its spritz, when it is mixed with either *prosecco*, or white wine and soda, is a classic *aperitivo* across the north, although in Lombardy, home of Campari, they use that instead. Predictably, I prefer the girlier Aperol version...

2oz Aperol
Generous 2oz *prosecco*
1 orange slice – blood, if in season

Fill a large tumbler with ice. Pour in the Aperol (with the ice, it should fill the glass two-thirds), add the *prosecco,* stir gently and tuck in the orange slice.

NEGRONI AND NEGRONI SBAGLIATO
TUSCANY / LOMBARDY

Invented by Count Negroni, who asked a Florentine bartender to strengthen an *Americano* with gin, *Negroni* is the other classic *aperitivo* drink. Campari, as a bitter, has an unusual property – the longer you sip it, the sweeter it tastes – so the uplifting bitterness gives way to a soothing sensation that is amplified drink after drink after drink. Martini Rosso, rather bittersweet and fabulous, is the oldest drink from the Martini stable, dating to 1863.

A *Negroni Sbagliato,* or 'mistaken Negroni', is made with dry sparkling wine in place of gin, and was invented in Milan. Its creation may have been accidental, but to make one is never a mistake. It is quite the most refreshing thing.

Negroni
1oz Martini Rosso
1oz Campari
1oz gin
1 orange slice – blood, if in season

Negroni Sbagliato
1oz Martini Rosso
1oz Campari
2oz *prosecco*
1 orange slice – blood, if in season

Fill a large tumbler with ice. Pour in the drinks (*prosecco* last, if making a *Sbagliato*, so it loses its bubbles less), and give the feeblest of stirs. Tuck in the orange slice, and get ready to make another round quickly...

COFFEE

In Italy *caffè*, 'coffee', is synonymous with espresso. Despite its foreign origins (coffee arrived from Latin America in the seventeenth century) it is perhaps *the* aroma that defines Italy. Most Italians go to a bar to get their first of the morning, as it just cannot quite be equalled. By the end of the day they resign themselves to one made at home – in a *moka* (or *macchinetta*, 'little machine'), one of the little stove-top pots that work so well.

Coffee should be deep and complex: like a fine chocolate, the bitterness should be balanced by richness, sweetness and acidity. Unless you are a geek and have an espresso machine at home, the best coffee you can brew will be in a *moka*: they are inexpensive, and can extract all the flavour of a commercial machine, if not the *crema* (chestnut-brown foam) that signals a great cup.

To make good coffee, buy good coffee, and make sure it is an 'espresso' or '*moka*' grind – coffee ground for filtering is too coarse. Fill the base of the *moka* with tapwater up to the steam valve. Put in the filter funnel, and fill it to the top with the coffee. Press down *lightly* with the back of a spoon, and top the coffee up again until level with the rim. Screw the top part of the machine on very tightly and put it over the highest flame of the smallest burner. The moment you hear boiling and spluttering, reduce the flame to minimum. When the coffee stops coming, take it off the heat quickly.

Most Italians drink their espresso with a little, or a lot of, sugar. Milky coffees – *cappuccino* and the like – are served only in the morning as the Italians, obsessed with their digestion, refuse to drink milk in the evening.

CORRETTO AND RISCIACQUINO VENETO

These two drinks are rather 'older gentleman', and both have charming names. Both involve coffee mixed with booze, probably a coarse grappa. This is not to say all grappa is coarse, but that drunk by grumpy old men is.

Caffè corretto, 'corrected' coffee, is taken in the morning by the brave. A shot of spirit, occasionally Sambuca or brandy but normally an unrefined, fearsome and firesome grappa, is added to a hot espresso. This is quite hard to take, as hot alcohol tastes strong.

A *risciacquino* is even cheekier. Sitting at a bar, having finished a coffee you might ask for *un risciacquino*, 'a little rinse'. The barman will pour a shot of grappa into your empty cup to swill around, rescuing the espresso *crema* that clings to the rim, and the sugar slurry at the bottom. The grappa, now delicately flavoured and slightly warm, is delectable.

BICERIN PIEDMONT

This drink – hot chocolate, whipped cream or foamed milk, and espresso – is the pride of Turin. A café there, also called Bicerin, has been making it for nigh on 250 years and knows its history better than I: 'Initially, there were three variations of the same theme: "*pur e fiur*" (today's *cappuccino*), "*pur e barba*" (coffee and chocolate), and "'*n poc 'd tut*" (a little of everything)...' Each café has its own recipe for the chocolate, a secret, never divulged. But I'm happy enough with my own, as I'm particular about my hot chocolate, and make it without milk (like my sorbet, page 416) for purity of flavour.

2oz bittersweet (70%) chocolate, room temperature, finely chopped
1½ tablespoons superfine sugar, plus ½ teaspoon

2 tablespoons heavy cream
¼ cup boiling water
A double espresso

Put the chocolate and 1½ tablespoons sugar in a glass. Whip the cream to soft billowing peaks with the remaining sugar. Pour the boiling water into the glass – it's just a little – and let it sit for a minute or two, it should have just enough heat to melt the chocolate – and stir well with a coffee spoon. Pour the hot espresso into the glass and stir again to incorporate. Top with the whipped cream and serve.

Variation For an 'Irish' *bicerin,* or *bicerin corretto*, which you'd never see in Italy but might see me drinking, add a shot of whisky, or brandy or rum or grappa, along with the espresso.

DRUNKEN BABY LOMBARDY

Alberto, inspiration for many a recipe in this book, told me that when he was a baby his granny would quieten him before bedtime with a little hot milk mixed with honey, and grappa if need be. It sounded like such a good idea that I named a cocktail after him.

1½oz grappa
1 rounded, dripping teaspoon honey

⅓ cup milk, steaming hot and frothed with a whisk

Put the grappa into a medium glass, or a champagne flute. Whisk the honey into the milk, making as much froth as you can, and use it to top the grappa glass to the rim, or to taste. Being rather soporific, this is best served towards the end of an evening.

CAFFÈ ALLO ZABAIONE

My mum waited until awfully late before making me my first espresso with *zabaione*, beaten egg yolks. I was in awe, so much so that I forgave her for all the years I had missed out on this creation. She tells me it is the sort of coffee Italian grandmothers make for themselves, when they need a little comfort.

For 4 little cups

2 egg yolks
¼ cup superfine sugar
4 double espressos

Combine the egg yolk and sugar with 2 tablespoons of water in a metal bowl and set it over a pan of simmering water. Whisk until the egg yolk is light, fluffy, and steaming hot; it's okay if the water underneath boils, but take care not to scorch your hand; the egg yolk won't curdle as long as you whisk constantly, and take it off when it will thicken no further. Spoon this dense *zabaione* on top of the hot coffee and serve.

CAFFÈ ALLA NOCCIOLA / HAZELNUT COFFEE
CAMPANIA

This coffee, sweet, nutty and rich, is typical of Naples, where small and badly drawn illustrations of coffee cups and hazelnuts on plastic signs behind the bar promise little. Looking at them, you'd think they were advertising the latest tourist gimmick, but the hordes of Neapolitans, each with a glass of *caffè alla nocciola*, indicate otherwise. In Naples, the bars use a special cream – I believe a mixture of whipped cream and egg yolks. I use a clean, cream-free *zabaione* – denser, richer, and even more unctuous.

1 cup *caffè allo zabaione* (see above)
1 good teaspoon hazelnut paste

Make the coffee exactly as for *caffè allo zabaione*, but put the hazelnut paste in the glasses before you start. Tell your guests to give their coffee a good stir before drinking, or they will not have the experience you intend.

LATTE DI MANDORLE / ALMOND MILK
SICILY

Sicily, exotic and perfumed, is covered in orange, lemon and almond trees. Between them, there is always a beautiful smell and beautiful sight: brightly coloured citrus fruits in red, orange and golden yellow cover the trees in winter like Christmas balls; rosy pink almond blossom is the first sign of spring; oranges and lemons blossom in summer, perfuming the hills. All three provide refreshing drinks – orange juice and lemonade are always welcome. But only ice-cold, ivory-white almond milk can quench the full heat of a Sicilian summer.

Almonds are not native to Sicily: they come from the Levant, as do sweet icy drinks like *jallab* and *badam kheer*. The drink became popular in the west, not only because it is so delicious, but it is also 'kosher' for Lent.

This recipe is in two parts. The first is to make an almond paste, which keeps for weeks in the fridge or months in the freezer – it is a good idea to have it on hand at all times in the summer months. The second is to blend the paste with water to make the drink.

Makes enough for 3 quarts almond milk

3/4 cup blanched almonds
1 1/2 cups superfine sugar

1/2 oz bitter almonds or apricot kernels, or 2 teaspoons almond extract

To make the paste, put the almonds, sugar and bitter almonds (if using) in the food processor and grind until they will get no finer, then add 1/3 cup water (and almond extract) and let the machine work it to a smooth paste. Feel the side of the processor bowl – when it is quite warm, you're done. Either continue to make a big batch of almond milk, or keep the paste for blending small batches later.

If you don't have a blender, you can carry on in the food processor, as long as you're happy to make a big batch. Measure out 2 quarts of water, and start to add this gradually to the food processor, with the motor running. When the mixer bowl seems full, tip the contents into a large bowl or massive jug. Add the rest of the water along with 4 cups ice, stir until chilled and serve. This will fill 10 very large glasses.

If you do have a blender, put in a scant cup ice and 1 1/2 cups water (the exact proportions aren't important – you just need the ice to make the drink cold, and a combined 2 cups), along with 2 very heaped tablespoons of the almond paste. Blend until white as chalk, and serve. This will fill 2 large glasses.

POSSO (A RECIPE FOR DISASTER)

At the end of a meal, when we have the energy, we play *Posso*. A hypercharged rummy, it finishes the work our dinner started – bringing us together around a table, even though at times it may threaten to drive us apart.

Alfred brought the game to us, having learnt it from a group of Franciscan nuns in California, in particular one Sister Ruth, who apparently always carried a gun to the table. It is played in a series of ten hands. In each hand one more card is dealt than in the previous. By hand six or seven you may find yourself holding more than half a deck in an ill-formed fan. The game requires a lot of cards, a lot of time (about an hour, once you get the hang of it), and a lot of rules. Here they are:

Serves 3–5, but up to 8

1 deck of cards *less* than you have
   players (i.e. 2 decks for 3 people, etc),
   which must include the jokers
1 piece of paper
1 pen

Someone you trust to keep score
Many drinks (page 442)
An ashtray (optional, depending
   on company)

The goal
The overall goal is to have the lowest score, which is cumulative over ten hands. In each turn, you pick up a card (from the top of the face-down *stack* or face-up *pile*), take it into your hand, then discard one, face-up on the *pile*. In each hand you try to get rid of your cards – any cards left over count towards your score. First you must *go down*, by putting a particular *requirement* (a combination of *runs* and *of-a-kinds*) down on the table. After you have *gone down*, you can get rid of your remaining cards on any *requirements* (your own *runs* or *of-a-kinds*, or someone else's) that are already down on the table. There are therefore two phases in each hand – trying to *go down* and trying to *go out*. Twos and jokers are wild – they can represent any card of any suit you like. You may have a lot of cards to get rid of if you have *Posso*-ed ('bought' extra cards) too often.

For the deal
Cut the deck – the player who draws the highest card is first to deal. The dealer shuffles the deck, the player to his right cuts, and the dealer deals clockwise, starting with the player to his left. In the first hand, 7 cards are dealt to each player. The turn to deal passes clockwise, and the next dealer deals 8 cards in the second hand, the next deals 9 in the third, and so on. The undealt cards are placed face-down in a *stack* in the middle of the table, and the top one turned face-up, starting the separate *pile*.

To play

Play passes clockwise, starting to the left of the dealer. You start your turn by picking up either the top card in the face-up *pile* or the top one in the face-down *stack*, and you end your turn by discarding a card on the face-up *pile*. During your turn, with luck, you may be able to do one of the following:

If you haven't already *gone down*, you may do so if you have the *requirement* in your hand, and as long as it is your turn. You haven't won the hand, though, until you have *gone out* – either put down or discarded your very last card. In the last hand, *going down* is a little different, and harder (we'll come on to this later).

If you have already *gone down*, in this turn or a previous one, you can *put down* – in other words, you can add – cards to *runs* and *of-a-kinds* already down on the table. You can put down on to your own *runs* and *of-a-kinds* **or anyone else's, as long as it is your turn and you've already *gone down*** – even in the same turn you *go down* yourself. You can't start a new *run* or *of-a-kind*, or move cards between them, but you can add to them – using the correct card, or a wild card (two or joker), which can go anywhere. You may also replace a wild card that is already down, in which case the wild card must stay in the same *run* – it can be moved up or down the *run*, but not into another run or your hand. (When a run is 'full', from three to Ace, no more cards can be added to it, wild ones included.)

You win the hand by getting rid of your last card – either by discarding it, or adding it to a *run* or *of-a-kind* – and *going out*. Of course, this can only be done after you've started your turn by picking up a card.

'Posso'

This happens between turns (and, usefully, immediately after the deal, before the first player has started his turn by picking up a card). After one player has discarded, but before the next has picked up, you may stake a claim to the top card in the face-up *pile* by shouting 'Posso?' ('May I?'). The person whose turn is next may either say 'no', in which case he **must** take the top pile card to start his turn, or 'yes', in which case you must take both the top pile card **and** the top stack card. It is not actually your turn: you have just 'bought' a card you wanted by taking another one you couldn't see, and you don't get to discard. Play continues with the player whose turn it was about to be before you called 'Posso'.

If more than one player calls 'Posso', priority is given to the one closest to the player whose turn it is, moving clockwise.

After someone has Posso-ed, 'Posso' may not be called again until the player whose turn it was anyway starts and finishes his turn.

If it is your turn to play, you neither want to, nor are you permitted to, call 'Posso'.

Going down

When you have made the *requirement* for the hand, but only after you have started your turn by picking up a card, you may *go down* by putting the *requirement* face-up on the table.

No part of the *requirement* may be more than half wild cards when you *go down*, although any number of wild cards may be *put down* on it subsequently. Here are the requirements:

Hand one	7 cards dealt	2 threes *of-a-kind*
Hand two	8 cards dealt	a three *of-a-kind* and a *run* of four cards
Hand three	9 cards dealt	2 fours *of-a-kind*
Hand four	10 cards dealt	a four *of-a-kind* and a *run* of five
Hand five	11 cards dealt	2 *runs* of five (each in a different suit)
Hand six	12 cards dealt	a *run* of eight and three *of-a-kind*
Hand seven	13 cards dealt	3 fours *of-a-kind*
Hand eight	14 cards dealt	2 fours *of-a-kind* and a *run* of five
Hand nine	15 cards dealt	2 *runs* of five (each in a different suit) and four *of-a-kind*
Hand ten	16 cards dealt	3 *runs* of five or more (each in a different suit) with no discard (see note under 'going out')

An '*of-a-kind*' is a group of cards with the same number or face (except twos and jokers, which are wild). A '*run*' is a series of consecutive cards in the same suit, with threes low (twos don't exist as they are wild) and Aces high.

Going out
You keep playing until your last card is gone and you have *gone out* – when you have won the hand all the other players, having cards left in their hand, need to add up their scores.

Hand ten, the last hand, is different. The *requirement* is not just that you make 3 *runs*, but that you are able to put them down with nothing left in your hand, and **no discard**. You must therefore, with 3 perfect *runs* in your hand, wait until you pick up the perfect card, when you can put down the lot. Having *gone down* and *out* in one fell swoop, everyone else has lost the hand and must add up their scores, which will be high.

Scoring
Only cards held in the hand (not 'down' on the table) count against you, and the score is cumulative from round to round. The lowest score after ten hands wins. Cards count thus:

Three to seven all score 5 points
Eight to King all score 10 points
Aces score 15 points
Twos score 20 points
Jokers are free (0 points)

If you end up with a score of over 500 you are deemed to be 'in the toilet', which someone normally is.

Alfred's rules

Alfred seems to make up the rules as he goes along. Here are a handful that have stuck:

'**Dead card**' After the top card in the face-up *pile* has been '*Posso-ed*', the next one is *dead*, and may not be taken by the player whose turn it is next, they can only pick up from the face-down *stack*. I never play this rule, unless I have to because I'm playing with Alfred.

'**No *Posso* down**' After you have gone down you may not call '*Posso*' in the remainder of the hand. I prefer not to play this rule, unless Alfred or Ginny insists.

'**Cutting to win**' When it is your turn to deal, you try to pick up the right number of cards for the deal, without counting cards or fidgeting with the deck. If you get it right (i.e. for round 2 among 3 people, you pick up 24 or 25 cards – 8 cards each, or 8 cards each plus 1 to turn over for the face-up *pile*), your entire score up to this point is cancelled, and you start again from zero. We always play this rule, as it offers a chance of reprieve to players who are 'in the toilet', and haven't a hope in hell of winning.

INDEX

ACKNOWLEDGEMENTS

Thank you to my family, who taught me to eat and are the best people to cook for. Victor, I couldn't do anything without you. Mum, Dad, Rachel, Clive, my late grandfather John and my very living grandmothers Agnes and Ginny, you make the world delicious. Ros, Dave, Olivia, Matthew and Adam, you have always been brilliant – and your belief in Bocca di Lupo has given me a kitchen in which to cook.

Thank you also to my other family at the restaurant, you make it what it is today, your efforts are superb and much appreciated – especially David Cook and Alberto Comai for all that inspiration (and perspiration). Thanks, too, to those of you who helped me with this book – Alberto Comai (doubly, for proofing also), Stefano Pingue, Angelo Guida and Daniele Ceforo in the kitchen and on location, and Massimo Allonzo for your work on the drinks. Sylvain Jamois, thank you so very much for testing most of the recipes – Adam, Adam, Adam, Alice, Marcelo, Massimo I., Nevio and Ollie too for testing the rest.

I owe a great deal to all who taught me to cook – Sam and Sam at Moro, Nancy at Boulevard and your husband Bruce especially – I can't tell you how much I appreciate all you've done for me. Gianni Figliomeni, you alone taught me so generously to make *gelato*, I hope one day I can repay you. Also thank you Gianni, and Dario Cecchini, for contributing your recipes – and Faith Willinger, for showing me the very best of Italy. Aljoscha and Antonia at Corzano e Paterno, and Ginny, thank you for the most beautiful locations.

Caz Hildebrand, you believed in my ability to write a cookbook long before I did, and have made this one an utter beauty. Howard Sooley, you have seen all the joy in the food, and captured it brilliantly on camera. Richard Atkinson, you have guided this book through every stage of creation, and me from cook to author. Together, we have been the Fantastic Four. Antony and Anouschka at Bacchus – you found me a publisher in the first place. My special thanks to Sarah Barlow, Penny Edwards and Natalie Hunt (for proofing, producing and editing respectively). Susan Fleming, thank you for your sage advice and expertise. Clive Sinclair, thank you for reading the text and helping to make it suitably unctuous.

Trattoria Valenza in Turin; Toni Del Spin in Treviso; Da Fiore and Al Mascaron in Venice; Al Merluzzo Felice and Masuelli San Marco in Milan; Autotreno, Anna Maria and Gelatauro in Bologna; Antico Forno del Ghetto, Caffè Sant'Eustachio, Da Enzo, Filetti di Baccalà, Marcello, Piperno and Dal Paino in Rome; Poco-Poco in Sperlonga, Masaniello by the old lion in Gaeta; Da Dora (and your beautiful chefs who grace pages 232–3) in Naples; Oasis and Pane e Salute in Puglia; La Casa del Brodo, Maria Grammatico and Mastrociliegia in Sicily – thank you all, and thanks to the many cooks in Italy, whose food I have enjoyed so much.

PASTE NUOVE
PER COMBATTERE
LA DEPRESSIONE
€ 2,00 L'UNA

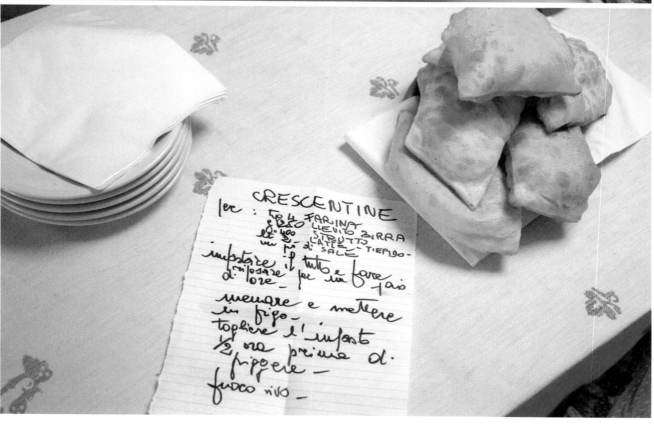

CRESCENTINE

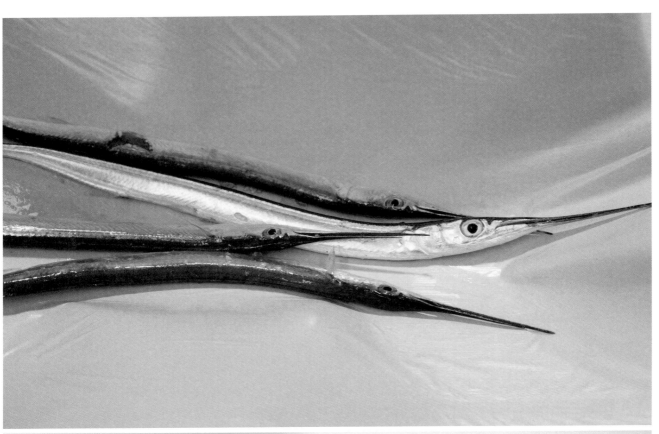

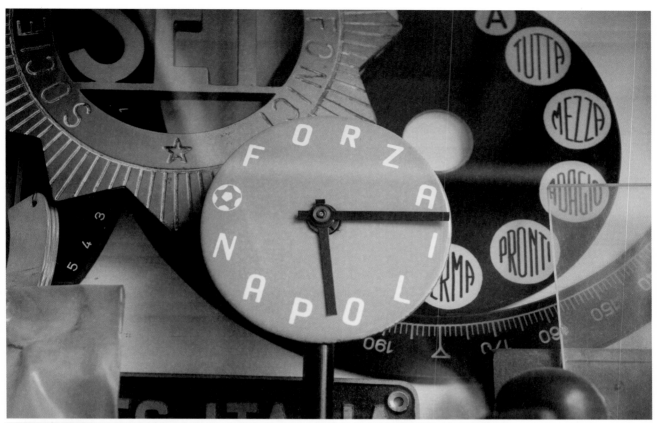